W9-CZM-666

Bloom's Modern Critical Views

African-American
  Poets: Volume I
African-American
  Poets: Volume II
Aldous Huxley
Alfred, Lord Tennyson
Alice Munro
Alice Walker
American Women
  Poets: 1650–1950
Amy Tan
Anton Chekhov
Arthur Miller
Asian-American
  Writers
August Wilson
The Bible
The Brontës
Carson McCullers
Charles Dickens
Christopher Marlowe
Contemporary Poets
Cormac McCarthy
C.S. Lewis
Dante Aligheri
David Mamet
Derek Walcott
Don DeLillo
Doris Lessing
Edgar Allan Poe
Émile Zola
Emily Dickinson
Ernest Hemingway
Eudora Welty
Eugene O'Neill
F. Scott Fitzgerald
Flannery O'Connor
Franz Kafka
Gabriel García Márquez

Geoffrey Chaucer
George Orwell
G.K. Chesterton
Gwendolyn Brooks
Hans Christian
  Andersen
Henry David Thoreau
Herman Melville
Hermann Hesse
H.G. Wells
Hispanic-American
  Writers
Homer
Honoré de Balzac
Jamaica Kincaid
James Joyce
Jane Austen
Jay Wright
J.D. Salinger
Jean-Paul Sartre
John Irving
John Keats
John Milton
John Steinbeck
José Saramago
J.R.R. Tolkien
Julio Cortázar
Kate Chopin
Kurt Vonnegut
Langston Hughes
Leo Tolstoy
Marcel Proust
Margaret Atwood
Mark Twain
Mary Wollstonecraft
  Shelley
Maya Angelou
Miguel de Cervantes
Milan Kundera

Nathaniel Hawthorne
Norman Mailer
Octavio Paz
Paul Auster
Philip Roth
Ralph Ellison
Ralph Waldo
  Emerson
Ray Bradbury
Richard Wright
Robert Browning
Robert Frost
Robert Hayden
Robert Louis
  Stevenson
Salman Rushdie
Stephen Crane
Stephen King
Sylvia Plath
Tennessee Williams
Thomas Hardy
Thomas Pynchon
Tom Wolfe
Toni Morrison
Tony Kushner
Truman Capote
Walt Whitman
W.E.B. Du Bois
William Blake
William Faulkner
William Gaddis
William Shakespeare:
  Comedies
William Shakespeare:
  Histories
William Shakespeare:
  Tragedies
William Wordsworth
Zora Neale Hurston

Bloom's Modern Critical Views

ANTON CHEKHOV
New Edition

Edited and with an introduction by
Harold Bloom
Sterling Professor of the Humanities
Yale University

BLOOM'S
LITERARY CRITICISM
An imprint of Infobase Publishing

Bloom's Modern Critical Views: Anton Chekhov—New Edition

Copyright © 2009 by Infobase Publishing

Introduction © 2009 by Harold Bloom

Bloom's Literary Criticism
An imprint of Infobase Publishing
132 West 31st Street
New York NY 10001

Library of Congress Cataloging-in-Publication Data

Anton Chekhov / edited and with an introduction by Harold Bloom.—New ed.
    p. cm.—(Bloom's modern critical views)
Includes bibliographical references and index.
ISBN 978-1-60413-576-3 (acid-free paper) 1. Chekhov, Anton Pavlovich, 1860–1904—
Criticism and interpretation. I. Bloom, Harold.

PG3458.Z8A523 2009
891.72'3—dc22
                              2009018267

Contents

Editor's Note

My introduction admires Chekhov's plays for their skill in humanizing change, and so in rendering us more humane.

The Cherry Orchard is interpreted by Savely Senderovich as Chekhov's tonal farewell to his art and to his auditors and readers.

Four essays examine the Chekhovian short story. Maggie Christensen stresses Chekhov's offering of shared meaning with his public, while Adrian Hunter describes Constance Garnett's achievement as a translator and its wide influence. Jefferson J. A. Gattrall and Kerry McSweeny center upon the role of subtexts.

Uncle Vania, in Kjeld Bjørnager's view, is a drama of masculine intersections, after which Cynthia Marsh analyzes the subtle temporal pattern of *Three Sisters*.

Mistranslating Chekhov intrigues Robin Milner-Gulland and Olga Soboleva, while "A Boring Story" receives another reading from Pekka Tammi.

Oliver Taplin juxtaposes Chekhov with Greek tragedy, after which Stuart Young concludes this volume by urging a theatrical restoration of Chekhovian skyscapes and vistas.

HAROLD BLOOM

Introduction

ANTON CHEKHOV (1860–1904)

I

Chekhov's best critics tend to agree that he is essentially a dramatist, even as a writer of short stories. Since the action of his plays is both immensely subtle and absolutely ineluctable, the stories also are dramatic in Chekhov's utterly original way. D. S. Mirsky, in his helpful *History of Russian Literature,* rather severely remarks upon "the complete lack of individuality in his characters and in their way of speaking." That seems unjust, but a critic who reads no Russian perhaps cannot dispute Mirsky, who also indicts Chekhov's Russian:

> It is colorless and lacks individuality. He had no feeling for words. No Russian writer of anything like his significance used a language so devoid of all raciness and verve. This makes Chekhov (except for topical allusions, technical terms and occasional catch-words) so easy to translate; of all Russian writers, he has the least to fear from the treachery of translators.

It is difficult to believe that this helps account for the permanent popularity of Chekhov's plays in the English-speaking theater, or of his stories with readers of English. Chekhov, as Mirsky also says, is uniquely original and powerful at one mode of representation in particular: "No writer excels in conveying the mutual unsurpassable isolation of human beings and the impossibility of understanding each other." Mirsky wrote this in 1926, presumably in ignorance of Kafka, before the advent of Beckett, but they

1

verge upon vision or phantasmagoria; Chekhov seems to represent a simpler and more available reality, but by no means a cruder one.

The best critical observation on Chekhov that I have encountered is a remark that Gorky made about the man rather than the stories and plays: "It seems to me that in the presence of Anton Pavlovich, everyone felt an unconscious desire to be simpler, more truthful, more himself." That is the effect upon me of rereading "The Student" or "The Lady with Dog," or of attending a performance of *Three Sisters* or *The Cherry Orchard*. That hardly means we will be made any better by Chekhov, but on some level we will wish we could be better. That desire, however repressed, seems to me an aesthetic rather than a moral phenomenon. Chekhov, with his artist's wisdom, teaches us implicitly that literature is a form of desire and wonder and not a form of the good.

II

As a modern version of *Hamlet, The Seagull* surpasses Pirandello's *Henry IV* and even Beckett's *Endgame,* precisely because its *Hamlet* is so hopelessly weak. I do not mean by this that *The Seagull* is of the dramatic eminence of *Endgame,* or even of *Henry IV;* it is not, and seems to me the weakest and most contrived of Chekhov's four major plays. Its use of *Hamlet,* however, is shrewd and effective, and despite *The Seagull's* limitations, few comedies stage better or remain as authentically funny.

Trigorin, in one of Chekhov's frightening ironies, appears to be a self-parody of Chekhov's own part. One hardly knows who is funnier, more outrageously deceptive, and ultimately self-deceived, the novelist or the actress. Trigorin begins by savoring Nina's naive but sincere offer to be ruined by him, which he, Arkadina, and we know he is going to take up anyway. That makes wholly and deliciously rancid Trigorin's deliberations: "Why do I hear so much sorrow in this cry sent by someone so pure in soul? Why does it wring so much pain in my own heart?" But even better is his address to Arkadina, beginning: "If you wanted to, you could be extraordinary." And yet better is the ferocious hilarity of the exchange after the actress has fallen upon her knees, with Arkadina assuring Trigorin that he is "Russia's one and only hope," and the submissive writer collapsing into: "Take me, carry me off, but just don't let me go one single step away from you." These beauties deserve, and will go on deserving, one another, and Chekhov has achieved the highest comedy with them, rather clearly modeling these extravagant charmers upon his own relation to various actresses.

Wherever it is pure comedy, *The Seagull* seems to me magnificent. Unfortunately, it has two aesthetic disasters, the unfortunate Konstantin, bad writer and mama's boy, who inconsiderately delays shooting himself until the very end of the play, and the aspiring actress Nina, Trigorin's eager victim, whose endless vows of high-mindedness always make me wish a director would interject a rousing chorus or two of Noel Coward's "Don't put your daughter on the stage, Mrs. Worthington—don't put your daughter on the stage!" One sees what Chekhov meant to do with Nina, and Ibsen might have gotten away with it, but Chekhov was too good a comedian not to subvert his own presentation of Nina's idealism. That does not quite save Chekhov, and us, from having to hear Nina proclaim, "Know how to bear your cross and have faith." Subtlest of writers, Chekhov did not make that mistake again in a drama.

III

Eric Bentley, in his superb essay on *Uncle Vanya,* observes that "what makes Chekhov seem most formless is precisely the means by which he achieves strict form—namely, the series of tea-drinkings, arrivals, departures, meals, dances, family gatherings, casual conversations of which his plays are made." This only apparent formlessness, as Bentley goes on to show, allows Chekhov to naturalize such unrealistic conventions as the tirade and "self explaining soliloquies" spoken with others present but with no reference to "Naturalizing the unrealistic" is indeed a summary of Chekhov's dramatic art except that Chekhov's deep wisdom is always to remind us how strange "the realistic" actually is. One might venture, quite naively, that Chekhov's most indisputable power is the impression we almost invariably receive, reading his stories or attending his plays, that here at last is the truth of our existence. It is as though Chekhov's quest had been to refute Nietzsche's declaration that we possess art lest we perish from the truth.

Uncle Vanya, as it happens, is my earliest theatrical memory except for the Yiddish theater, since I saw the Old Vic production when I was a teenager. Alas, I have forgotten Laurence Olivier as Astrov, and even those three extraordinary actresses—Joyce Redman, Sybil Thorndike, Margaret Leighton—but that is because I was so permanently mesmerized by Ralph Richardson as Vanya, a performance eclipsed in my memory only by seeing Richardson, years later, as Falstaff. I have seen *Uncle Vanya* several times since, but in less splendid productions, and like *The Seagull,* it seems to survive any director. The audience discovers what Vanya and Sonya and even Astrov discover: our ordinary existence has a genuine horror in it, however we make the recognition lest we become mad or violent. Sonya's dark, closing tirade can neither be forgotten nor accepted, and makes us reflect that *The Seagull* and *The Cherry Orchard* are subtitled as comedies in four acts, and *Three Sisters* as a drama in four acts, but *Uncle Vanya,* a play where all life must be lived vicariously, has the ironic subtitle "Scenes from Country Life in Four Acts."

Serebriakov is an effective if simplistic representation of all those qualities of obtuseness, vainglory, and ignorance that are the curse of the academic profession at all times and in all places. We are confronted again by the singular power of Chekhov's armory of ironies; it is the low intellectual and spiritual quality of Professor Serebriakov that helps reveal to Vanya and Sonya, Astrov and Yelena, their own lucid consciousnesses and ranges of significant emotion, a revelation that only serves to make a bad enough life still worse for all of them. You shall know the truth and the truth shall make you despair would be the gospel of Anton Chekhov, except that this gloomy genius insists upon being cheerful. As Bentley says, your fate is unsettled because that is how Chekhov sees the truth.

The highest tribute that can be made to *Uncle Vanya* is that the play partakes of the madness of great art; to describe it is to believe that attending it or reading it would be depressing, but the aesthetic dignity of this drama produces a very different effect, somber but strong, a dirge for the unlined life. If *Uncle Vanya* is not quite of the order of *Three Sisters* and *The Cherry Orchard*, still it surpasses *The Seagull* and is imperishable.

IV

Three Sisters seems to me, as to many other readers, Chekhov's masterpiece, outdoing even the grand epilogue to his work in *The Cherry Orchard* and such magnificent stories as "The Darling," "The Lady with Dog," and "The Bishop." But *Three Sisters* is darker even than *Uncle Vanya*, though more vitalistic in that darkness. Howard Moss, in a preternaturally Chekhovian essay on the play, began by noting that "the inability to act becomes the action of the play." That suggests to me a particular tradition in tragedy, one that includes the *Prometheus Bound* of Aeschylus and the Book of Job, and Job's inheritors in Milton's *Samson Agonistes* and Shelley's *The Cenci*. Since *Three Sisters* is not a tragedy, but deliberately only "a drama," of no genre, we are left, perplexed by the play's final effect upon us, which does appear to be a Chekhovian ambiguity.

Moss's comparison to *Hamlet* applies throughout *Three Sisters* far more adequately than in *The Seagull*, though there the use of *Hamlet* is overt. Chekhov's three sisters Olga, Masha, and Irina—together with their brother Andrey, make up a kind of fourfold parody of the prince of Denmark, rather in the way that the Karamazov brothers Ivan, Mitya, Alyosha, and the bastard Smerdyakov—make up a sort of necessarily indeliberate parody of Blake's primordial man, Albion, by way of the Four Zoas who constitute him. Moss justly remarks that Olga is the least interesting of the three sisters, but that is only because Masha and Irina are so profoundly fascinating, and are more at home in the erotic realm than she is. Yet Olga has her own enchantments for the playgoer or reader, being both motherly and exceedingly fragile, incarnating the good, but unable to defend it, whether in herself or others.

An Ibsenite terror, much as we adore her, Masha gives everyone, on stage and in the audience, more truth than anyone can hope to bear, and she certainly is almost too much for her lover, the weak but imaginative Vershinin, who seems to be another of Chekhov's remarkably unflattering self-portraits. We do not know very much about some of the greatest writers of the past, but what we do know about some of the titans, such as Milton and Wordsworth, does not make us love them. Chekhov, of all the major writers, would appear to have been the best human being, something we could hardly know from his various self-presentations.

Masha is more intricate than Irina, but matched by her in vitality. What we remember best about Irina though is her grim metaphor in which she calls herself a locked piano to which she herself has lost the key. She is very young, but maturation will not make her able to return the passions that she so frequently provokes, and even if she reached the Moscow of her visions, her heart would not spring open there. Greatly deluded, Irina takes the erotic place of her dead mother, being her visual representative in the play, yet otherwise strangely unconnected to her. As for Andrey, he is less than his sisters, being little more than an amiable aesthete and his fierce wife's willing victim. Yet he is the artist among the four, even as Masha is the intellectual, Irina the dreamer, and Olga the benign embodiment of maternal care. All of them self-defeating, all worthy of love, all yearners for culture, kindness, and the spirit, the four Prozorovs are quite enough to break the heart of any playgoer.

Hamlet, particularly in Act 5, is beyond our love, and very nearly beyond even the most transcendental of our apprehensions. The sisters' suffering affects us so greatly because, unlike Hamlet, they are within the limits of the possible for us. Alas, they are incapable of learning to live to the full within the limits of the possible for themselves. The sisters' self-frustration remains as much a mystery as their failure to resist their rapacious sister-in-law, Natasha. Moss, again almost more Chekhovian than Chekhov was, insists that they are survivors and not losers, too alive to be quite mortal: "They may languish in life but they refuse to die in art, and with a peculiar insistence—an irony only good plays manage to achieve because it is only on the stage that the human figure is always wholly represented and representative." Chekhov would have agreed, but Tolstoy, as Moss well knows, would not. The sisters lament that they do not know enough, which Moss translates as their stasis, their inability to be elsewhere, to be different, to be in Moscow or in world of open vision. So profound is Chekhov's play that I suspect the sisters must be right. They embody the truth but cannot know it, yet surely that is just as well. Unlike Vanya, they go on living not wholly without hope.

V

The Cherry Orchard is far less intricate in texture than *Three Sisters*, but like that greater play it is of no genre, though Chekhov insisted upon his subtitle: "A Comedy in Four Acts." Whatever Chekhov's intentions, we attend or read the drama now and are compelled to find in it the author's pastoral elegy both for himself and his world. There are strong elements of farce in *The Cherry Orchard*, and the merchant Lopakhin, though he has some complex elements, could be at home in a relatively pure farce. But the distinguished and doom-eager protagonist, Lyubov Andreevna Ranevsskaya, who is fated to lose the cherry orchard, is a figure of immense pathos, stylized yet intensely moving, and she prevents the play from being farce or pure comedy. *The Cherry Orchard* is a lyric meditation—theatrical through and through but a theater-poem, as Francis Fergusson usefully called it.

Genre hardly matters in Chekhov anyway, since like Shakespeare he excelled in the representation of change, or even impending change, and the dramatic image of a crossing or transition necessarily participates in the nature of what Emerson splendidly termed "shooting the gulf" or "darting to an aim." Chekhov is not much interested in the aim or in change as such, so I am impressed by Fergusson's complete phrase for *The Cherry Orchard:* "A Theater-Poem of the suffering of change." The pathos of change in this play is strangely similar to the pathos of stasis in *Three Sisters*, so it seems clear that Chekhov by "change" does not mean anything so vulgar or reductive as social and economic, let alone political metamorphoses. Lopakhin, before the play ends, is almost as much a figure of pathos as Lyubov. It is true that her life has been one long disaster: an alcoholic husband, dead of drink; an endless love affair with a scoundrel, who stole from her and abandoned her; the death by drowning of her little boy; the coming sale of her ancestral property. In contrast to this self-destructive and charming gentlewoman, Lopakhin is a very tough soul archetype of the self-made man. Son of a muzhik, Lopakhin has considerable cruelty in him, but his deep feeling is for Lyubov, with whom we can surmise he always will be, quite hopelessly, in love. But then, so are we, with its endlessly mobile and magnificent woman, this large-souled vision of passion on the old, grand, high scale. In his elegy for himself, the lover of women Anton Chekhov has given us his most vivid representation of an embodied Sublime in Lyubov.

Yet Lopakhin is even more interesting, and perhaps enables us to encounter a more profound pathos. The one respect in which *The Cherry Orchard* could be termed an advance over the astonishing *Three Sisters* is that in his masterpiece, Chekhov had to give us Natasha as a very negative figure. I do not agree with Robert Brustein when he sees Natasha's victory as "the triumph of pure evil" and says she is "without a single redeeming trait." Unlike the sisters, whose vitality is thwarted, the uncultured Natasha is extending the life of the Prozorov family; she is peopling the house with babies, though it is unclear whether they are Prozorovs or the children of her offstage lover, one Protopopov, whose splendid name is that of a contemporary literay critic whom Chekhov despised. In any case, Lopakhin is no Natasha; he is not a villain, but a good man, though clownish and hard, and there is something curiously Shakespearean in his complex mixture of force and nostalgia, his pragmatic workmanship and his reverence for, almost awe of, the glorious Lyubov.

It is almost as frustrating to attempt a description of the aesthetic effects of *The Cherry Orchard* as it is to venture an analysis of the almost absurdly rich *Three Sisters*. Chekhov, in his two finest plays, writes a theatrical poetry that relies upon perspectives unlike any achieved before him. Consider only the famous and weirdly poignant end of Act 3, Lopakhin's great moment, which calls for an extraordinary actor. Chekhov wrote it for Stanislavsky himself, who declined the part. Charles Laughton played it in London in 1933, and I always envision him as Lopakhin when I reread the play. One sees him handling that persuasive antithetical movement from Lopakhin proclaiming, "Music, start playing!" to his tenderly rough reproach to the bitterly weeping Lyubov, until he himself passes to tears, with an immense, "Oh, if only this would pass by as quickly as possible, if only we could hurry and change our life somehow, this unhappy, helter-skelter way we live." The change he wants he cannot have—to be married to Lyubov, eternally too high above him—and his clownish exit ("I can pay for everything!") reverberates darkly as we listen to Anya's ineffectual and self-deceiving but sincere and loving consolation of her mother. We see why Chekhov, in his letters, described Lopakhin as a gentle and honest person, and as a man who did not shout. Chekhov, confronting change, humanized it, and goes on humanizing us.

SAVELY SENDEROVICH

The Cherry Orchard:
Chekhov's Last Testament

As concerns Chekhov's dramatic works, the contemporary criticism is lagging far behind the contemporary theater. Nothing significant has been said about *The Cherry Orchard* for years while new performances, one fancier than the other, are currently mushrooming after many years of drought. Remarkable is not the quantity but the diversity of stage interpretations all of which, however, are aimed in one and the same direction: as far from Chekhov as possible in attempt to reclaim the play by a director. No wonder: this is in the nature of theater. As a good translator is a rival of a poet, so an imaginative director is a rival of the playwright. Be it so: theater is entertainment. Against this background, the task of a literary scholar is modest: how to return the play to the author?

Let me without further ado advance a thesis which would set the desired course. The last work of great poets tends to be his artistic last testament. I think this is very much true in regard to *The Cherry Orchard*. The play has never been looked at from this point of view, meanwhile this is a must if we understand that Chekhov was a great lyrical poet, his choice of genres notwithstanding. Indeed, Chekhov was one of the greatest lyrical writers in Russian literature but not in the trite sense of habitual praises for his mastery in touching the strings of human soul and creating the atmosphere of heart-to-heart talk. What I mean is lyricism in the direct and precise sense.

Russian Literature, Volume 35 (1994/2009): pp. 223–242. Copyright © 1994/2009 Savely Senderovich.

Chekhov was a lyrical poet in the same sense as Pushkin and Byron, Goethe and Verlaine: he was an introspective writer, master of profound individual reflection. As he matured, his personal plight increasingly more defined his choice of problems and ways of their treatment. Chekhov has been rightly compared to Proust.[1]

Although I cannot address here the nature of the whole lyrical, self-expressive perspective in Chekhov, at least a few words must be said. This perspective in Chekhov is intimately related to the components of his texts pointing to and reflecting on his own life and art of writing and his own situation in literature. The presence of this element—ubiquitous indeed— has yet to be acknowledged on its true scale.[2] As concerns Chekhov drama, this feature has drawn some more attention. Having noted that writers and actresses are the main characters in *The Seagull*, Richard Peace convincingly argues, that both Trigorin and Treplev are comical and one-sided mirrors of Chekhov's self-image, such that "[t]he artistic 'duel' between Trigorin and Treplev is the reflection of an argument within Chekhov himself".[3] Helena Tolstoy has persuasively demonstrated that Chekhov's *Ivanov* reflects the inner experience associated with his engagement to Evdokia Efros.[4]

Another feature of Chekhov's poetics, which is particularly relevant here, is the much discussed role of the incidental in his work. Presence of seemingly incidental details in Chekhov's writings has traditionally puzzled critics and has been seen as a salient feature of his style. Already Chekhov's contemporary N. K. Mikhailovsky noticed strange, incidental details in his texts.[5] A century later, A. P. Chudakov pronounced the incidental to be the key feature of Chekhov's style. According to him, Chekhov inserted details functionally irrelevant in the narrative but pointing to the broad open context of the surrounding world; he supposedly favored the incidental in order to reject the positivist view of the world as rationally and neatly organized system.[6] This is one of the crudest misconceptions in Chekhov scholarship, but it gained a wide currency.

The presence of seemingly incidental details in Chekhov's texts is a fact of a paramount significance. They do, indeed, point beyond the immediate context of his narrative or drama, however, not to the open surrounding world but, on the contrary, to the depth of his own world, toward a second context masterfully constructed beyond the one which takes place in the foreground. What looks incidental in Chekhov is incidental only on the surface but actually is an invitation to step into the region of deeper meaning. Seemingly incidental details are superdetermined in regard to the motives of the surface invents. Chekhov's incidental is the most non-incidental that can be in a work of literary art. The proof is in the pudding.

* * *

On October 14, 1903, A. P. Chekhov let his wife, the actress Olga L. Knipper, know by telegraph that the manuscript of *The Cherry Orchard* had been mailed to the directors of The Moscow Art Theater. No sooner was the play received by K. S. Stanislavsky and V. I. Nemirovich-Danchenko than bizarre misunderstandings began to take place. The very next day, October 15, an Odessa newspaper observed of the new Chekhov play: "... *The Cherry Orchard* is the leitmotif of the drama. In the act one, it is in bloom. In bloom are also the young people populating it," and so on.[7] As Chekhov summed it up: "No slightest resemblance" (letter to O. L. Knipper of October 19, 1903). Chekhov took this one philosophically. Then, on October 19, Nikolai Efros, his acquaintance, published an account of the play in the widely read *The Daily News*[8] (it was then reprinted in other papers) containing again a number of distortions. He wrote, as Chekhov himself reported, "that Ranevskaia lives with Ania abroad, lives with a Frenchman; that the act three takes place in an inn [*gostinitsa* instead of *gostinnaia,* living room,—S.S.]; that Lopakhin is a *kulak* (an exploiter), a son of a bitch, etc. etc." (letter to V. I. Nemirovich-Danchenko of October 23). This time Chekhov was furious as seldom happened. In a rather lengthy telegram sent to Chekhov in the 20's of October, in response to an angry telegram by Chekhov, Nemirovich speaks of "an outburst." Few people knew that Chekhov was capable of an outburst. "If I only knew that the Efros's escapade would affect me so badly, I wouldn't have given my play to The Art Theater for anything in the world," wrote Chekhov to Olga Knipper (October 25). This reaction is surprising and seems out of proportion. After all Efros's account was just a brief newspaper correspondence meant to live one day, whereas the play was going to be produced and be judged firsthand by the public. It was going to be produced by Chekhov's friends and admirers, highly talented and well known directors V. I. Nemirovich-Danchenko and K. S. Stanislavsky. It is precisely the incongruity of this reaction that bespeaks its misplaced character. In Chekhov's life as in his work, what seems to be patently incidental often upon scrutiny turns out to be not at all incidental but a metonymic expression of something quite important and profound thus mis- or displaced.

There was nothing extraordinary in the episode of Efros's correspondence, save perhaps a little farcical twist, but such were and are the ways of newspaper journalism and Chekhov knew that as well as anybody—he began his writing career in newspapers. And yet it was, in fact, a rather typical new episode in the chain of customary misapprehensions: Chekhov's fame notwithstanding, he was the most misunderstood Russian writer—be it his prose or drama. Everybody misread him—be it friends, admirers, or arrogant ideologues and the public at large. A graduate of a classical gymnasium, Chekhov surely knew the origin of the word *farce* from the Latin *farcio, farcire* 'to stuff' and presented its symbol—a stuffed bird—in the last act of his *The Seagull*.[9] Chekhov took it for granted that his admirers, friends, collaborators understood him no better than anybody else. Why then his outburst?

It is a well documented and widely cited fact that Chekhov participated in the production of *The Cherry Orchard* and in course of rehearsals introduced a number of changes on directors' and actors' requests. We also know that there were some disagreements between the author and the directors concerning the interpretation of the play. While Chekhov tried to accommodate the needs of friendly directors and actors out of kindness, he was deep down dissatisfied with the whole enterprise. The day after the premiere he wrote to a friend: "My play was played yesterday, therefore my mood is lousy" (to I. L. Shcheglov, January 18, 1904). The directors were not inclined to understand Chekhov's intentions. They saw the play as a *lyrical drama* in the most trite, sentimental sense of the notion and meant to affect a tearful reaction from the public, while Chekhov insisted—in vain—that it was a *comedy*. This discrepancy is well known; it has been widely discussed . . . and largely misinterpreted by historians of theater as well as by Chekhov scholars. It has been habitually explained away as a difference in degree, in the accentuation of various elements of the play, and in the ideological take. The traditional ideological interpretation of this difference can be summed up like this: Chekhov viewed the future of the society more optimistically than Stanislavsky and Nemirovich, therefore he preferred to laugh where they were inclined to shed tears. In order to avoid blaming someone in particular, I shall adduce a summary of typical views given by the commentators in one of the prestigious Chekhov editions:

> Chekhov's dissatisfaction with the Moscow Art Theater was caused apparently by a distortion of necessary proportions on stage. The writer saw in *The Cherry Orchard* both the sad and the ridiculous in a certain combination. The theater did not succeed in finding a suitable measure for each element.[10]

I believe the case was different: the meaning of the play was missed altogether. Chekhov's friends from The Art Theater did not hear the play in his voice and did not heed his hints. He exploded ostensibly on account of N. Efros, but what he actually said was that if he knew that things could turn out this way, he . . . would have not given his play to The Art Theater for anything in the world. He definitely associated the kind of understanding he found in Efros with what he anticipated to happen in The Art Theater. He must have known for himself the real reason of his explosion and—being a kind of permanently guilt-ridden person—expiated it through his faithful collaboration with The Art Theater.

But his mood was justified: the misunderstandings which started then seem to have never ended.

* * *

As *The Cherry Orchard* was written specifically for the Moscow Art Theater, Chekhov was thinking about who should play what role even before he started putting words on paper (letter to O. Knipper of 12.28.1902). Later, he wrote about his concerns in a number of letters addressed to his wife, to Stanislavsky, and to Nemirovich-Danchenko. In the end Chekhov had very little input in the production, and in regard to the most important issues, none whatsoever.

One of Chekhov's main concerns was Lopakhin. He wrote this character with Stanislavsky in mind. The significance of this fact is greater than meets the eye. "The merchant ought to be played by Const. Serg. [Stanislavsky]. This is not a merchant in the vulgar sense of the word, one must understand" (to O. Knipper, 10.28.1903). It must be explained to the unaware non-Russian reader that among Russian educated class the word *merchant*—as well as anything associated with trade or commerce—until the last decade of the 20th century used to have a vulgar ring. Clearly, Chekhov intended to break with the stereotype. His appeal at times sounds like a cry of desperation. Chekhov again: "The Lopakhin role is central one indeed. If it is not played successfully, the whole play would fail" (to O. Knipper, 10.30.1903).

It may seem that Chekhov was wrong. The Lopakhin role was played neither by the performer for whom he intended it nor as the central one, but the play did not fail; on the contrary, it was a success. However, Chekhov's anxiety actually has nothing to do with the failure in the eyes of the public. He speaks of a different, more substantial failure—failure of *his intended meaning* in the play. In the letter to O. Knipper just quoted he goes on: "Lopakhin must be played not by a loud mouth, there is no necessity to make him a merchant." In a letter addressed to Stanislavsky the same day he wrote:

> When I was writing Lopakhin, I thought it was your role . . . Lopakhin, true, is a merchant, but he is a decent man in all regards; he must act in a dignified manner, as an educated person, without trifling or tricks, and thus I was thinking that this role, central in the play, would be a success by you.

Stanislavsky did not heed. The merchant's son Alekseev (Stanislavsky's real name) did not want to play a merchant Ermolai Alekseevich: he preferred to play the gentleman Gaev and by this very choice—Stanislavsky's presence on the stage was an imposing one—made him a figure more central than Lopakhin. He set up a tradition according to which the gentry,

Ranevskaia and Gaev, have been considered the main figures of the play. *The Cherry Orchard* appeared on stage as a play different than it was intended by its author.

It is difficult to blame the followers of Stanislavsky who followed in his footsteps: he had the benefit of the author's participation in the production of the play. And there is no slightest indication in the play that Lopakhin might be an educated person—the signs are rather to the contrary. Besides, there was a realistic canon of presenting a merchant on stage. Chekhov's contemporaries loved recognizing types in literary works. "To follow the routine" *("Dut' v rutinu")* was Chekhov's sarcastic definition of the course taken by a critic who explains his, Chekhov's, characters as types. The typical merchant on stage was everything Chekhov did not want Lopakhin to be. Chekhov's suggestions to the directors seemed to be odd, they were culturally mute.

Let us now summarize what Chekhov said about Lopakhin: 1. He is the central figure in the play. 2. The success of the play depends on the performance of this character. 3. He is not at all a merchant in the stereotypical sense. 4. He is a soft-spoken, intelligent, well-mannered man, he acts as an educated man.

If Lopakhin, according to Chekhov, little resembles a merchant, then he definitely resembles someone else familiar to us. At the very opening of the play Lopakhin says:

> I remember when I was a youngster about fifteen, my father—he's dead now, but at that time he was a shopkeeper in the village here—hit me in the face with his fist, blood ran out of my nose . . . Little peasant . . . [He repeats here a word dropped by Liubov Andreevna Ranevskaia.—S.S.] It's true my father was a peasant, and here I am in the white waistcoat and yellow boots. Like a pig's nozzle showing up in a row of wedding cakes . . . [11]

And at the close of the Act Three he says: "I bought the estate where my grandfather and my father were slaves, where they weren't even allowed to go into the kitchen."

If that resembles anybody, *it is Chekhov himself,* who made a lot of his family story, of the fact that his grandfather was a serf and his father a shopkeeper and a harsh disciplinarian in whose shop he himself worked as a boy. These facts loomed in Chekhov's mind so large that, as we know from his letters, they grew into his familial mythology.

The disclaimer Chekhov puts into Lopakhin's mouth at the beginning of the play comically points to this similarity precisely by denying it in an exaggerated manner:

> Like a pig's nozzle showing up in a row of wedding cakes . . .
> It's just that I am rich, lots of money, but if you really think about
> it and sort things out, you'll know I'm just a peasant through and
> through . . . *(Turns the pages of the book.)* I read this book and didn't
> catch on to a single thing. I was reading and fell right to sleep.

Another comic disclaimer, driven even closer to home, concerns theater:

LOPAKHIN. What a play I saw at the theater yesterday. Really <u>a lot to laugh
at.</u>

LIUBOV ANDREEVNA. <u>And probably there wasn't anything funny in it.</u> Going
to see plays isn't what you people should do. You'd better <u>look at your-
selves</u> a little more often and see what gray lives you all lead, how much
of what you say is unnecessary. (Emphasis added.—S.S.)

Chekhov repeats here what he once said about his own plays to his friend
the writer A. Serebrov (A. N. Tikhonov):

> You say you wept watching my plays . . . You are not
> alone. However, I wrote them not to this end? It was Alekseev
> [Stanislavsky] who made them tearful. I wanted something
> different . . . I wanted only to say to people: <u>look at yourself,</u> look
> how poor and dull is your way of life! (Emphasis added.—S.S.)[12]

Of course, Chekhov would first say so to himself before he reproached
others. Lopakhin takes Ranevskaia's cue seriously. He does look back at himself, which he is inclined to do anyway. This is the cue to the whole play. In
a few minutes of stage time we learn that the funny play was . . . *Hamlet,*
Chekhov's favorite reference in *The Seagull* and other works. This is a cue to
the farcical nature of *The Cherry Orchard.*

At this point we get—at last—an inkling of why Chekhov insisted that
The Cherry Orchard is a comedy. I don't think any explanation of that up to
now has touched on the real nerve of the comic in the play. It is a comedy in
a very special sense: it is a self-referential game in disguise, a travesty, a burlesque. At this point we can surmise an additional reason behind Chekhov's
desire to see Stanslavsky playing Lopakhin: Stanislavsky had an uncanny resemblance to Chekhov, especially on stage—just look at his photograph in
the role of Dr. Astrov in *Uncle Vanya.*

The element of travesty, however, is not limited to the strictly biographical allusions. The fun just begins at that point.

* * *

As much as the merchant is not a usual merchant, the cherry orchard is something else, too. It is too easy to turn it into a symbol. It is Trofimov who does not miss this banal opportunity: "The whole Russia is our orchard," he solemnly proclaims. Chekhov shunned solemn proclamations. Alas, too often this one was taken for granted in spite of the simple fact that Lopakhin had no design concerning the whole Russia.

In the 1980s, at the time of Russian *perestroika*, a leading economist M. Shmelev explained *The Cherry Orchard* in terms of economic reconstruction.[13] Indeed, let us recall Lopakhin's project for the *perestroika* of the cherry orchard; it is the issue on which all the events hinge. A large gentry estate is bankrupt. The cherry orchard is no longer profitable. Lopakhin suggests dividing it into small parcels and building on them summer cottages *(dachi)*. The gentry is distraught by the project, but Lopakhin fulfills it anyway. This reading of the play is indisputable, it makes a lot of sense but falls short of Chekhov's meaning which is a language of economic travesty.

What Chekhov says about Lopakhin's plan presents in economic terms what he himself, in his own understanding, did in Russian literature. Chekhov was the most representative figure for the new developments in Russian literature, which were a change from the literature of gentry to that of the third estate and a transition from the age of the great Russian novel, spacious and cozy like a gentry seat, to the age of the short story. It happened in the early 1880s that the aristocratic tradition of great Russian novel ended, and a new literature of unpretentious and often uncouth short prose came to supplant it. Turgenev, Leo Tolstoy, Dostoevsky, Goncharov were replaced by Leikin, Bilibin, Potapenko, Albov, and in the first place by Chekhov. It became habitual to speak of the decline, decadence in literature. Chekhov did not share this view. The writer A. Serebrov (Tikhonov) recalled: "'There were or are no decadents,' Chekhov mercilessly dealt me a blow. 'Where did you find them? . . . Maupassant in France and I in our country began to write short stories—that is the entire new trend in literature'".[14]

But the novel still remained in contemporaries' minds a symbol of high literary prestige. Chekhov, the author of hundreds of motley stories[15], throughout his life experienced what can be called a complex of *novel-lessness*. His letters profusely testify to his dream of writing a novel. At one point he was even informing his friends that he was writing one. But he could not write a novel. Quite consistently, he considered himself a champion of the whole new breed of short prose writers. He made a point of it. Having received the Pushkin Prize of the Academy of Sciences, he wrote to the publisher A. S. Suvorin:

> I repeat once more: The second and third rate writers who
> publish in newspapers should erect a monument in my honor or at

least present me a silver cigarette-case; I have cleared for them a path to the big magazines, to the laurels and to the hearts of decent people. So far it is my only virtue; as concerns whatever I have written and was awarded the prize for, it won't last in the human memory even ten years. (10.10.1888)

The economic feasibility of short story writing was also not irrelevant in Chekhov's career.[16] Moreover, in a quite bizarre manner, language of economics broke into Chekhov's thinking about the genre re-orientation in literature. Literature and economics were intertwined in Chekhov's mind in a particular odd manner. For years Chekhov dreamt of buying an estate. Having learned that a friend had bought one, he wrote him: "Congratulations on the purchase. I awfully love everything which in Russia is called estate. This word has not yet lost its poetic connotation." (Emphasis added.—S.S. To N. A. Leikin, October 12, 1885.) Besides the application of the epithet *poetic* to the *estate*, a sign of cultural value and the admission of emotional investment in it, there is here also a note of anticipatory nostalgia ("has not yet").

A prefiguration of the theme of *The Cherry Orchard* appears in the fall of 1888, in a letter to brother Alexander:

If our book trade goes well, we'd buy a farm. Save money: for 600 rubles I can buy you a piece of land in such a location that you couldn't have dreamt of. If I buy a farm, I would divide it into plots with the price of each no more than 500–600 rubles. A bearable structure, quite livable, costs also no more than 500–600 rubles depending on the number of rooms. Reckon 100 rubles per room. (October 13, 1888)

Except for the *book trade* (NB a notion which unites literature and trade) as the source of capital, this passage hilariously resembles Lopakhin's project.

The association of such a project with the literary life seems to have been steady in Chekhov's mind. In the summer of 1888, amidst negotiations about the purchase of a farm *(khutor)* on the river Khorol, near Poltava, he wrote to a friend, the poet A. N. Pleshcheev: "If I indeed succeed in buying, I'd build cottages on the banks of the river Khorol and lay the basis of a literary colony" (August 27, 1888).

Thus, long before *The Cherry Orchard*, an association between literature and types of land owning accompanied by strange, indeed, chimerical projects forms in Chekhov's mind. Should we understand this episode literally or as spontaneous bursts of comedic enaction of his obsessive idea?[17]

There was also in Chekhov's mind an association—apparently shared by his contemporaries—of the concept of genre with the forms of land ownership and corresponding social classes. While the landlords and the peasants were favorite subjects of the great Russian novelists, the inhabitants of summer cottages, the summering urbanites *(dachniki)* were among the favorite subjects of the early Chekhov and were never totally forgotten by the later.[18]

In Chekhov's mind, the gentry estates are associated with the novel to such an extent that when one of his protagonists writes novels, he writes of nothing but those estates although he is an urbanite and knows very little about his chosen subject: "In his novels he described only the countryside and gentry estates, although he seldom saw the countryside, only when he visited friends in their summer cottages, while he had visited a gentry seat just once in his entire life." ("Three Years"). Hence the double meaning of a Lopakhin's remark: "Until now, in the country side, there were only landlords and peasants, but recently also summering urbanites have appeared." What Lopakhin says about social life is perfectly true about literature. The dominant genres in literature changed like the forms of land ownership.

Of course, the above adduced quotations from Chekhov which show the association of economic and literary notions in his mind don't do full justice to the writer's world, for they present only the eccentric side of it. This association seems to have a deeper meaning: working land and creating literature presented for Chekhov two parallel spheres of human culture.[19] Here we touch on Chekhov's implicit philosophy; but pursuing this theme would take us too far afield.

The understanding of the play I am trying to offer might have seemed too far fetched, if it did not have an antecedent. At least one perceptive reader took a similar view of *The Cherry Orchard;* the poet Vladimir Mayakovsky wrote in 1914:

> Literature before Chekhov is an orchard by an opulent mansion of a "gentry man." . . .
>
> Almost for a hundred years, writers conjoined by the way of life spoke the same language. The notion of beauty stopped to grow, got detached from the life, and proclaimed itself to be eternal and immortal.
>
> As a consequence, their writing turns into a worn photo of a rich and quiet estate. . . .
>
> Meanwhile, beyond the fence, a little shop has grown into a motley and noisy market place. A discordant crowd of Chekhovian lawyers, excisemen, clerks, and ladies with lap dogs has encroached on the quiet life of estates. . . .
>
> The old beauty began to go to pieces like a corset on a three-hundred-pound priest's daughter.

Under the accompaniment of axes in the cherry orchards? The wardrobe of worn out words was sold out along with gobelins, mahogany in the styles of half-a-dozen Louises.[20]

True, Chekhov's words are not worn out because they don't follow trodden paths, and one has to learn their unique ways.

* * *

The Cherry Orchard is interlaced with literary allusions which might seem to be incidental or ornamental. Who does not remember the funny episode of Gaev's speech to a bookcase? Listen to what Gaev says:

GAEV. Dear, highly honored bookcase! I hail your existence, which for more than one hundred years has been in the service of the shining ideals of goodness and justice. Your silent appeal to fruitful labor has never lessened in the course of a hundred years, upholding *[through tears]* in the generations of our family high spirits and faith in a better future and nurturing in us the ideals of goodness and civic consciousness.

The figurative mode of this passage can be defined as a metonymic substitution: the bookcase stands for any writer who on the occasion of his anniversary appears at the butt of bombastic speeches. And it is what the Russian formalists would later call *obnazhenie priëma,* the laying bare of the device prominent in the play. Actually there is a double metonymic shift here, for not just Gaev's speech but Gaev's very figure is a device. The speech is not a marginal poking of fun at the nincompoop Gaev. It is the *key* to the figure of Gaev which, in turn, is a key to the equivocal language of the text. The very functional justification of the figure of Gaev in the economy of Chekhovian dramatic dialogue lies in his giving cues, in his "incidental" references to literature, which can alert the spectator to the undercurrents, to the travesty of the literary context and Chekhov's own place in it surreptitiously put forward. Besides the speech to the bookcase, Gaev talks to restaurant waiters about the decadents and paraphrases Pushkin's "Whether I walk noisy streets ..."); but above all, he *is* a figure of speech *par excellence* by his whole manner of speech: his "whom?" instead of "what?," his series of remarks like "you smell of chicken" instead of "I detest you," and his jargon of a pool-player. His part is nothing but a series of quasi-quotations which signify presence of a contiguous context. Above all, he speaks a language of duality, of *double-entendre* under any pretext. In his own words, he is getting "a **doublet** sunk in the corner pocket," or sends a ball "off **two** banks into the middle pocket." The pool-player's jargon of Gaev has been of course considered as a totally incidental and marginal element in the verbal texture of the play, a kind of flowery embellishment. It must be noted that the figure of Gaev is drawn unevenly; it carries the imprint of Chekhov's growing infirmity; its functional charge largely fades away in Acts Three and Four.

To what extent precisely the incidental plays a key role in Chekhov's construction of meaning can be seen in the example of a pronouncedly incidental figure, a Passerby in the Act Two. The surface function of this figure is to provoke Ranevskaia's generosity, disproportionate and unbecoming in her situation. But this is a point too trivial and quite redundant. The straightforward and properly dialogic input of the Passerby is his reciting lines of the populist poet Nekrasov and the decadent poet Nadson in such a way as to reveal their manner of expression: their high-blown rhetoric—something which Chekhov couldn't hear without a smile. Facing him even Gaev for once says a sensible thing:

PASSER-BY. May I ask whether I can go from here straight to the railroad station?

GAEV. You can. Take this road.

PASSER-BY. I thank you from the bottom of my heart. *(Having coughed.)* Superb weather . . . *(Recites.)* "O my brother, my suffering brother . . . come out to the Volga; whose moan . . ." *(To Varia.)* Mademoiselle, could you allow a starving Russian thirty kopeks . . .

There is also in the play one Petia Trofimov, a spoof on a literary figure. He is at one remove from being a writer: he makes his living as a translator; more importantly, he speaks like a typical representative of populist literature and is fixated on social problems in their crudest form. He also has a claim on sophistication to which end echoes Nietzsche in the avant-garde style. As far as I know, Chekhov uses ideological positions not so much to paint an ideological picture of society, but rather for two purposes: for psychological characterization, as in "Name Day Party" which is clearly not the case here, or with respect to art, as in "A House with a Mansard." In Chekhov's *Three Years*, his last large prose work, the same set of ideas as announced by Trofimov is discussed precisely in relation to literature to indicate a type of literature:

"A work of fiction is significant and useful only if it contains a serious social problem in its idea," Kostia was saying while angrily looking at Yartsev. "If there is in a literary work a protestation against serfdom or the author is in arms against high society with all its banality, such a work is significant and useful. Novels and tales in which one finds only sentiments—she fell in love with him and he loves her no more—such works, I say, are insignificant and God damn them."

And yet Trofimov's literary sensibility is justified for once when he tells Lopakhin: "Your fingers are delicate and gentle <u>like an artist's</u>." Nobody else is aware of Lopakhin's being not quite a merchant.

* * *

The very embodiment of the incidental in *The Cherry Orchard* is, of course, Charlotte, who has no tangible part to play in the events. She has no points of contact whatsoever with the central figure of Lopakhin. She is an eccentric foreign body and repeatedly says that she does not know where she is from or what she is for. She is German, a former circus performer and a governess without children to educate.

Chekhov attached to the seemingly marginal role of Charlotte a significance which may seem exaggerated and inexplicable. He was concerned with the problem of who would play her before *The Cherry Orchard* was finished (see a letter to O. Knipper of 10.8.1902) and grew more and more concerned with that upon its completion (to O. Knipper of 10.9 and 10.21.1903). In a letter to Nemirovich-Danchenko (11.2.1903) he indicated: "Charlotte is an important role . . . It is a role for M-m Knipper," that is, his wife who was a leading actress in the Art Theater! However, everything that concerned the cast of characters went contrary to his design, and Olga Knipper did not play Charlotte, she played the leading role of Renvskaya opposite Gaev-Stanislavsky.

The association of Charlotte with Olga Knipper is only one of its kind. Chekhov's wife was of German extraction and Chekhov, in his correspondence with her, affectionately calls her "a German," "dear German lady," "little German". The very name Charlotte comes up in Chekhov's correspondence in association with Olga Knipper at the time when early references to *The Cherry Orchard* appear. Chekhov's letters of April–June 1902, that is, on the eve of the period when he actually wrote the play, reveal that at that time Olga was pregnant, then fell seriously ill and lost the child through miscarriage or abortion.[21] On September 10 he wrote to her:

> O, my darling, time is running out on us! When our child will be a year and a half, I will be, in all probability, already bald, gray haired, toothless, and you will be like your aunt Charlotte. [A reference to the real Olga Knipper's aunt Charlotte.—S.S.][22]

The following episode in *The Cherry Orchard* looks like an echo of this letter: "CHARLOTTE. *(Picks up a bundle which resembles a baby in swaddling clothes.)* My baby, sweet dreams . . . (*The crying of a baby is heard,* "Wah, Wah!)" [Emphasis added.—S.S.]. Of course, this is an illusionist trick: there is no child there. This is Charlotte's finale in the play, she appears no more after that.

And again, in Chekhov's mind, Charlotte is not a typical German on the Russian stage. In a letter to Nemirovich-Danchenko quoted earlier he explained:

> Charlotte speaks not broken but pure Russian; only seldom instead
> of a soft consonant at a word's end she pronounces a hard one and
> mixes up the masculine and feminine adjectives.

She was a hard character. Amazingly, Chekhov, closely associated himself with Olga to an extraordinary degree—to a paradoxical swap of inseparable characteristics with her. In his letters, we find him calling her not only the common "my dear half," but referring to himself as "your German husband." Her Germanness becomes his, in view of which his remark about Charlotte's mixing up genders, hardly is accidental.

Charlotte's moment of glory comes in the Act Three, when she shows a cascade of her tricks—here her circus past is justified:

CHARLOTTE. I beg your attention, one more trick. *(Takes a lap robe from a chair.)* Here you see a very fine lap robe, I'd like to sell . . . *(Shakes it.)* Isn't there anyone who'd like to buy it?

PISHCHIK *(surprised).* What do you think of that!

CHARLOTTE. *Ein, zwei, drei!* (*Quickly raises the lap robe which she had low-ered and held like a curtain: behind it stands ANIA, who curtsies, runs to her mother, embraces her, and runs back into the ballroom amid general excitement.)*

LIUBOV ANDREEVNA *[applauds].* Bravo, bravo! . . .

CHARLOTTE. Now once more. *Ein, zwei, drei!* (*Raises the lap robe and behind it stands VARIA, who bows.)*

Besides personal intimations, isn't this a charade presenting the magic power of transformation possessed by a dramatic actress? or, perhaps, present-ing the absolute power of a playwright over his personages? a power of artistic sleight of hand?

So much for a totally "incidental" episode. We really don't know how far Chekhov's jokes go, but a limited attempt at deciphering seems to be worth risking for the simple reason that Chekhov's meaning *is* involuted by its very nature, makes its way through associations and intimations and manifests suggestively and elusively through both the art of expression and the game of hiding.

* * *

It should be clear by now that *The Cherry Orchard* speaks a double language. Behind the references to the commonly familiar and easily comprehensible social reality, this language—by means of odd details, manipulation of polysemy, *sous-entendu*, and private allusions—opens up another field of reference. Such structure of artistic utterance unmistakably exhibits presence of an authorial intention. It would be nice if the fields of secondary reference in the play comprised a perfect ensemble in the manner of instrumental parts within an orchestral score. But they present a welter of undercurrents flowing, however, in one and the same direction. They amount to a referential sphere which concerns literature and literary life, a scene in the center of which stands a figure of one who radically reformed it, whose origins and life are relevant to this reform, who is successful, but acutely feels being misunderstood and lonely.

We are facing here a particularly tricky interpretative problem, and the following question is unavoidable: haven't we gone too far by eliciting Chekhov's private language? To what extent can we take into account the uncommon, esoteric usage of language and hints at intimate circumstances of the author's life which are inaccessible to the common spectator? In the last two centuries European literary sensibility takes it for granted that an artistic expression may bring out from the depth of artists psyche contents which remain hidden in the subtle folds of a text and elusive to such an extent that the artist himself might be not aware of their arrival. In this regard there is no borderline between the dual language accessible to the audience and strictly intimate references. The Moebius strip of artistic expression makes such distinctions irrelevant. By delving into the references inaccessible to the common reader we only confirm that the second perspective has deep roots. After all, Chekhov explicitly insisted that Lopakhin and Charlotte be treated as main characters and that they be played by Stanislavsky and Knipper. By giving Lopakhin his own famous biographical features and unexpected physiognomy ("Your fingers are delicate and gentle like an artist's") the playwright clearly indicated that things are not as they seem to be, that there is a perspective reaching beyond the obvious. The difficulty comes with the question: whom is it addressed? If what is going beyond the obvious shades into the private language of the author, it must be the author himself who is his own primary audience.[23] Could it be that Chekhov did not want the audience to recognize his intimate allusions? This is quite a conundrum.

Let us look into the nature of the double perspective in the play. Double perspectives have place in various kinds of symbolic expressions. The simplest of them is allegory; but what we have in front of us in *The Cherry Orchard* is not an allegory. The façade imagery in the allegory effortlessly yields the second meaning. The façade of *The Cherry Orchard* or its field of primary reference is not transparent: it does not blend with the secondary field of reference; and the total double perspective resists totalization. The foreground perspective, the story of a gentry estate, is self-contained, well inscribed into the ordinarily known and thus easily satisfies the common sense without any further questions. The other perspective lurking behind it breaks in impishly yet in a subtle and unimposing manner. The tension between two perspectives remains unresolved and dramatically played out. If this is not an allegory, then it is a travesty—insofar as we can recognize the author's double in the merchant Lopakhin. It is a grotesque, a preposterous association of irreconcilable elements: the innovative ways in literature presented in the guise of capitalist venture, and the inaccessibly private dressed as the commonly known, even topical. It is as well a burlesque. The disparate and comical invocations of the second reality remind a variety show, a sequence of amusing vignettes emerging in fits and starts. It mockingly strips the author in front of the unaware audience who takes the surface for granted. Chekhov seems to enjoy speaking to the public in his private language imperceptible to the public, and yet he weaves into the score of his play discordant sounds which should convey a sensation of a different music nearby.

This design, apparently incongruous, is anything but senseless. Taking into account the lyrical, expressive aspect in Chekhov shines the necessary light at the play. If we look at readers' and critics' responses to Chekhov's writings, we come to the conclusion that he is the most misunderstood writer in Russian literature—misunderstood and at the same time highly successful, broadly popular! *The Cherry Orchard*'s stage history is a case in point. By presenting Lopakhin's plight, Chekhov makes a statement about his own dual existence in the cultural atmosphere of his time, about his contemporaries who were incorrigibly beyond hearing what he had been saying throughout his whole writing career. And having chosen to tell about his own role on the scene of Russian literature, Chekhov tells it as a private joke, stages a—masochistic?—experiment in being unheard.

The burlesque, the travesty of Chekhov's last play in part lies in plain view while in part it is a private joke. Chekhov was a good judge of his audience and took pleasure in playing a—sadistic?—joke on his audience which remained unaware of his joking on his own account. I put the accent on this circumstance. He was profoundly unhappy with being famous without being understood. The standard public discourse was situated in the socio-economic sphere, and a writer was expected to expose relevant problems. This sphere wasn't alien to Chekhov, a keen observer of social life, but his task was to go deeper, into the existential problems of human life, and that was what the public turned a deaf ear to. He was systematically misread by the most prestigious critics. He never forgot or forgave the failure of the first performance of *The Seagull* on the stage of the Imperial Alexandrine theater. Translation of the personal plight into the language of socio-economic peripeteia amounts to his ironically saying: this is the only language you understand, then, please, have it your way.

An acute bitterness in regard to his situation in literature and at the same time the intention to counter the sadness of it with a joke, to present his own situation as a comedy of misunderstanding—such is the attitude of Chekhov, the lyrical poet, in his final work. Chekhov's last joke is paradoxical: it is a private gag, but not quite hermetic—it cries out for the acknowledgment of its eccentricity. While it remains unrecognized, it is a sad joke, but it is situated in plain view and thus is not entirely hopeless . . . or perhaps even more sad?

The mode of writing displayed by Chekhov in *The Cherry Orchard* was a harbinger of a new epoch in Russian arts which blossomed out in the beginning of the 20th century and is known today as the Silver Age of Russian arts. People of Russian avant-garde theater of that period not by chance felt Chekhov as their predecessor. The epitome of the artistic culture of the period, the play *The Fairground Booth* by Alexander Blok, displayed a mysterious world of one lyrical poet in a sequence of eccentric scenes. The reflection of the poet's self was here no more comprehensible than in Chekhov, but it was foregrounded in its oddity as if the poet were saying to the public: you wouldn't understand my view of myself but that is what I am about. Blok wrote his play just three years after the last Chekov's. One of the most brilliant figures of the period, the playwright, director and theorist N. N. Evreinov introduced the notion of "theater for oneself."[24] His one time associate and an eminent critic in his own right, A. R. Kugel (pen name Homo Novus) reflected somewhat later: "The most typical Chekhov work combining Chekhov's poetry and his world view is *The Cherry Orchard.* The entire play is permeated by <u>ironically sad smile directed at himself</u>" (emphasis added.—S.S.).[25] The aforementioned interpretation of the play by the poet Vladimir Mayakovsky belongs to the same short lived culture. Alas, the disposition allowing an insight into the Chekhov's play was soon lost as a mirage in desert.

In conclusion here is a Chekhov's own comment on how misleading the concentration on the foreground referential plane in art can be. We find it in his last large prose work *Three Years* (the main protagonist of which, one Laptev, is, like Lopakhin, a variation on the theme of the grandson of a slave and the son of a shopkeeper; both carry peasants' names close in sounding, too). It concerns the ways of watching and perceiving painting:

Yulia Sergeevna watched paintings like her husband, through the fist or binoculars, and was overjoyed that people in the picture looked live, and the trees looked real; but she was far from understanding: she thought that there were at the exhibition many similar paintings and that the whole task of art consisted exactly in making sure that the people and things would stand out like real when you were watching them through the fist.

Well, it is up to us whether we choose to view Chekhov "through the fist"—that is, to keep recognizing in *The Cherry Orchard* a faithfully captured conflict between the gentry, the bourgeoisie and the socialist radicals—or to read him with wide-open eyes and hear his unique tone of voice.

NOTES

1. See: Robert L. Jackson, "Chekhov and Proust: A Posing of a Problem" // *The Supernatural in Slavic and Baltic Literatures. Essays in Honor of Victor Terras,* Emy Mandelker and Roberta Reeder, eds. (Columbus, Oh.: Slavica Publishers, 1988), pp. 200–213.

2. See the first profound study of this kind: Michael Finke, "Chekhov's 'Steppe': A Metapoetic Journey" // *Anton Chekhov Rediscovered: A Collection of New Studies with a Comprehensive Bibliography,* S. Senderovich and M. Sendich, eds. (East Lansing, Mich.: Russian Language Journal [Press], 1987) pp. 93–134.

3. Richard Peace, *Chekhov. A Study of the Four Major Plays* (New Haven: Yale University Press, 1983), p. 29.

4. Helena Tolstoy, "From Susanna to Sara: Chekhov in 1886–1887" // *Slavic Review,* v. 50, no. 3 (1991), pp. 590–600.

5. N. K. Mikhailovsky, *Literaturno-kriticheskie stat'i* (Moscow: GIKhL, 1957), p. 559.

6. A. P. Chudakov, *Chekhov's Poetics,* transl. by E. J. Cruise and D. Dragt (Ann Arbor, Mich.: Ardis, 1983).

7. Al. Voznesensky, "Iz Moskvy" // *Odesskie novosti* (1903, no. 6111).

8. [No signature], "'Vishnevyi sad' (novaia piesa A. P. Chekhova)" // *Novosti dnia* (1903, no. 7315).

9. See: Ellen Chancis, "Chekhov's *Seagull:* Ethereal Creature or Stuffed Bird" // *Chekhov's Art of Writing: A Collection of Critical Essays.* Paul Debreczeny and Thomas Eekman, eds. (Columbus, Ohio: Slavica Publishers, 1977), pp. 27–34.

10. A. P. Chekhov, *Sobranie sochinenii* in 12 vv. (Moscow: GIKhL, 1960), v. 9, p. 706.

11. The quotations from *The Cherry Orchard* follow the edition *Anton Chekhov's Plays,* translated and edited by Eugene K. Bristow (New York: W.W. Norton & Co., 1977), sometimes with slight corrections.

12. *Chekhov v vospominaniiakh sovremennikov,* 2nd amended ed. (Moscow: GIKhL, 195), p. 566.

13. Mikhail Shmelev, "Klass, kotorogo net, i klass, kotoryi budet" // *Moskovskie novosti,* 1990, no.8/25, p. 2.

14. *Chekhov v vospominaniiakh sovremennikov,* p. 560.

15. *Motley Stories* is the title of one of Chekhov's collections.

16. This motive was well documented by Laurence Senelick (Tufts University) in the paper "Chekhov and Money" presented at the FIRT International Congress in St. Petersburg on May 23, 2004.

17. One possibility to understand these associations of land broken in parcels and genres of short prose can be found in Chekhov's psychic economy of "partial instincts" which are perspicaciously described in Michael Finke, *Seeing Chechov: Life and Art* (Ithaca Cornell University Press, 2005, "Looking the Part"), pp. 51–98.

18. See Chekhov short stories: "Who out of Three," "The Summering Lady," "The Summering People," "At the Summer Cottage," "The Romance with the Double Base," "Superfluous People," "Calamity," "Talent," "In the Dark," and others.

19. See: Wallace Sherlock, *The Pastoral Theme in the Short Stories of A. P. Chekhov*, A doctoral dissertation (Cornell University, 1996).

20. V. V. Maiakovskii, *Polnoe sobranie sochinenii* (Moscow: GIKhL, 1955), v. 1, p. 298 ("Dva Chekhova").

21. See Chekhov's letters to Olga Knipper and her mother of April through June 1902.

22. Two days earlier, on September 8, Chekhov wrote to Vukol Lavrov: "I will not write play this year," which means that he already thought of it.

23. Vladimir Nabokov, the only true heir to Chekhov's legacy, offered a memorable opinion: "I don't think that an artist should bother about his audience. His best audience is the person he sees in his shaving mirror every morning. I think that the audience and artist imagines, when he imagines that kind of thing, is a room filled with people wearing his own mask" (Vladimir Nabokov, *Strong Opinions,* New York: Vantage International, 1973, p. 18).

24. N. N. Evreinov, *Teatr dlia sebia* in 3 vv. (St. Petersburg: N.I. Butkovskaia, 1911–1917).

25. A. R. Kugel (Homo Novus), *Russkie dramaturgi: Ocherki teatral 'nogo kritika* (Moscow: Mir, 1933), p. 119.

MAGGIE CHRISTENSEN

Re-examining the "Coldly Objective" Point-of-View in Chekhov's "The Bet" and "A Trifle from Life"

Much has been written about Anton Chekhov's "coldly" objective narrative style in his short stories, in which his stories appear to be snapshots of life, with seemingly nothing in between the reader and the story's characters. Conrad Aiken, who calls Chekhov "possibly the greatest writer of the short story who has ever lived" (21), characterizes Chekhov's stories in the "slice of life" tradition. Aiken notes that Chekhov's stories depict the mood of an "actual" moment: "his picture is to be frameless and immediate, so close to us that we can touch it" (23). With Chekhov there is seldom any meddling, opinionated narrator distracting the reader's attention. Chekhov believed his "objective" narrative technique made his short stories more effective. He wrote, "When you depict sad or unlucky people, and want to touch the reader's heart, try to be colder—it gives their grief as it were a background, against which it stands out in greater relief" (qtd. in Friedland 97). He added later: "The more objective the telling, the more powerful the effect produced" (qtd. in Yarmolinsky 210). Chekhov's stories appear simple and "easy to read," and students respond well to what they perceive as his "straightforward" writing style, his interesting characters, and his glimpses into everyday life.

It might seem quixotic, then, to try to use a Chekhov story to discuss narrative point-of-view in stories in which the narrator's presence appears

Eureka Studies in Teaching Short Fiction, Volume 3, Number 1 (Fall 2002): pp. 56–63.

29

muted or even non-existent. Yet in Chekhov's carefully crafted stories, we see his purposeful use of perspective to deftly direct his readers where he wants us to go. The narrative voice in Chekhov's stories, although tangible and palpable, is often so smoothly inserted that we may not immediately notice it. Carefully examining Chekhov's uncluttered narrative style in his short stories can provide students with a clearer understanding of point-of-view and narrative perspective.

Much to the chagrin of their instructors, students often cling to their misguided insistence that a story written in the third-person voice must necessarily be either completely objective or entirely omniscient. In the abstract, students understand "limited omniscience," in which the narrator is inside one or two characters' minds, but somehow students struggle with a story written in third person voice that may exhibit only one perspective (especially if it is an unreliable or selfishly motivated perspective). In addition, a narrator may deliberately disagree with a protagonist, or may try to engage the readers to think differently about a character, further complicating a student's understanding of narrative point-of-view. Many of Chekhov's stories employ this type of narration. Two stories, "The Bet" and "A Trifle from Life," are especially useful examples for examining how the narrative voice is clearly drawn from one particular moral perspective, which is often not the protagonist's. Students can learn, through careful reading and analysis, that Chekhov's narrators often disagree with their characters or function to highlight a character's weakness or foible.

"The Bet" (1888) is the story of a wealthy banker who, after a heated discussion about capital punishment, bets a young lawyer two million rubles that the lawyer cannot remain in solitary confinement for fifteen years. The lawyer agrees to live in captivity in a lodge in the banker's garden under "strictest supervision," and the banker agrees to meet all the lawyer's requests for food, books, musical instruments, wine, and so on, which are to be passed through a small window to prevent any contact with the outside world. The arrangement goes on for fifteen years, until the night before the bet is up. The banker, whose fortunes have taken a downturn and who would be ruined by paying off the bet, slips into the prisoner's room unnoticed, intending to kill the lawyer. He finds a transformed man, aged beyond his years, hunched over a letter, asleep. The banker reads the letter and learns that the lawyer, through his studies over the years, has renounced all worldly possessions and intends to leave early to deliberately forfeit the bet. The banker leaves the room, and the next morning the guards report seeing the prisoner run away.

Although "The Bet" is written in third-person voice, most students recognize (sometimes after prompting) that the story is told from the banker's point-of-view. We are inside the banker's head, hearing his thoughts and intentions and following his actions. In fact, the only places the reader can peek at the lawyer's perspective are in his book requests, the short note he writes around year six, and most important, in his final vitriolic letter in which he reveals he will leave his prison early, thus forfeiting the money. Chekhov's prose may be clean and uncluttered, but this story is no objective 'newspaper' account.

And even though "The Bet" is written from the banker's point-of-view, clearly the narrative voice does not sympathize with the banker. Notice the narrator's choice of words in describing the books selected by the lawyer: "Then after the tenth year, the prisoner sat immovably at the table and read nothing but the Gospel. It seemed strange to the banker that a man who in four years had mastered six hundred learned volumes could *waste* nearly a year over one thin book *easy of comprehension.*" [emphasis added]. (All the primary quotes are taken from the eldritchpress.org web site.) The narrator shows not only the banker's dismissal (or disregard) of Christianity, but also that the banker, looking back after fifteen years, does not, and could not, understand the change in the lawyer.

As the banker contemplates murdering the lawyer to prevent his own financial ruin, the narrator comments:

> Fifteen years before, his millions had been beyond his reckoning; now he was afraid to ask himself which were greater, his debts or his assets. Desperate gambling on the Stock Exchange, wild speculation, and the excitability which he could not get over even in advancing years, had by degrees led to the decline of his fortune, and the proud, fearless, self-confident millionaire had become a banker of middling rank, trembling at every rise and fall in his investments.

Through the narrator's ironic stance here, the reader does not feel sorry for the banker. Rather, we see the narrator's disparaging description of the banker: greedy and desperate enough to consider murder. In fact, the more closely students examine the narrative voice in "The Bet," the more it seems to become a blunt object knocking us on the head to show us how the narrator perceives the banker.

At the end of the story, after the banker reads the lawyer's letter and leaves the lodge weeping, the narrator states, "At no other time, even when he had lost heavily on the Stock Exchange, had he felt so great a contempt for himself. When he got home he lay on his bed, but his tears and emotion kept him for hours from sleeping." Initially students may view the banker's weeping, self-contempt, and sleeplessness as a change in attitude, as some sort of reform in the banker—he has become a changed man. Students should recognize, however, that the banker never strays far from thinking about the stock market and his own fortunes. Furthermore, it is "tears and emotion" that keep him from sleeping, not some sense of guilt or remorse for what he had contemplated. One senses the banker feels relief more than anything. In fact, he does get back to sleep, after crying only a few hours. He is fine in the morning as he gets back down to business: he completely forgets about any potential murder, and he has the foresight to put the letter in a protected place.

So the banker's remorse, if there ever was any, is short-lived. And the banker's actions the next morning support the reading that the banker returned to his same-old-self. After the watchmen tell the banker of the lawyer's escape, he goes to the lodge. The story's last sentence reads, "To avoid arousing unnecessary talk, he took from the table the writing in which the millions were renounced, and when he got home locked it up in the fireproof safe." Rather than referring to the lawyer's letter as the writing that changed the banker's life or enlightened his perspective on the world, the narrator dryly refers to the letter as that document in which the banker's fortune is spared. Some students argue if the banker was a reformed man, he might have kept the letter to remind himself of how close he came to murder or how much the lawyer influenced his life. The problem with this view is that the banker would not have had to lock the letter up; he may even have wanted to share this letter with everyone, to shout it from the mountaintop. A more realistic reading, one supported by the narrative voice, suggests that the banker locks the letter safely away to protect himself in case the lawyer returns to dispute the bet. Once students read carefully, it is difficult to find much sympathy for the banker.

Chekhov's inconclusive ending allows students to speculate on the original question posed by "The Bet," regarding capital punishment versus life imprisonment, or even what happens to someone in solitary confinement. The life imprisonment issue is clouded by two features of this bet: 1) the confinement was not for life, rather a set period of time—fifteen years and 2) his confinement was voluntary—he could leave at any time, which may have changed the dynamics of imprisonment. These issues present good discussion material. In, addition, students love to write on the question, "Who won the bet?" Many argue persuasively that even though the banker kept his money, the lawyer really won since he gained knowledge, wisdom, and so on. They like the idea of having time to lie around, be waited on, read and just think about life as the lawyer did. (Anyone who pursues this train of thought for too long is directed to the passage describing the lawyer's wretched physical deterioration at age 40.) Furthermore, after a bit of discussion, someone inevitably points out that the lawyer did not sound happy, peaceful, or fulfilled in his letter, and close inspection of the bitter tone of the letter (in which he uses the word "despise" at least five times) raises additional questions. The students speculate, and even write on, what will happen to the lawyer once he leaves confinement. Many suggest he will become a hermit or throw himself off a cliff in despair. So, we ask again, who really won the bet. In answer, we plunge into further discussion, critical thinking, and textual analysis.

At some point in an advanced discussion, I mention that Chekhov originally published an additional section at the end of "The Bet," in which the lawyer returns after a year to demand some money, and the banker has meanwhile made yet another foolish bet. This addition reveals even more woes of the banker, especially his gambling trouble, and ends on a more conclusive and definitive note. Chekhov chose to cut the ending and stop the story where we see it now, but students can read the original ending in Koteliansky (236–239), which can be a valuable assignment for students to gain insight into Chekhov's writing process and, perhaps, his motives.

Another useful story to demonstrate Chekhov's narrative technique is "A Trifle from Life" (1886). In this story, Nikolay Ilyitch Belyaev comes to visit his romantic interest, Olga Ivanovna, a married woman who is separated from her husband and has two children. Since Olga is not home, Nikolay sits down to wait and encounters her eight-year old son Alyosha, whom he had never really noticed before. As they visit, Nikolay learns that Olga's servant Pelagea secretly takes the children to meet their father twice a week. Nikolay is surprised at the news, but indignant that the father seems to blame Nikolay for the break-up of their marriage. Alyosha begs Nikolay not to say anything to his mother, and Nikolay promises, only to immediately break his pledge and proceed to tell Olga when she enters. Of course, Alyosha is crushed at Nikolay's betrayal.

In "Trifle" Chekhov demonstrates his interest in the dramatic narrative, in that this story is almost completely dialogue. Critic Ronald L. Johnson, referring to "Trifle," notes that "this story shows [Chekhov] at his strongest in the sparser, more objective, dramatically focused narrative" (29). The narrator appears almost non-existent, so readers just watch the action unfold before us, "objectively." Yet the story is not *completely* dialogue, and the narrator has ample opportunity, particularly in the first and final paragraphs of the story, to shape and direct the readers' responses. Although "Trifle" is narrated primarily in third-person voice, early in the story the narrator refers to Nikolay as "my hero." The narrative perspective seems to be from Nikolay's point-of-view, and initially readers may feel sorry for Nikolay and his rather boring romance: "And, indeed, the first interesting and enthusiastic pages of this romance had long been perused; now the pages dragged on, and still dragged on, without presenting anything new or of interest." We observe the sitting room incident through Nikolay's eyes, but if readers ever felt sorry for Nikolay, by the middle of the story it becomes clear that Nikolay is not a sympathetic character since he betrays the boy's trust and shows himself to be completely self-centered. In fact, Nikolay becomes downright repulsive, and the narrator's early reference

to Nikolay as "my hero" now seems sarcastic. Moreover, the narrator continues to underline how indignant and hurt Nikolay felt, even to the point of
absurdity. When Nikolay drops the bomb on Olga Ivanovna, he still can only
worry about himself: "Your Pelagea, like a regular fool, takes them about to
restaurants and arranges meetings with their papa. But that's not the point:
the point is that their dear papa is a victim, while I'm a wretch who has broken up both your lives . . ." His whiney tone is outweighed only by the shock
he gives to the various characters, as well as to the reader. The description of
his final interaction with Alyosha drips with irony:

> "Nikolay Ilyitch," moaned Alyosha. "Why, you promised on
> your word of honour!"
> "Oh, get away!" said Belyaev, waving him off. "This is more
> important than any word of honour. It's the hypocrisy revolts me,
> the lying! . . ."

By this time the reader is dumbfound at the sheer gall of Nikolay to
mention hypocrisy when he had just promised on his honor to keep Alyosha's
secret. The narrative voice, which initially appeared to sympathize with Nikolay, closes the story with a completely ironic tone: "Belyaev dismissed him
with a wave of his hand, and went on walking up and down. He was absorbed
in his grievance and was oblivious of the boy's presence, as he always had
been. He, a grownup, serious person, had no thought to spare for boys." As
readers we recognize (and applaud) the biting tone the narrator uses toward
Nikolay's indefensible actions, and we are brought into consort with the narrator against Nikolay.

In "Trifle" students quickly pick up on the idea of innocence lost; that
is, Alyosha's trust is shattered through Nikolay's betrayal. The narrator notes
that Alyosha "was trembling, stammering, and crying. It was the first time
in his life that he had been brought into such coarse contact with lying." The
recognition carries even more weight because the reader participates in making meaning, that is, the narrator allows the readers to observe the casualness
with which Nikolay betrays the boy—immediately, and with absolutely no regard for the boy's feelings. In addition, the effects of the mother's relationship
with Nikolay (when her husband is still alive and around) are never addressed
directly, but certainly and deliberately left for the reader to piece together.
Johnson suggests that Chekhov "illustrates the painful, forced involvement of
the other family members in the situation" (29). Early in the story the narrator notes that Nikolay "had completely ignored [Alyosha's] existence; the boy
had been before his eyes, but he had not cared to think why he was there and
what part he was playing." Close readers will realize that the narrator points
out that Nikolay never really thought about (or didn't want to admit to) the

effects of his adulterous relationship on the children. Students also will want to discuss the ironic title as well, since the incident was not trifling for either Nikolay or Alyosha, but for vastly different reasons.

A close reading of "The Bet" and "A Trifle from Life," with attention to narrative voice, gives students a good idea not only of Chekhov's mastery of storytelling, but also a sense of the possibilities of narration. Chekhov's narrators may seem to be "coldly objective," yet they help readers construct meaning of the stories. Students can vividly see how a third-person narrator may disagree morally with a protagonist, or point the reader in a specific direction, without meddling or sermonizing. In this way, Chekhov allows readers to become part of the conversation, which continues into class discussion and student writing. Students will become more attuned to the value of paying attention to how a story is told, especially the narrative perspective and motivation.

NOTE

Two hundred and one of Chekhov's short stories are available online, in Constance Garnett's translations, at the following web address: www.eldritchpress. org/ac/jr/ allowing instructors to make selections and decide how they wish to cover this influential short story author.

WORKS CITED

Aiken, Conrad. "Anton Chekhov." *Critical Essays on Anton Chekhov.* Ed. Thomas A. Eckman. Boston: G.K. Hall, 1989. 21–25.

Chekhov, Anton. "The Bet." (1888). Trans. Constance Garnett. Online. www.eldritchprcss. org/ac/jr/154.htm

———. "A Trifle from Life." (1886). Trans. Constance Garnett. Online. www.eldritchpress. org/ac/jr/083.htm

Friedland, Louis S., Ed. *Letters on the Short Story, the Drama, and Other Literary Topics by Anton Chekhov.* New York: Benjamin Blom, 1964.

Johnson, Ronald L. *Anton Chekhov: A Study of the Short Fiction.* New York: Twayne, 1993.

Koteliansky, S. S., Ed. *Anton Tchekhov. Literary and Theatrical Reminiscences.* New York: Benjamin Blom, 1965.

Yarmolinsky, Avrahm. *Letters of Anton Chekhov.* New York: Viking Press, 1973.

ADRIAN HUNTER

Constance Garnett's Chekhov
and the Modernist Short Story

Writing in 1974, the critic Roberta Rubenstein complained that Constance Garnett had not received proper recognition for her contribution to the literature of the English-speaking world. Determined to 'find out more about the woman who had translated such an astonishing number of books',[1] Rubenstein approached Constance's son, David Garnett, who furnished her with a portrait of a retiring, easily amused woman, inclined to vanity only in respect of her own intelligence, and firmly convinced of the value of free love, early sexual experience for women, and a doctrine of economic self-reliance. The world has since learned much more about Constance Garnett from her grandson, Richard, who in 1991 published her biography under the title *A Heroic Life*.[2] Yet the tendency to overlook Garnett persists, and the neglect is nowhere more evident than in the study of how her translations have affected anglophone literary culture. It is widely understood that Garnett's work was fundamental in introducing English speakers to the Russian masters and that the course of European and American modernism was altered by her rapid output of some sixty volumes of Tolstoy, Gogol, Dostoyevsky, and Chekhov, among others: but this is to say little of the nature of the work itself, or of precisely how it affected the English writers who read it. In this essay, I want to examine the response to Garnett's translations of Chekhov's stories by modernist writers, and to argue that it was in

Translation & Literature, Volume 12, Number 1 (Spring 2003): pp. 69–87. Copyright © 2003 Adrian Hunter.

fact the particular qualities of her renderings that shaped the development
of the short story in English.

Reviewing Garnett's achievement in 1947, the Russian historian Edward
Crankshaw claimed that, having 'entered in their full stature into English literature', her translations of Chekhov's stories decisively altered it: 'in effect
... Mrs. Garnett gave us a new literature'. Crankshaw went on to describe
how Garnett's work 'completely revolutionized the English short story' by
bringing off the central feature of the Chekhovian text, its 'faultless, matter-
of-fact rendering of the complex states of mind and being of ordinary people'.
In the absence of such a sensitive and faithful translator, he concluded, the
stories of D. H. Lawrence, Katherine Mansfield, A. E. Coppard, and H. E.
Bates would be 'unthinkable'.[3]

Crankshaw's large claims are borne out by the response of the modernist writers themselves to the Chekhov volumes as they appeared in the
years 1916–1922. Taken together, their comments amount to a remarkable
study in the emergence of a new literary form and the evolution of a set of
aesthetic criteria for describing it. For John Middleton Murray, writing in *The
Athenaeum* in 1922, the effect of Garnett's Chekhov was nothing less than
revolutionary, marking off his generation from its predecessors as decisively
as the writings of Darwin had separated out the Victorians. In particular, it is
Chekhov's 'plotlessness' which emerges as the most significant aspect of the
stories for Murray, and he singles out they way in which Garnett brings over
this 'bewildering' absence of conventional narrative organization:

> Tchehov's breach with the classical tradition is the most significant
> event in modern literature ... Tchehov wanted to prove nothing,
> because he profoundly believed there was nothing to be proved.
> Life was neither good nor bad; it was simply Life, given, unique,
> irreducible.[4]

Murray's interest lies in the way the Chekhovian story stops short, and in
the implications of this refusal to fulfil casual expectations in narrative.

Virginia Woolf and Katherine Mansfield also light upon what may be
termed the 'interrogative' quality of Chekhov's fiction. Mansfield's attachment
to Chekhov has long been the subject of controversy, owing to the accusa-
tion, first levelled by Elisabeth Schneider in 1935, that her story 'The Child-
Who-Was-Tired' plagiarized Chekhov's 'Sleepyhead'.[5] Whatever the extent
and nature of the debt in that particular story, Mansfield's critical observations reveal the importance of Chekhov to her developing sense of the form
the short story might take. She writes to Woolf (27 May 1919) of a letter
of Chekhov's published in *The Athenaeum:* 'what the writer does is not so
much *solve* the question but *put* ... the question. There must be the question

put. That seems to me a very nice dividing line between the true and the false writer.'[6] The following month she is reflecting to S. S. Koteliansky (with whom she translated some of Chekhov's correspondence) that this refusal to 'solve' seems 'one of the most valuable things I have ever read, It opens—it discovers rather, a new world' (*Letters*, II, 324). In her readings of Garnett's Chekhov it is this irresolute quality above all that interests Mansfield, and particularly the way in which consequential relationships between elements in the Chekhovian narrative are suppressed. She writes, again to Koteliansky, of Garnett's translation of 'The Steppe' (from *The Bishop and Other Stories*) that it has apparently 'no beginning or end', and she marvels at the compositional method by which Chekhov 'touche[s] one point with his pen—and then another point—enclos[ing] something which had, as it were, been there for ever' (*Letters*, II, 353).

Woolf, too, admires the way in which Chekhov's narratives so bravely advance towards irresolution and even misapprehension, the way the reader is left hanging, 'asking questions in mid air . . . giddy, uncomfortable'. Like Mansfield, she notes the blatancy of Chekhov's refusal to supply answers to the very questions his stories pose:

> The recurrence of th[ese] question[s], not only in the form of an actual note of interrogation but in the choice of incidents and of endings, produces at first a queer feeling that the solid ground upon which we expected to make a safe landing has been twitched from under us . . . But imperceptibly things arrange themselves, and we come to feel that the horizon is much wider from this point of view; we have gained an astonishing sense of freedom.[7]

Both Woolf and Mansfield are intrigued by the apparent discrepancy between what is said and what is implied in the Chekhovian story. Despite the restricted articulation, there is no corresponding reduction in complexity or implication, indeed quite the reverse: meaning seems to amplify outward from the curtailed centre. Their enthusiasm for this effect is reminiscent of Henry James, who, in the Preface to *The Lesson of the Master*, envisages a kind of short story in which it will be possible 'to do the complicated thing with a strong brevity and lucidity—to arrive, on behalf of the multiplicity, at a certain science of control'.[8]

The idea of a 'science of control', in which the 'shortness' of the short story is more than a matter of condensation or compression, recurs throughout definitions of the form by its key practitioners in English. Elizabeth Bowen, in her 1936 introduction to *The Faber Book of Modern Short Stories*, conceives of the modern story as one proving an 'urgent aesthetic necessity' in which 'shortness' is a 'positive' quality, rather than merely 'non-extension'.[9]

In similar terms, Frank O'Connor distinguishes between a brevity motivated by 'convenience' and one motivated by 'its own necessities'.[10] And H. E. Bates, addressing Garnett's Chekhov, defines the 'art of distillation' as a matter of withholding what may amount to crucial orientational material from the narrative, thereby placing 'immense responsibility on the reader'.[11] In all these comments, what is envisaged is a species of short fiction distinct from the plot-bound Victorian tale, a form which was dependent on novelistic compositional conventions. When, in his apologetic preface to the 'Charles Dickens' edition of *Christmas Stories* (1852), Dickens complained that the 'narrow space' within which it was necessary to confine his Christmas stories meant that he 'could not attempt great elaboration of detail, in the working out of character',[12] he was reflecting the widespread Victorian difficulty in conceiving of an aesthetic of the short story which was distinct from novelistic practice. Dickens was certainly aware that condensation necessitated a different approach, but considered this a confinement and limitation of his full expressive capacity. That the form did not allow him to individuate character through 'great elaboration of detail' was for him a privation rather than a stimulus to a new conception of characterization. As Henry James later observed in an essay on Maupassant, the Victorians preferred their fiction 'rather by the volume than by the page'.[13] Short pose works tended to be considered uncertain fragments of a meaningful whole, and emerged from the English novelist, as H. E. Bates describes, laden with novelistic tropes 'like a baby fed on a diet of two-inch steaks and porter'. It is Bates' contention that no English nineteenth-century writer applied to the short story 'a technique different from that of the novel'. Rather, they tended to construct their tales around the twin axes of historical sequence and social survey—what Wendell Harris terms a 'longitudinal tracing of sequence and the latitudinal or comprehensive survey of interrelationships'.[14] Failing to appreciate the formal distinctiveness of the short story, the Victorians simply applied to it the rules of novel writing, and to no great effect.

It is in their encounter with Garnett's Chekhov that Woolf and Mansfield, and later Frank O'Connor and Elizabeth Bowen, discover how the short story can distinguish itself as something other than a miniaturized novel by resisting novelistic strategies of continuity and identification, seeking an 'open', interrogative effect rather than a 'closed', declarative one. For Woolf, this breakthrough is significant in terms of her thinking about the new operative principles of modern fiction. She explains how Chekhov's short stories offer a form into which she can escape from the burden of Victorian narrative convention:

Where the tune is familiar and the end emphatic—lovers united, villains discomfited, intrigues exposed—as it is in most Victorian fiction, we can scarcely go wrong, but where the tune is unfamiliar and the end a note of interrogation or merely the information that they went on talking, as it is in Tchehov, we need a very daring and alert sense of literature to make us hear the tune.[15]

That ultimate 'note of interrogation' is precisely what the Victorian story is shy of; what Woolf saw in Garnett's Chekhov was a kind of short fiction in which it could be sounded at every level in the text. In such a story, narrative elements would not be reduced to a functional role in the unravelling of plot, but would be able to float free of determinate structures. Individual scenes—what Woolf elsewhere termed 'evanescent moments'[16]—could come and go with no obligation to sustain narrative unity or even continuity. As Elizabeth Bowen was later to describe it, the Chekhovian story introduced a species of short fiction ungoverned by the 'astringency' and 'iron relevance' of plot, and able instead to 'let in what might appear inchoate or nebulous' (*Collected Impressions*, p. 39). In her review of Garnett's volume *The Bishop and Other Stories* (1919), Woolf remarks that 'inconclusive stories' are made 'legitimate' by the way in which, despite leaving the reader feeling 'melancholy and perhaps uncertain', they nevertheless 'provide a meeting point for the mind—a solid object casting its shade of reflection and speculation'.[17] By abandoning formal closure, such stories liberate that multiplicity of meaning which James envisaged for the short form: by their very brevity they excite the co-productive capacity of the reader. Woolf uncovers in Garnett's Chekhov a new kind of transaction between writer and reader in which the author is released from the obligation to provide any interpretative content in the narrative.[18]

We can see Woolf experimenting with the 'note of interrogation' in a story written contemporaneously with the Garnett review. 'An Unwritten Novel' concerns an encounter between an unnamed narrator and a woman on a train, with the narrator composing an imaginary identity and set of relationships for the strangers, as though she were a character in a novel being written by the narrator. The narrator conjures up novelistic scenarios for the woman, whom she names Minnie Marsh, in keeping with various storytelling conventions. So, she speculates, Minnie must have 'committed some crime!'; she must be susceptible to psychoanalytic explication ('They would say she kept her sorrow, suppressed her secret—her sex, they'd say—the scientific people'); and when she walks on the beach 'there must be preachers along the sands'.[19] And once a narrative detail is specified, the narrator is burdened with the obligation to reveal its significance for the narrative as a whole:

> But what I cannot thus eliminate, what I must, head down, eyes shut, with the courage of a battalion and the blindness of a bull,

charge and disperse are, indubitably, the figures behind the ferns, commercial travellers. There I've hidden them all this time in the hope that somehow they'd disappear, or better still emerge, as indeed they must, if the story's to go on gathering richness and rotundity, destiny and tragedy, as stories should.

(pp. 31–32)

As stories should, but this one won't. The narrator is conscious of the contract binding on any act of storytelling that causal expectations will be fulfilled, that anything which gains admittance to the narrative—even the figures behind the ferns—will finally be made to count. But Minnie's story refuses to come to order. At the end, she alights from the train to be met by her son, thereby ruining the narrator's speculations on her character. But even then, doubt as to the woman's identity remains; there is room yet for imagination: 'A strange young man . . . There's something queer in her cloak as it blows. Oh, but it's untrue, it's indecent' (p. 36). The story ends with the narrator acknowledging the failure of her conventional narrative aspirations, but descrying a new set of compositional possibilities:

And yet the last look of them—he stepping from the kerb and she following him round the edge of the big building brims me with wonder—floods me anew. Mysterious figures! Mother and son. Who are you? Why do you walk down the street? Where tonight will you sleep, and then, tomorrow? Oh, how it whirls and surges—floats me afresh! I start after them. People drive this way and that. The white light splutters and pours. Plateglass windows. Carnations; chrysanthemums. Ivy in dark gardens. Milk carts at the door. Wherever I go, mysterious figures, I see you, turning the corner, mothers and sons; you, you, you. I hasten, I follow. This, I fancy, must be the sea. Grey is the landscape; dim as ashes; the water murmurs and moves. If I fall on my knees, if I go through the ritual, the ancient antics, it's you, unknown figures, you I adore; if I open my arms, it's you I embrace, you I draw to me—adorable world!

(p. 36)

Like Poe's man of the crowd, the populace of Woolf's story is finally inscrutable. Elizabeth Bowen once said that she tried to render in her stories the sense of 'human unknowableness'.[20] Even though 'Minnie' and her son take on flesh, become, in the phrase Woolf uses in the Garnett review (and which provides the title of another of her stories), 'solid objects', they are unknowable, objects not of definition but of 'reflection and specula-tion'. They are perceived rather than interpreted. This method of rendering perception without interpretation is what Woolf admired so much in Garnett's Chekhov, and in her own short fiction she experimented with ways in which similar interrogative effects might be produced. Her understanding of this disruptive potential in the short story has its origin in her sensitivity to the implications of 'plotlessness' in the Chekhovian text.

Dominic Head argues that in her short stories Woolf can be seen 'continually reacting against, revolving around, conventional story types'.[21] But more explicitly in 'An Unwritten Novel', Woolf is writing against what she sees as a specifically novelistic burden of plot and character convention, and setting the radically interrogative short story off against that. It is useful to acknowledge the critical relationship between the two forms, because it is Woolf's experiments in short fiction which lead her out of the 'exercise in the conventional style' of her early novels. She writes to Ethyl Smyth of 'An Unwritten Novel':

> [That] was the great discovery . . . That—again in one second—showed me how I could embody all my deposit of experience in a shape that fitted it—not that I have ever reached that end; but anyhow I saw, branching out of the tunnel I made, when I discovered that method of approach, Jacobs Room, Mrs Dalloway etc—How I trembled with excitement; and then Leonard came in, and I drank my milk, and concealed my excitement, and wrote I suppose another page of that interminable Night and Day (which some say is my best book).[22]

Woolf's diary entry for 26 January 1920 (a few months before she began work on *Jacob's Room*) confirms the importance of her discoveries in the short story for the writing of her novels. She tells there of how she 'arrived at some idea of a new form for a new novel. Suppose one thing should open out of another—as in *An Unwritten Novel*—not only for 10 pages but for 200 or so.' This new kind of novel will be marked by its interstices and structural occlusions: it will bear 'no scaffolding; hardly a brick to be seen':

> Then I'll find room for so much—a gaiety—an inconsequence—a light spirited stepping out at my own sweet will. Whether I'm sufficiently mistress of things—that's the doubt; but conceive 'Mark on the Wall', 'Kew Gardens' and unwritten novel taking hands and dancing in unity.
>
> (*Diary*, II, 13–14)

As with her observations on Chekhov, it is the freedom of inconsequence that so engages Woolf about this kind of short fiction. Indeed, it is not too much to say that her discovery of the episodic narrative structure came largely through her experimentation with the short story. That individual episodes could remain as self-sufficient narratives in Woolf's mind is borne out by the story 'A Woman's College From Outside' which originally formed a chapter in *Jacob's Room* but which was subsequently removed and allowed to stand as a story in its own right. That it could do so suggests a process of composition in which the interrogative short fiction was the controlling generic model in Woolf's manner of seeing, remembering, and writing.

Clearly, Garnett's Chekhov is crucial to the modernist project of defining and developing the theory and practice of the short story, and, in the case of Woolf, the effort to transform narrative generally. But oddly, recent criticism which accounts for the impact of Chekhov on the form in English tends to remove Garnett from the picture. The leading short story critic Charles E. May, for example, in an essay which surveys various aspects of the Russian's influence, takes no notice of the fact that he is citing from Garnett's translations, despite the detailed claims he makes based on specific effects of the writing.[23] Likewise, Eudora Welty, discussing the importance of Chekhov in her own story-writing, fails to acknowledge Garnett even though her observations of how Chekhov 'revolutioniz[es] . . . the short story' are based on Garnett's translations of 'The Privy Councillor' and 'The Steppe'.[24] The question is, does this matter? Can we say that the enthusiastic response to Chekhov by English-speaking writers, and their subsequent theorizing about short story form, is in any meaningful way the result of particular qualities in Garnett's renderings? Garnett herself seemed happy to be overlooked in her texts: indeed, her son, David, comments on how she 'found it an agony to write anything original', hesitating even over the composition of reviews and biographical notes on the authors she translated.[25] But, faced with the fact that Woolf, Mansfield, and numerous short story theorists and critics throughout the twentieth century are reacting specifically to her versions, we have to ask whether there is anything to be gained from making Garnett visible in the story of Chekhov's legacy. I think there is, and I would argue that the aspects of Chekhov to which the modernists respond, and upon which so much of their thinking about the short story depends, are communicated more forcefully in Garnett than in any other translator of the time.

The special qualities of Garnett's work can be demonstrated, to begin with, by a comparison of her translation of 'The Bishop', which Woolf read and reviewed, with a version by her contemporary, Marian Fell, whose two volumes of Chekhov stories were published in London by Duckworth in 1914–1915. 'The Bishop' tells of Bishop Pyotr ('Reverend Peter' in Fell's version), a young ecclesiastic, who, in poor health, undertakes a punishing schedule of Easter week services which leads ultimately to his demise. The story begins on Palm Sunday, when the bishop, conducting evening worship in a crowded and overheated church, begins to feel unwell. Garnett's translation continues:

> And then all of a sudden, as though in a dream or delirium, it seemed to the bishop as though his mother Marya Timofyevna, whom he had not seen for nine years, or some old woman just like his mother, came up to him out of the crowd, and, after taking a palm branch from him, walked away looking at him all the while good-humouredly with a kind, joyful smile until she was lost in the crowd. And for some reason tears flowed down his face. There was peace in his heart, everything was well, yet he kept gazing fixedly towards the left choir, where the prayers were being read, where in the dusk of evening you could not recognize anyone, and—wept. Tears glistened on his face and on his beard. Here someone close at hand was weeping, then someone else farther away, then others and still others, and little by little the church was filled with soft weeping. And a little later, within five minutes, the nuns' choir was singing; no one was weeping and everything was as before.[26]

For immediate comparison, here is Fell's version of the same scene:

> And now, as a climax, his Reverence saw, as in a delirium, his own mother whom he had not seen for nine years coming toward him in the crowd. She, or an old woman exactly like her, took a palm leaf from his hands, and moved away looking at him all the while with a glad, sweet smile, until she was lost in the crowd. And for some reason the tears began to course down his cheeks. His heart was happy and peaceful, but his eyes were fixed on a distant part of the chapel where the prayers were being read, and where no human being could be distinguished among the shadows. The tears glistened on his cheeks and beard. Then someone who was standing near him began to weep, too, and then another, and then another, until little by little the chapel was filled with a low sound of weeping. Then they convent choir began to sing, the weeping stopped, and everything went on as before.[27]

As well as the general awkwardness of Fell's expression—'And now, as in a climax, his Reverence saw, as in a delirium'—an obvious point of difference between these passages is that Garnett refuses to allow trivial connections, particularly in the final sentences. Fell, by contrast, employs a simple causal logic to explain how one thing leads to another in the scene. The weeping that fills the church, Fell's rendering implies, is triggered by the weeping of the bishop: 'Then some one who was standing near him began to weep, too.' Garnett, in contrast, has the bishop come upon the weeping, and focuses through his uncertain apprehension of how, why, or when it began. In other words, Garnett's version provides more of an interior perspective. The final sentence in the Fell is similarly hidebound in its tripartite logic: the choir sings, this causes the weeping to stop, with the result that normality is resumed. Garnett disrupts that narrative simplicity: in her version the choir music neither stems the weeping nor brings the kirk to order. She suppresses causal connections, presenting contiguities rather than continuities. In Mansfield's terms, one has the sense of questions posed rather than answers given. Where the Garnett is scrupulously perceptive, the Fell is glibly interpretative.

More substantially, Fell tends to trivialize important adjectival phrases. The mother's 'glad, sweet smile' (Fell) is far less suggestive of the woman's actions and, moreover, of the bishop's emotional susceptibility to her, than Garnett's fuller rendering in which the mother looks at her son 'good-humouredly with a kind, joyful smile'. Given that the story centres around the bishop's anxiety that he has lost intimacy with his mother since being ordained, and that she is intimidated into politeness in his company, Garnett is careful to convey an impression not just of the mother but of the son's need for her 'kindness'. Fell's brisk 'glad, sweet smile' carries none of this, and hence misses out early in the story on what will prove a significant aspect of the characterization of the bishop. Here again, as throughout her translations, Garnett is more successful in conveying interiority. Charles E. May observes that the technique of creating 'an illusion of inner reality by focusing on external details' is one of Chekhov's most important contributions to the short story in English ('Chekhov', p. 202). More precisely, one might say that Chekhov's narratorial observations frequently carry within them traces of his characters' points of view. This is decisive in the case of 'The Bishop', as we shall see, because it is by this device that Chekhov introduces a crucial element of irony into the presentation of his central character—an irony entirely lacking in Fell's translation. More generally we might note that one of the principal means by which the modernist short story achieves its interrogative effect is by the occlusion of an 'objective' third-person point of view, and the persistent infiltration of character interiority into the narrational discourse. Dominic Head, in his study of the modernist short story, has shown how particularly Joyce and Mansfield use the technique of free indirect discourse in their stories, often insidiously to qualify apparent moments of insight or self-realization by admitting the possibility that the character was self-dramatizing, Although Chekhov does not deploy free indirect style nearly as extensively as Mansfield, he nevertheless, in Garnett's rendering, consistently suppresses the omniscient point of view in favour of a perspective filtered through a character, and, as we shall see, this is the key to how 'The Bishop' achieves its complexity of effect.

In Garnett's translation, the muting of the explanatory voice occurs at key moments in the text. Fell, on the other hand, is inclined to fill in the gaps, to explain and resolve ambivalence rather than conduct it intact to the reader. Often she will do this by omitting complex or ambiguous passages in order to achieve clarification of what she takes to be the story's meaning. In doing so, Fell misses crucial dimensions in Chekhov's presentation of the bishop which Garnett is careful to preserve. One such omission occurs during the bishop's reminiscence about his early religious life. In this recollection, he is sent one day from clerical school to the post office. We are told in the Garnett that he 'stared a long time at the post-office clerks and asked: "Allow me to ask, how do you get your salary, every month or every day?"'(p. 8). We might read this as an indication of the bishop's chronic unworldliness, or it might suggest that he has a tendency to be distracted from his studies by inappropriate interests. Either way (and the narrative doesn't propose to tell us *which* way), this passage has the effect of imposing an ironic distance between the narrative voice and the character, raising doubt over the bishop's commitment to his vocation. This irony gathers force in the Garnett version, as suggestions are made that the bishop's unhappiness is fuelled by his longing for a past which never existed in the terms he recalls it:

> And he was carried back in thought to the distant past, to his childhood and youth, when, too, they used to sing of the Bridegroom and of the Heavenly Mansion; and now that past rose up before him—living, fair, and joyful as in all likelihood it had never been. And perhaps in the other world, in the life to come, we shall think of the distant past, of our life here, with the same feeling. Who knows? The bishop was sitting near the altar. It was dark; tears flowed down his face.
>
> (p. 18)

In Fell's translation of this passage the bishop's relationship to his past is greatly reduced and, we may say, sentimentalized:

> He sat by the altar where the shadows were deepest, and was swept in imagination back into the days of his childhood and youth, when he had first heard these words sung. The tears trickled down his cheeks.
>
> (p. 309)

Fell omits the crucial qualification that in all probability the bishop's past had not been as he remembers it. In the Garnett, this qualification connects with other suggestions that the bishop is self-deluding. For, example, in his desire for someone in whom he can confide, he lights on the figure of Father Sisoy, an elderly, disaffected, and outspoken former housekeeper. In Fell we are told: 'his Reverence felt at ease with Sisoi, even though he was, without doubt, a rough and quarrelsome person' (p. 308). This is far more favourable to the bishop than Garnett's translation: 'And so the bishop was at ease with him, although, of course, he was a tedious and nonsensical man' (p. 17). In Garnett, this sense of the bishop as chronically dissatisfied with other people, despite his repeated claims that all he wants is familiar company, is reinforced by the recollection the priest has that he was happiest when alone abroad, spending his time in his room surrounded with books, cut off from his family and countrymen (p. 14). Fell again omits this passage, with the effect that the bishop's encounter with his mother and niece appears to be merely a matter of his coming into contact with the values of simplicity and intimacy from which his higher vocation has distanced him. Garnett's is a darker, sadder story in which the bishop's unhappiness is not such a straightforward affair. The final words the bishop speaks are (in Garnett's version): 'I ought to have been a village priest, a deacon . . . or simply a monk . . . All this oppresses me . . . oppresses me' (p. 24). In Fell, that longing for simplicity comes across as entirely genuine, unqualified by any irony. In her telling, the story is composed around a reliable opposition between past and present in the bishop's mind. As Garnett has it, the past is not such a simple place, and rather than being fatally severed from it, the implication persists that the bishop is a man inclined to nostalgia, chronic dissatisfaction, and even anti-social feeling. Despite the fact that Fell reports of the same events in much the same order as Garnett, her version of 'The Bishop' communicates none of this complexity concerning the central character. Garnett's story by no means resolves easily, as Fell's does, into a tale of a man, the victim of his own success, whose true happiness was lodged somewhere beyond him in his past. What success, what happiness, what past? These crucial matters hover interrogatively in the Garnett translation.

In an essay comparing Garnett's Chekhov with translations by S. S. Koteliansky and Ronald Hingley, Craig Raine, the editor of the recent Oxford Chekhov, praises the way in which Garnett manages to remain 'perfectly invisible' in her work, 'as effective and insubstantial as the Holy Ghost, a divine nobody'.[28] Hingley, Raine suggests, tends to simplify and explicate the text (he cites 'The Lady with the Dog' as an instance) by translating 'Chekhov's hints and guesses into four-square certainties' (p. 138). The same error clearly blights Marian Fell's rendering of 'The Bishop', but it is evident too in Koteliansky's highly respected translations, which he made in collaboration with

Middleton Murry and Gilbert Cannan respectively. Though clearly superior to Fell's, Koteliansky's versions nevertheless show the same tendency to trivialize character, and are markedly less successful than Garnett's in conveying interiority in third-person narrative.

Koteliansky's translation of 'In Exile' is a case in point. The story, about a group of petty criminals exiled in Siberia, centres on the nihilistic figure of Old Semyon (in Koteliansky he is referred to by his nickname 'Brains'), whose philosophy of endurance, stated repeatedly, is to want nothing. However, Koteliansky's heavy-handedness greatly simplifies Semyon's character when compared with Garnett's text. Like Fell's, Koteliansky's adjectival and adverbial phrases frequently have a synthetic literary quality—the young Tatar in the opening paragraph is 'miserable' where in Garnett he is 'weary'[29] —or are perfunctory and lacking in implication, as when at the end of the story Garnett describes how Semyon and his mates 'sauntered' back to their hut (p. 112) after the impassioned speech by the young Tatar, whereas in Koteliansky they merely 'went slowly' (p. 68). Koteliansky's phrase conveys none of the studied indifference of the men to the Tatar's display of emotion; indeed, their going 'slowly' might suggest that his words had made some visible impression on them. The Koteliansky also removes the suggestion of performance or even affectation in the men's response which 'sauntered' carries. Garnett is careful to communicate the idea that Semyon's recalcitrance is the result of his constant vigilance over his feelings. Telling of how he survived his early days in exile, Garnett has him remark: 'I stuck to it, and here you see I live well, and I don't complain' (p. 101). In the Koteliansky, he says simply, 'I stuck to it, and, you see, I live happily and have nothing to grumble at' (p. 57). Garnett's version allows that Semyon has plenty to grumble at, but that he decides not to; and her living 'well' falls short of living 'happily'. The Garnett admits the possibility that Semyon's buoyancy is an act of will, a performance that must never falter, thereby opening up an interpretative space in the story between what Semyon says and what he is really convinced of. In the Koteliansky, Semyon appears to owe his ability to endure merely to his thick-skinned insensitivity to suffering.

Garnett's willingness to preserve ambiguity and even contradiction in characterization means that her stories are less susceptible of summary than Koteliansky's. In 'Gooseberries', for example, Koteliansky's version reads as a story in which the central character, Ivan Ivanich, narrates a moment of profound change in his life. Telling the story of his brother, who has found happiness on a rural estate growing gooseberries, Ivan describes how he himself has come to understand that contentment in material things has effected a hypnosis on the Russian people which leaves them unwilling and unable to pursue revolutionary change in their country. 'Don't be satisfied', he entreats his listeners, 'don't let yourself be lulled to sleep . . . Do good!' (*The House,*

p. 53). The men who have heard Ivan's story and his passionate appeal are left dissatisfied, for the sort of story they enjoy tells of ladies and generals and the romance of the past. However, in Garnett's translation, the character of Ivan is considerably more complex than Koteliansky allows, and the dismissal of him by his auditors at the end of the story takes on a deeper significance. The main difference between the translations lies in Garnett's fuller realization of Ivan through his speech. What comes across in his account of his brother's life are traces of envy mixed with sardonic contempt, as well as a tendency to rhetorical pomposity, that are largely absent from the Koteliansky. Concerning the brother's marriage, for example, Koteliansky has Ivan say: 'he married an elderly, ugly widow, not out of any feeling for her, but because she had money' (p. 46). Garnett, on the other hand, has Ivan condemn both the brother and his wife, so revealing more general aspects to his contempt: 'he married an elderly and ugly widow without a trace of feeling for her, simply because she had filthy lucre'.[30] The broad sweep of Ivan's condemnation here fits with the portrait Garnett draws throughout the text of a man fond of rhetorical excess. On the death of his brother's wife, Ivan, in the Koteliansky, relates how his brother 'never for a moment thought himself to blame for her death' (p. 47). Garnett, on the other hand, shows Ivan to be more commanding and manipulative of his audience: 'And I need hardly say that my brother never for one moment imagined that he was responsible for her death' (p. 282). Garnett similarly conveys Ivan's tendency to sarcasm in his speech more forcefully than Koteliansky. For instance, of his brother's acts of benevolent paternalism, Ivan says: 'And, like a good landowner, he looked after his soul and did good works pompously, never simply. What, good works? He cured the peasants of all kinds of diseases with soda and castor oil' (Koteliansky, p. 48). Garnett gives us: 'And he concerned himself with the salvation of his soul in a substantial, gentlemanly manner, and performed deeds of charity, not simply, but with an air of consequence. And what deeds of charity! He treated the peasants for every sort of disease with soda and castor oil' (p. 284). Elsewhere in the Garnett we see Ivan straining for effect as he tells of how his brother made grand speeches to the peasants in which he said the same thing 'twenty times over' (p. 285), rather than 'constantly' as Koteliansky has it (p. 49). And Garnett's Ivan, in his peroration to the other men, presumes to use 'you' and 'we' as he comments on the state of Russian society (pp. 286–287), where in Koteliansky he limits himself to the first-person singular (pp. 50–51). This allows Garnett to lodge a subtle insinuation against Ivan which Koteliansky omits altogether, because earlier in the story Ivan has criticized his brother for his use of the phrase 'we noblemen' when addressing the peasants (p. 285). Ivan's presumptuousness is also picked up by Garnett in the final words he speaks in the story, when, taking himself to bed, he says, 'Lord forgive us sinners!' (p. 290), as though praying on account of the failings of all the men in the room, whereas in Koteliansky he confines himself to the appraisal of his own soul: 'God forgive me, a wicked sinner' (p. 54).

The significance of these differences between the two versions becomes apparent when Ivan's story reaches its emotional climax with his revelation of how his brother's way of life triggered a profound change in his own view of the world. His speech gets an indifferent reception from his listeners, which in the Koteliansky version appears to be simply a matter of political apathy among the men and a lamentable desire for sensationalism in their storytelling. But in Garnett, the reasons for Ivan's rejection by the men are not so straightforward, because of the suggestions made that Ivan is pompous, manipulative, and self-aggrandizing in his speech. His sincerity is open to doubt in a way it is not in Koteliansky's rendering. This doubt is vividly expressed in the Garnett version early on in Ivan's narrative. One of the listeners intervenes when Ivan wanders from his point to complain: 'That's a story from a different opera' (p. 283). In the Koteliansky, Ivan is merely warned: 'Keep to your story' (p. 47). It is as though, in the Garnett, the listeners' confidence in Ivan has already failed. As Koteliansky has it, 'Gooseberries' is a story about a political idealist whose sincere desire to 'do good' is confounded by the ignorance and indolence of his countrymen. The Garnett rendering, on the other hand, while permitting that reading, provides for another, much more characteristically Chekhovian interpretation, in which political commitment is shown to be subject to, rather than above, the designs of personality, even when it is proclaimed a politics of self-effacement, benevolence, and rationalism.

For Elizabeth Bowen, personality was the essence of Chekhov's realism: 'he made subjectivity edit and rule experience and pull art, obliquely, its way' (*Collected Impressions*, p. 39). Garnett's translations are likewise devoted to the preservation of every dissonance and awkward detail of character, however threatening these may be to principles of narrative unity. Her version of 'Gooseberries' gives out contradictory signals about its central character which it studiously refuses to resolve: the story stops short of full disclosure, producing the effect of 'interrogation' celebrated by Mansfield, Woolf, and the others in their comments on Chekhov. One senses that Koteliansky, by contrast, is determined to make gestures of rounding off and summing up. In this respect, he resembles the many readers and critics of the modernist short story who see it as their task to provide the missing parts to these oblique, interrogative texts.[31]

Even with a story like 'Misfortune' (the title of which Garnett gives as 'A Misfortune'), in which the inner turmoil of the central character is rendered in passages of free indirect style, Koteliansky nevertheless produces a text which is more resolute than Garnett's. The difference between the translations lies in their treatment of what motivates Sofya Petrovna as she struggles with her own feelings in response to the amorous advances of her friend, Ilyin. Koteliansky registers the fluctuations in Sofya's mind and mood, from protesting outrage at Ilyin's attentions, to courting him and taking pleasure in his devotion to her, and, ultimately, feelings of self-abasement as she realizes that she has been seduced by him and surrendered her belief in the sanctity of marriage and the family. However, Garnett complicates Sofya's story by casting doubt on the extent of the self-awareness she attains by the end of the story. Garnett persistently undermines Sofya's high opinion of herself as she considers her own conduct. For example, feeling shame at having allowed Ilyin to embrace her knees in the forest, Koteliansky has Sofya reflect as she rushes away from him that she is a 'good, respectable woman', motioning to her suitor as she goes 'to let her be'.[32] In the Garnett, Sofya thinks of herself as 'a chaste and high-principled woman', but her anxiety appears to have more to do with a fear of detection as she waves to signal to Ilyin to 'drop behind'.[33] What lingers in the Garnett is the suggestion that even in her moments of apparent shame, Sofya maintains a sense of herself as a woman of exceptional virtue, and that her self-abasement is far from absolute. Garnett maintains this doubt about Sofya through the many fluctuations in her thoughts about Ilyin. In the Garnett, Sofya's understanding of virtue is questionable: she defines her power over Ilyin in terms of 'her youth, her beauty, and her unassailable virtue' (p. 287). In the Koteliansky, 'unassailable virtue' is replaced by 'inaccessibility' in this statement (p. 155), so failing to register the way in which Sofya's much-protested notion of ideal feminine conduct is available to her as a tool of seduction and cruel teasing. When she arrives at her lowest point, and realizes that she has been turned from her own high principles, the Koteliansky version has her damn herself as the worst of women: 'You disgraceful woman', she calls herself, and later, 'immoral woman' (pp. 150, 161).Crucially in the Garnett, Sofya never scolds herself in terms of her femininity: 'You low creature', she says by contrast, 'Low wretch' (pp. 282, 292). It is as though she stops short of full condemnation, will not call herself the worst of names, as though she clings to the belief that she is still superior to the prostitutes and other women of ill repute to whom she has compared herself throughout the story. As with the characterization of Ivan Ivanich in 'Gooseberries', Koteliansky's Sofya achieves a clear moment of self-awareness. Garnett, by contrast, leaves us doubtful that any such transcendence of personality has taken place.

In her essay 'The Russian Point of View', Woolf says that reading Chekhov is a matter of getting used to his 'shades' of meaning, and when one is acclimatized, 'half the "conclusions" of fiction fade into thin air; they show like transparencies with a light behind them—gaudy, glaring, superficial' (*Essays*, IV, 185). But these shades, and this radical inconclusiveness—so important in accounts of the modernist short story in English—are very much dependent on which translation of Chekhov one reads. Transparent conclusions are what Garnett never allows in her Chekhov, at any level. Conceivably, had the anglophone modernists been deprived of her work, the development of the short story would have been different. In accounting for Chekhov's contribution to the development of the modernist form in English, therefore, it is important to say whose Chekhov we mean.

NOTES

1. Roberta Rubenstein, 'Genius of Translation', *Colorado Quarterly*, 22 (1974), 359–368.

2. Richard Garnett, *Constance Garnett: A Heroic Life* (London, 1991).

3. Edward Crankshaw, 'Work of Constance Garnett', *The Listener*, 30 January 1947, pp. 195–196 (p. 196).

4. J. Middleton Murry, 'The Method of Tchehov', *Athenaeum*, 8 April 1922, pp. 57–58 (p. 58).

5. Elisabeth Schneider, 'Katherine Mansfield and Chekhov', *MLN*, 50 (1935), 394–397. For a response to this piece see R. Sutherland, 'Katherine Mansfield: Plagiarist, Disciple, or Ardent Admirer?', *Critique*, 5.ii (1962), 58–76. Claire Tomalin reprints correspondence from the *TLS* on the plagiarism charge in her *Katherine Mansfield: A Secret Life* (London, 1987), pp. 261–272.

6. *Collected Letters of Katherine Mansfield*, edited by Vincent O'Sullivan with Margaret Scott, 4 vols (Oxford, 1984–1996), II, 320.

7. Virginia Woolf, 'Tchehov's Questions', in *The Essays of Virginia Woolf*, edited by Andrew McNeillie, 4 vols (London, 1987), II, 244–248 (p. 245).

8. Henry James, *The Art of the Novel: Critical Prefaces*, edited by R. P. Blackmur (New York, 1934), p. 231.

9. Elizabeth Bowen, *Collected Impressions* (London, 1950), p. 39.

10. Frank O'Connor, *The Lonely Voice* (London, 1963), p. 28.

11. H. E. Bates, *The Modern Short Story: A Critical Survey*, revised edition (London, 1972), pp. 80, 89.

12. Charles Dickens, *The Christmas Books*, edited by Michael Slater, 2 vols (Harmondsworth, 1971), I, xxix.

13. Henry James, *Partial Portraits* (London, 1905), p. 264.

14. Bates, pp. 41, 23; Wendell V. Harris, 'Vision and Form: The English Novel and the Emergence of the Short Story', in *The New Short Story Theories*, edited by Charles E. May (Athens, OH, 1994), pp. 182–191 (p. 183).

15. Woolf, 'The Russian Point of View', *Essays* (n. 7), IV, 181–190 (p. 184).

16. *The Diary of Virginia Woolf*, edited by Anne Oliver Bell, 5 vols (London, 1977; hereafter 'Diary'), III, 157.

17. Woolf, 'The Russian Background', *Essays*, III, 83–86 (p. 84).

18. In letters on short story composition, Chekhov himself repeatedly stated the importance of authorial neutrality. As he wrote to the publisher A. S. Suvorin (30 May 1888), 'I think that it is not for writers to solve such questions as the existence of God, pessimism, etc. The writer's function is only to describe by whom, how, and under what conditions the questions of God and pessimism were discussed . . . Let the jurors, that is to say, the readers, evaluate it.' Quoted in *Anton Chekhov's Short Stories*, edited by Ralph E. Matlaw (New York, 1979), p. 270. See also the

letters to Suvorin (27 October 1888), Alexander Chekhov (10 May 1886), and Lidia Avilova (29 April 1892).

19. Woolf, *Selected Short Stories*, edited by Sandra Kemp (Harmondsworth, 1993), pp. 29–30.

20. Elizabeth Bowen, *After-Thought: Pieces About Writing* (London, 1962), p. 94.

21. Dominic Head, *The Modernist Short Story: A Study in Theory and Practice* (Cambridge, 1992), p. 79.

22. *The Letters of Virginia Woolf*, edited by Nigel Nicholson and Joanna Trautmann, 6 vols (London, 1975–1980), IV, 231.

23. Charles E. May, 'Chekhov and the Modern Short Story', in May, *New Short Story Theories* (n. 14), pp. 199–217.

24. Eudora Welty, *The Eye of the Story: Selected Essays and Reviews* (London, 1987), p. 62. Nor is the Garnett translation specified by Jan Nordby Gretlund in an essay on Welty's reponse to Chekhov. See 'The Terrible and the Marvelous: Eudora Welty's Chekhov', in *Eudora Welty: Eye of the Storyteller*, edited by Dawn Trouard (Kent, OH, 1989), pp. 107–118.

25. Quoted by Richard Garnett (n. 2), pp. 306–307.

26. Anton Tchehov, *The Bishop and Other Stories*, translated by Constance Garnett (London, 1922), p. 4.

27. Anton Tchekoff, *Russian Silhouettes: More Stories of Russian Life*, translated by Marian Fell (London, 1915), p. 296.

28. Craig Raine, 'Constance Garnett—Translator', in *In Defence of T. S. Eliot: Literary Essays* (London, 2000), pp. 134–144 (p. 142).

29. Anton Tchekoff, *The House with the Mezzanine and Other Stories*, translated by S. S. Koteliansky and Gilbert Cannan (New York, 1921), p. 55; Anton Tchehov, *The Schoolmistress and Other Stories*, translated by Constance Garnett (London, 1920), p. 99.

30. Anton Tchehov, *The Wife and Other Stories*, translated by Constance Garnett (London, 1918), p. 282.

31. Elaine Baldeshwiler, for example, argues that in every short story can be detected its 'emerging emotion'—that unifying condition to which 'all other narrative elements must be subordinated' ('The Lyric Short Story: The Sketch of a History', in May, *New Short Story Theories* (n. 14), pp. 231–241; p. 239). Suzanne C. Ferguson, similarly, suggest that when we read an elliptical story we recognize 'a story that has not been fully told lying behind the one that *is* told' and that we therefore construct a 'hypothetical plot' in order to 'rationalize' the text ('Defining the Short Story: Impressionism and Form', in May, pp. 218–230; p. 223). See also John Gerlach's notion of an 'underlying narrative grid' applied to the short story in his *Toward the End: Closure and Structure in the American Short Story* (University, Alabama, 1985), p. 6.

32. Anton Tchekhov, *The Bet and Other Stories*, translated by S. Koteliansky and J. M. Murry (Dublin, 1915), p. 150.

33. Anton Tchehov, *The Party and Other Stories*, translated by Constance Garnett (London, 1917), p. 281.

JEFFERSON J. A. GATRALL

The Paradox of Melancholy Insight: Reading the Medical Subtext in Chekhov's "A Boring Story"

> Why is it that all men who are outstanding in philosophy or politics or poetry or the arts are melancholic, and some to such an extent that they are infected by the diseases arising from black bile, as the story of Heracles among the heroes tells?
>
> —Aristotle, Problem XXX.1

Throughout his "notes," Nikolai Stepanovich, the renowned professor of physiology and fictional author of Anton Chekhov's novella "A Boring Story," describes the symptoms and signs of a disease that he believes will kill him within half a year. Psychological symptoms figure prominently in his self-examination. He complains that since the onset of his illness he has undergone a change in his personality, his moods, and his "worldview" *(mirovozzrenie)*. It is his search for the origins of a new and uncharacteristic pessimism that initiates the crisis of identity around which the plot of the novella is largely structured. In a conversation with his adopted daughter Katia, Nikolai Stepanovich describes how his life has changed before asking a series of probing questions:

> day and night evil thoughts fester in my head, and feelings I've never known before have built a nest in my soul. I hate, I despise,

Slavic Review: American Quarterly of Russian, Eurasian, and East European Studies, Volume 62, Number 2 (Summer 2003): pp. 258–277. Copyright © 2003 University of Illinois.

I'm indignant, I'm exasperated, and I'm afraid. I've become excessively strict, demanding, irritable, unobliging, and suspicious. Even things that would have once given me occasion to make an unnecessary pun and laugh amiably now only produce a sense of weariness in me. My sense of logic has also changed. . . .

What does this mean? If these new thoughts and new feelings have arisen from a change in my convictions, then where could this change have come from? Has the world really grown worse, and me better, or was I just blind and indifferent before? If this change has arisen from a general decline in my physical and mental powers— I'm sick, after all, I'm losing weight every day—then my situation is pitiful; it means that my new thoughts are abnormal, morbid, that I should be ashamed of them and consider them worthless.[1]

In this passage and elsewhere in the novella, several possible reasons for the change in Nikolai Stepanovich's view of life are evoked: illness, the world around him, new insight. Of particular importance for an understanding of the professor's crisis is that he establishes a mutually exclusive choice between illness and insight in a search for the origin of his pessimism. Either his new thoughts are "abnormal" *(nenorml'ny)* and "morbid" *(nezdorovy)* or he has only now ceased to be "blind and indifferent" *(slep i navnodushen)*. Interrupting Nikolai Stepanovich's speech, Katia repeats this opposition even as she seeks to answer his questions: "Sickness hasn't got anything to do with it. . . . Your eyes have simply been opened, that's all." As a physician treating himself, however, Nikolai Stepanovich seriously weighs the merits of the opposing, psychopathological explanation. If his new pessimistic thoughts are symptoms of his illness, then they must be, as he suggests in another passage, "accidental, fleeting, and not deeply rooted within me." If these new thoughts are not just symptoms, on the other hand, but the result of a deeper penetration into the general lack of meaning in his life, then "the sixty-two years I've lived through must be considered wasted."[2]

Literary critics, following the lead of the novella's two main characters, have weighed in on both sides of this debate. Among those who stress the importance of illness for an understanding of Nikolai Stepanovich's predicament, M. M. Smirnov argues, "it is useless to analyze the judgments of the hero-narrator, because they are only a symptom of his disposition *[mirooshchushenie]*."[3] Carol A. Flath, in a recent article, defends Nikolai Stepanovich against those critics who would "condemn [his] behavior in the present": "For all of the professor's perceptions are colored by his pain and suffering. . . . I would like to suggest [his disease] is primarily physical in the sense that the crisis is provoked by the illness, not the reverse."[4] On the opposing side, several critics have emphasized how penetrating, if not always reliable, Nikolai

Stepanovich's insights can be. Lev Shestov leans heavily on the "originality" of the professor's pessimism in "A Boring Story" to justify his famous claim that Chekhov is the "poet of hopelessness," and Marina Senderovich considers Nikolai Stepanovich "an existential thinker" who faces his existence "as a vital necessity of his own being." In a statement that contradicts Smirnov's and Flath's views almost point by point, Leonid Gromov writes: "The hero of the novella, having understood the [futility] of his work and not having found the meaning of life, loses the ground under his feet, loses the mark of a 'living person,' and senses the approach of death. Precisely in this lies the terrible tragedy of the old scientist—whose life changes into a 'boring story'—and not in his physical illness."[6]

What has not yet been undertaken in the critical literature on "A Boring Story," despite some steps in this direction by Flath and Evgenii Meve, is a thorough examination of the novella's medical subtext.[7] Cribbing the cryptic title Nikolai Stepanovich gives to his own romance with his wife, it can be said that the novella depicts, among many other parallel and often loosely connected plot lines, a "Historia morbi."[8] Significantly, Nikolai Stepanovich informs neither the reader nor Katia what disease he believes himself to be suffering from. He does not even consult other physicians to confirm his own, unnamed diagnosis. This omission provides the impetus for the present article. From the few offhand comments he makes concerning the symptoms and signs of his disease, I have attempted not so much to render a scientifically precise diagnosis as to historically reconstruct, by drawing on contemporary medical intertexts, the diagnosis he himself seems to have made.[9] Nikolai Stepanovich scatters many symptoms and signs of an unnamed disease throughout "A Boring Story." If the conceptual leap that he himself makes from these signs and symptoms to his own self-diagnosis entails a movement from the surface of the body to deep organic structures, then an examination of his condition on the part of a literary critic involves a similar movement from the body of the text to an underlying medical subtext. This medical subtext is not directly visible in "A Boring Story," yet the novella does trace a network of signs that evoke the outline of a specific, contemporary disease concept. Since psychopathology plays an integral role in the novella's argument, determining the disease from which Nikolai Stepanovich believes himself to be suffering places the implications of his crisis in a new critical light.

At first glance, such a diagnostic undertaking might appear to be of little scholarly interest. A precise diagnosis of Nikolai Stepanovich's illness would demonstrate what is already a commonplace in Chekhov criticism, namely, that his medical portraiture is rigorously realistic. Conversely, an overreliance on the method of differential diagnosis would superficially resolve the philosophical problems that the novella presents.[10] These pitfalls aside, there nevertheless remains room for balanced comparative analysis of the intersection

between medicine, poetics, and epistemology in Chekhov's "A Boring Story."
As literary critics since Lev Tolstoi have noted, there is in Chekhov's prose
an "impressionistic" quality; or, as Aleksandr Chudakov puts it, an "incidental
wholeness."[11] In "A Boring Story," symptoms and signs are abundant, but the
professors own self-diagnosis, which might unite them into a coherent clinical picture, is lacking. Instead, these symptoms and signs appear as discon-
nected and often incidental details in Nikolai Stepanovich's broader literary
self-portrait. His notes are filled with many other "boring" matters ostensibly
unrelated to his medical condition, ranging from his digressions on various
topics in contemporary Russian society to his reflections on Katia's tragic life.
This lack of a unifying diagnosis seems structurally strategic, for the novella
not only withholds a disease whose name might have upset the balance between the two main, conflicting interpretations of its protagonist's crisis—
illness and insight—but this omission also creates a certain affective ambivalence. Does not the professor's propensity for digression, ellipsis, and surface
details, as well as his inability to draw on his life experience to say something meaningful to Katia in her despondency, reflect some of the speech
patterns of melancholia? In an observation that has wider stylistic relevance
for Chekhov's so often melancholy prose, Nikolai Stepanovich confesses of
his thoughts that "I have lost the sense of their organic connection."[12]

Shifting from literary to clinical portraiture, it is nonetheless possible
to provide a reasonably exhaustive list of the symptoms and signs to which
Nikolai Stepanovich alludes. At the beginning of the novella, he complains
of an "incurable tic" (*neizlechimyi* tic). This tic appears again in the last section: "There's a dull pain in my cheek—the tic has started" (*V shcheke tupaia
bol'—eto nachinaetsia* tic).[13] He is also suffering from chronic insomnia, which
he wryly claims has become the "chief and fundamental feature of my existence" (*glavnuiu i osnovnuiu chertu [moego] sushchestvovaniia*).[14] Elsewhere
he notes that he loses weight daily, that he often feels chilled, and that his
head and hands "shake from weakness" (*triasutsia ot slabosti*).[15] While lecturing he experiences an "unconquerable weakness in [his] legs and shoulders"
(*nepobedimuiu slabost' v nogakh i v plechakh*), his "mouth becomes dry" (*vo
rtu sokhnet*), his "voice grows hoarse" (*golos sipnet*), his "head spins" (*golova
kruzhitsia*), and he "incessantly drinks water" (*to i delo p'iu vodu*).[16] At one
point during the novella he faints; at another he wakes during the night in a
sweat, tries to take his pulse, and begins to hyperventilate.[17] In a particularly
revealing passage, he expresses the hope that he is mistaken "about the albumin and sugar I find, about my heart, and about the edema I've now twice
seen in the morning" (*naschet belka i sakhara, kotorye nakhozhu u sebia, i naschet
serdtsa, i naschet tekh otekov, kotorye uzhe dva raza videl u sebia po utram*).[18]
Nikolai Stepanovich's psychological symptoms are more difficult to isolate
and categorize than these physical ones. In broad terms, his psychological

symptoms include withdrawal from family and friends, irritability, uncontrollable sadness and fear, weakness in memory, pessimistic thoughts, and paralyzing indifference, a condition he calls "premature death" *(prezhdevremennaia smert')*.[19]

Since the argument of the novella is based upon the very nature of these psychological symptoms, however, any attempt to summarize them is inherently problematic. Indeed, the search for a diagnosis of Nikolai Stepanovich's disease in "A Boring Story," far from resolving his crisis, opens onto an expanse of further problems, ranging from the reliability of self-analysis in mental disease to the lingering dualism in nineteenth-century materialist psychiatry. First, as the Russian psychiatrist Sergei Korsakov writes in the introduction to his *Course on Psychiatry* (1893), a textbook Chekhov owned, "the manifestations of mental diseases in separate cases are extremely varied, but what is common to all them is that the 'personality' *[lichnost' cheloveka]* alters."[20] Yet, as is the case with several of Chekhov's medically inflected stories and plays, "A Boring Story" opens *after* a change in Nikolai Stepanovich's personality has apparently already taken place.[21] The reader is directly familiar only with the character of an altered, dying Nikolai Stepanovich. From a purely clinical perspective, his tendency for most of the novella to contrast his dreary present with a happier past might thus be seen as itself symptomatic of a pervasive melancholia. In a related manner, the reader is never able to step outside the shadow cast by Nikolai Stepanovich's melancholy prose, and thus it remains difficult to gauge the merit of his increasingly self-critical judgments on his own life, which he claims had earlier seemed to be "a beautiful and ably made composition" *(krasivoi, talantlivo sdelannoi kompozitsiei)* but whose "finale" *(final)* he now fears he is spoiling.[22]

Second, this question of the reliability of the narrator-protagonist's self-examination has an epistemological dimension arising from the superimposition of two central dualities in modern medicine; namely, those of mind and body and of physician and patient. Nikolai Stepanovich reveals to the reader his symptoms, which as a patient he experiences directly, as well as the clinical signs that he has gathered as a physician. In his hypochondriacal attention to medical textbooks, however, he seems troubled by more than just the clinical dimensions of his self-diagnosis: "Now, when I diagnose and treat myself, I have the hope every now and then that my ignorance is deceiving me . . . when, with the zeal of a hypochondriac, I reread my textbooks on therapy and daily change my medications, it always seems to me that I'll come across something comforting."[23] Nikolai Stepanovich's hypochondria would seem to result in part from the conflation of roles that arises, not only as his professional impartiality breaks down during the course of self-treatment, but also as his diseased body begins to infect the thought processes of his medically trained mind. In Chekhov's realist aesthetic, an aesthetic that is arguably more phenomenological than materialistic, it is not just the objective fact of a disease that is portrayed, but a character's subjective experience of illness.[24] The physiological processes that govern the progression of his disease acquire meaning inasmuch as Nikolai Stepanovich strives, as a physician, to understand their psychopathological consequences. Conversely, and more pressingly, Nikolai Stepanovich's "new" and "evil" thoughts—which have provoked a reevaluation of his long and illustrious life—become an existential problem to the extent that he grapples, as a patient, with the question of whether they derive from recent illness or belated insight.[25]

Nikolai Stepanovich's role as a renowned physiologist during the rise of materialism in psychiatry further renders the crisis occasioned by his illness all the more acute. As the soul gradually disappeared as an explanatory principle in mental disease throughout the nineteenth century, the humanist attributes of the soul—the immaterial intellect and free moral agency—began to lose their epistemological footing. Nikolai Stepanovich's anxiety about the origin of his pessimism can be interpreted against the background of the tendency in materialist psychiatry to dissolve the mind into physiological processes as well as the philosophical and ethical problems that this reduction—which preceded Freud and now, in the "Age of Prozac," seems to be outliving him—has long engendered. Caught between the options of illness and insight, which had become mutually exclusive in mainstream psychiatry by the end of the nineteenth century, Nikolai Stepanovich follows the course of his own spiraling thoughts, which seem to grow more penetrating the more his marasmus advances, yet unearth less meaning from his life the deeper they penetrate.

Diabetes

One of the clinical signs that Nikolai Stepanovich mentions in passing in his notes is glycosuria. Glycosuria, or sugar in the urine, was the definitive sign of diabetes in the second half of the nineteenth century. Yet, as the celebrated French physiologist Claude Bernard suggests in one of his seminal midcentury studies on diabetes, "the existence of sugar in the urine does not constitute diabetes. It is the proportion of this material that is important." Indeed, the difficulty in distinguishing between a glycosuria that is "in a certain sense normal" and the glycosuria of diabetes presents a diagnostic dilemma: "the majority of physicians do not render a diagnosis of diabetes until glycosuria becomes permanent."[26] In "A Boring Story," Nikolai Stepanovich mentions the sugar he "finds" *(nakhozhu)*, presumably in his urine, using an imperfective verb in the present tense. This would seem to indicate a recurring clinical result, but he does not mention for how long or how many times this sign has presented itself. Moreover, in the same passage, he even compares himself to a hypochondriac, a comparison it would be at least possible to take at face value. If on the one hand hypochondria (as a subtype of melancholia) was often cited as a concomitant condition of diabetes, then on the other hand, as the British pathologist William Dickinson notes in his 1877 monograph on diabetes, "in acute mania and in melancholia a trace of sugar is the rule rather than the exception."[27] While a diagnosis of hypochondriacal melancholia would not necessarily preclude one of diabetes, it is nevertheless typical of the clinical portrait that follows that a single clinical sign evokes both physical and psychological conditions.

In terms of differential diagnosis, however, the evidence in favor of diabetes is much more substantial than simply glycosuria. A second clinical sign especially indicative of the terminal stages of diabetes, and which Nikolai Stepanovich mentions alongside glycosuria, is albuminuria, or albumin in the urine. Dickinson explains that this "later complication" is often the only visible sign of an underlying "renal change": "When sugar and albumen are together, the sugar as a rule is primary, the albumen consequent. The kidneys, goaded by the diuretic action of the sugar, after a time show signs of irritation and allow a little albumen to escape as the result of congestion or tubal disturbance."[28] The presence of albuminuria suggests that one of the sequelae of Nikolai Stepanovich's diabetes maybe what was known as "Bright's disease." In the second half of the nineteenth century, Bright's disease was a common diagnosis that covered a variety of forms of nephritis (inflammation of the kidneys) and that was often noted alongside diabetes. In his 1872 treatise *Des terminaisons du diabète sucré*, Pierre Costes, for example, describes how in many cases the patient dies as a "result of Bright's disease, which comes to complicate the preexisting diabetes. . . . The two ailments march in tandem and precipitate the *dénouement* . . . in such cases it is difficult to determine precisely what should be attributed to Bright's disease and what to diabetes." In terms of diet, furthermore, Nikolai Stepanovich mentions not only that he drinks water "incessantly" (polydipsia), a characteristic symptom of diabetes, but also that he suffers from "daily" weight loss (autophagia), indicating that his illness has likely reached an advanced stage. As Costes writes, after the commencement of "the stage of autophagia" further complications arise and "the patient is lost": "In the midst of diverse impairments, the marasmus particular to the diabetic *[le marasme particulier au diabétique]* imperceptibly prepares itself."[29]

Nikolai Stepanovich's cardiovascular complications can also be situated in this clinical portrait of diabetes. The edema that he has twice seen (likely in his extremities) further suggests the onset of the serious heart congestion typical of Bright's disease. Even more ominously, Nikolai Stepanovich seems to suffer from what Flath calls a "panic attack" and Meve "angina pectoris" *(grudnaia zhaba)* when he awakes during a "sparrow's night" *(vorob'inaia noch')* in section five.[30] As Nikolai Stepanovich writes, "in my body there was not one sensation that might indicate that the end was near, but my soul was oppressed by horror, as if I had suddenly seen a vast, ominous glow." Having awakened, the professor becomes immediately concerned with such bodily functions as his breathing and heart rate: "I feel for my pulse and, not finding it in my wrist, search for it in my temples, then under my chin, then again in my wrist. . . . My breathing becomes more and more rapid" *(shchupaiu u sebia pul's i, ne naidia na ruke, ishchu ego v viskakh, potom v podborodke i opiat' na ruke. . . . Dykhanie stanovitsia vse chashche i chashche).*[31]

In terms of etiology, the relationship between heart congestion and Bright's disease, although clinically evident to nineteenth-century researchers, had not received a commonly accepted explanation. Taken in the context of the history of medicine, however, Nikolai Stepanovich's nervous symptoms do suggest a possible, if speculative, origin for his illness. The tic and pain in his cheek, which he mentions three times, mostly likely represent trigeminal neuralgia or, as it is commonly known, "tic douloureux." If glycosuria is the sign that most supports a diagnosis of diabetes, then trigeminal neuralgia is perhaps the most important clue in determining the historical form of diabetes from which Nikolai Stepanovich suffers. In the second half of the nineteenth century, the pathology of diabetes was a matter of considerable controversy. One of the main theories postulated what would become commonplace in the twentieth century, namely, that the anatomical anomaly responsible for diabetes lies in the pancreas. In 1889, the same year that "A Boring Story" was published, Joseph von Mering and Oskar Minkowski were able to induce permanent diabetes in a dog by removing its pancreas. The French clinician Apollinaire Bouchardat, who gained renown for his dietary treatment of the disease, argued instead that diabetes has its source in the stomach.[32] In contrast to these theories based on localized organ failures, Nikolai Stepanovich's trigeminal neuralgia tentatively evokes the then widespread theory that diabetes is a disease of the nervous system. This "angioneurotic" theory of diabetes originated with Bernard's famous (and retrospectively notorious) *piqûre* of the fourth ventricle of a dog's brain. In an influential 1857 article, Bernard argued that excess secretion of glucose by the liver into the bloodstream (hyperglycemia) can be caused by a lesion in this supposed "sugar center" in the brain, by a lesion in the nerves from this sugar center to blood vessels in the liver, or by stimulation of the nerves that dilate these vessels. In other words, as Bernard concluded, "one can thus consider diabetes to be a nervous disease."[33] As late as 1892, the French pathologist J. Thiroloix could still argue that "the grand varieties of diabetes that have been established . . . are all 'functions of an impairment of the central nervous system.'"[34] While not all contemporary researchers and clinicians would have been comfortable with the scope of Thiroloix's generalization, many sought and found evidence of lesions in the fourth ventricle of the brain during autopsies of patients who had died of diabetes. As Horst and Joseph Schumacher write concerning the angioneurotic theory of diabetes: "The clinician saw in numerous phenomena—disturbances of sensation and motility, reflex anomalies, occipital and *trigeminal neuralgias, physical and mental fatigue, frequent depression,* etc.—genuine manifestations of a disorder of the nervous system in line with the theory."[35] This level of physiological and clinical detail, of course, extends beyond the range of "A Boring Story." Nikolai Stepanovich's tic is directly present in the text, yet the move from this symptom to a particular etiology, from text to subtext, remains a speculative one. Nikolai Stepanovich's tic might instead represent a symptom only incidentally related to his diabetic condition. Francis Anstie, for example, in a contemporary monograph on neuralgia, observed that late onset trigeminal neuralgia, "are almost invariably connected with a strong family taint of insanity, and very often with strong melancholy."[36] Once again, a single symptom evokes the possibility of an ailment of either body or mind.

Without insisting that a single disease concept accounts for all of Nikolai Stepanovich's symptoms, it is nevertheless significant that trigeminal neuralgia suggests that he may be suffering from a diabetes of nervous origin. There is evidence that Nikolai Stepanovich himself supports a nervous explanation for his general condition. In a passage that provides a link—one typical of diabetes—between his diet and his moods, he writes, "it is especially after dinner, in the early evening, that my nervous excitation *(moe nervnoe vozbuzhdenie)* attains its highest pitch"; at a later point in the novella he also alludes to his "violent nervous tension" *(sil'noe nervnoe napriazhenie).*[37] In the context of nervous disease, trigeminal neuralgia represents a possible bridge between Nikolai Stepanovich's physical symptoms and signs—glycosuria, albuminuria, polydipsia, autophagia, heart congestion, and edema—and the psychological symptoms so crucial to the story's argument. In the late nineteenth century, symptoms of a psychological nature were situated in a complex, dual relationship with the physical symptoms of diabetes. On the one hand, sadness, apathy, and despondency were commonly observed during the terminal stages of diabetes. Costes's psychologically nuanced depiction of "le malheureux diabétique" resembles Nikolai Stepanovich's self-portrait in several suggestive ways: "The patient complains of various problems, which are no more than precursory or concomitant phenomena, such as a loss of strength, a certain general malaise, a greater sensitivity to external cold, apathy, and an aversion to movement. . . . [A] nonchalance he finds hard to overcome sentences the unfortunate diabetic to rest. Despondency and sadness take hold of him."[38] On the other hand, the angioneurotic theory made it possible to include diabetes among the many ailments thought to be influenced by what was known as the "neurotic diathesis" (that is, neurosis as predisposing cause). In a popular contemporary Anglo-American medical textbook, for example, William

Osler notes of diabetes that "persons of a neurotic temperament are often affected."[39] And although Dickinson insists that diabetes "clearly belong[s] to the body and not its surroundings," he, too, suggests, "Of all the causes of diabetes mental emotion is the one which we can most often trace and which we must believe to be the most frequent. . . . Grief, anxiety, protracted intellectual toil, violent anger and mental shock, might all be shown to be directly productive of this disease."[40]

It is precisely at this pathological threshold between physical and psychological symptoms that the question of whether Nikolai Stepanovich's pessimism is symptomatic or insightful becomes meaningful. His symptoms and signs can be placed, without undue strain, into this historically reconstructed portrait of diabetes. Moreover, his own bleak prognosis would seem to be warranted: his heart and kidneys are failing; his body is wasting away. What is at stake in the novella's argument, however, is whether his pessimism results from this decline in his health. Reflecting on the relationship between the medical evidence in "A Boring Story" and Nikolai Stepanovich's crisis of identity, I would like to suggest that certain features of diabetes, as it was understood in the nineteenth century, make it an artistically nuanced and epistemologically unsteady source for the professor's pessimism. First, Bernard's work on diabetes belonged to his broader effort to establish the legitimacy of a physiological approach to the study of disease (his term for this approach, *la médecine expérimentale*, came to live a fortuitous existence in literary criticism after Émile Zola). In particular, Bernard's interest in the pathology of diabetes was closely related to his groundbreaking research on the metabolism of the liver and helped illustrate his contention that "physiology and pathology now march in an ever more intimate union." As Bernard writes, diabetes presents a problem for those "doctor-nosologists" who would consider all diseases as "morbid entities" and classify them "as objects of natural history, as if they were living beings like plants or animals." Diabetes does not exist as an independent entity within the body, as if it were a microbe, but results from "a simple functional disruption that, from our point of view, represents nothing beyond the realm of physiology."[41]

In "A Boring Story," Nikolai Stepanovich, a famous physiologist in his own right, neither names his disease nor burdens it, as something foreign to himself, with responsibility for his pessimism; instead, he faults the "general decline in my mental and physical powers" *(obshchii upadok fizicheskikh i umstvennykh sil).*[42] His loss of health is not sudden and localized, like the blow to Ivan Il'ich's side in Tolstoi, but insidious and multifaceted. Accordingly, Nikolai Stepanovich, rather than being haunted by the name of a particular disease, feels compelled to read and reread, across a range of different body functions, his disparate symptoms and signs. Such clinical diligence, moreover, reflects the scientific reserve typical of the ethos of experimental medicine. In advising the practitioner to be "an observing physician," Bernard writes, "if we take advantage . . . of a few possible connections between pathology and physiology, to try to explain the whole disease at a single stroke, then we lose sight of the patient, we distort the disease";[43] or, as Nikolai Stepanovich suggests, the physician should "individualize each separate case."[44] Far from making hasty or reifying judgments, Nikolai Stepanovich reads his body as thoroughly as his textbooks and reads both to the point of hypochondria, in a perpetual medical hermeneutic—literally, a *sémiologie*, which in the nineteenth century referred solely to the interpretation of clinical signs.[45]

Lastly, in his search for the cause of his pessimism, Nikolai Stepanovich struggles physically, intellectually, and spiritually with a disease whose etiology remained elusive throughout the nineteenth century. Even were it granted that he is suffering from diabetes—which I would conclude is what the professor himself suspects, given the clinical signs he selectively presents to the reader—the question of whether his pessimism has been caused by illness or insight would remain unresolvable. If the change in his moods and thoughts can be regarded as part of the marasmus wrought by diabetes, then it is nevertheless possible to take this causal regress one step further by attributing diabetes itself to an underlying neurotic diathesis. Yet if his pessimism derives from a diabetes of nervous origin, then what, in turn, causes neurosis? While the causal relationships between neurosis and diabetes cannot be resolved diagnostically in "A Boring Story," an epistemological exploration of Nikolai Stepanovich's crisis of identity in the context of a nineteenth-century understanding of nervous disease is nevertheless fruitful. It is important not only to assess the question of whether Nikolai Stepanovich's pessimism is symptomatic in light of the novella's medical evidence but to consider what such a question means within the context of nineteenth-century medical thought. In short, how could the professor's question have taken the historical form that it does?

The Anatomy of Thought

The gradual shift in the locus of mental disease from the soul to the body over much of the nineteenth century proved crucial to the formation of modern psychiatry. At the risk of oversimplifying this history, it can be argued that the writings of the German "somaticists," active especially in the 1830s and 1840s, provide the first clear traces of the question that will later haunt Nikolai Stepanovich; namely, whether his thoughts are insights or symptoms. While the "psychicists" considered the soul to be the seat of mental illness, their opponents the somaticists argued that, by definition, only the body could ever become diseased. The somaticism of the German psychiatrist Maximilian Jacobi can serve here as a representative example: "all morbid psychical phenomena can only be considered as symptomatic, as concomitant to states of disease formed and developed elsewhere in the organism."[46] Later in this somaticist tradition, Wilhelm Griesinger, aware of the successes of physiology in neurology, transferred the site of mental disease from the organism as a whole to the brain in particular. For Griesinger, the "father of modern psychiatry," the study of cerebral pathology is largely confined to insanity, which is "only a complication of symptoms of various morbid states of the brain."[47]

In the closing pages of "A Boring Story," Nikolai Stepanovich echoes this somaticist tradition: "When nothing within a person rises higher and stronger than all the external influences around him, then, it is true, a good head-cold is enough to make him lose his equilibrium . . . all his pessimism or optimism, all his thoughts, big or small, have in that case the meaning of a mere symptom and nothing more [imeiut znachenie tol'ko simptoma i bol'she nichego]."[48] The relegation of mental phenomena to a secondary order of being with respect to their primary material causes has had profound epistemological and ethical implications for modern psychiatry. As a result of the reduction of soul to body in mental disease, thought does not disappear but is instead rendered passive and silent. The psychiatrist interprets a patient's morbid thoughts as pathological effects, not as insights requiring a response in their own terms. Near the end of "A Boring Story," Nikolai Stepanovich similarly regards his pessimism as a mere symptom, yet he avoids a naive materialism by holding out the possibility that a person's thoughts can rise above "external influences." In this he differs from his colleague Ivan Sechenov, the most famous Russian physiologist of the second half of the nineteenth century. In his 1867 essay "Reflexes of the Brain," Sechenov argues that all thought—diseased or otherwise—is the result of external processes: "A psychological act . . . cannot appear in consciousness without external sensory excitement. It follows that thought [smysl'] is subordinate to this law. With thought there is the beginning of a reflex, its continuation, but not, evidently, its end result—movement. *Thought is the first two-thirds of a psychological reflex.*"[49] By contrast, Nikolai Stepanovich, who has a fondness for such Stoic philosophers as Marcus Aurelius and Epictetus, considers his pessimistic thoughts in physiological terms only inasmuch as he is ill. Instead of the thoroughgoing monism of Sechenov, Nikolai Stepanovich maintains a dualism between sickness and health on the one hand and, on the other, between those who are governed by a "general idea" (obshchaia ideia) and those who are not.[50] For the latter group, in which he includes himself by the end of his notes, the onset of disease initiates a descent into the impersonal laws of nature. Nikolai Stepanovich claims his thoughts are "stinging [his] brain, like mosquitoes" (zhalit' moi mozg, kak moskity). Elsewhere he calls them "Arakcheev thoughts" (arakcheevskie mysli), alluding to the brutal war minister under Alexander I.[51] In as intimate a manner as Nikolai Stepanovich responds to his own deteriorating body, he tends throughout his notes to treat his thoughts as if they were foreign objects. Even in their most lucid forms, such thoughts are incapable of being vehicles of genuine insight.

Nikolai Stepanovich's habit of deflecting responsibility for his thoughts away from himself toward his illness reflects not just the norms of modern psychiatry in general but a popular fin-de-siècle understanding of nervous disease in particular. Among contemporary disease concepts, it is perhaps neurasthenia, which its American "discoverer" George Beard defined as a "deficiency or lack of nerve-force," that best exemplifies the pervasive élan of "nervosity" among the European middle class near the turn of the twentieth century.[52] After a German translation of Beard's *A Practical Treatise on Nervous Exhaustion (Neurasthenia)* appeared in 1881, neurasthenia rapidly spread across Europe, reaching Chekhov's plays and short stories by the end of the decade.[53] While Nikolai Stepanovich suffers from a condition grounded much less contentiously in the body than the disease concept neurasthenia would ever manage to become, the professor's facial tic, his irritability, his appeals to his "nervous tension" and "nervous excitability," as well as the broader evidence suggesting that he is suffering from a diabetes of nervous origin, all make it possible to situate "A Boring Story" alongside other works by Chekhov involving nervous disorders, such as "An Attack of the Nerves," "Ivanov," "The Duel," and "The Black Monk."[54]

In terms of what might be called the "poetics of nervosity," nervous disease in the late nineteenth century not only served as an artistic means for reworking, along materialist lines, the traditional thematics of the mind-body divide but also enabled writers and critics to transform social commentary into an extended symptomology in which the nervous system acted, literally or metaphorically, as an interface between society and the individual. Concerning neurasthenia, for instance, Beard argues that its many forms "are diseases of civilization, and of modern civilization, and mainly of the nineteenth century, and of the United States."[55] Chekhov expresses a somewhat more circumspect view on the social pathology of neurasthenia in a letter to Aleksei Suvorin, whose son appears to have been diagnosed with the trendy disease: "[He] has a disease that is mental, socioeconomical, and psychological, which perhaps does not exist at all, or, if it does exist, then perhaps does not have to be considered a disease."[56] In "A Boring Story," Nikolai Stepanovich generally rejects the arguments that Katia and her suitor, Mikhail Fedorovich, put forward to support their bleak assessment of contemporary society. In a remarkable passage near the beginning of the novella, however, Nikolai Stepanovich implicitly raises the possibility that one of the causes of his pessimism, its "diathesis," may lie in the decay of Russian society around him: "On the whole, the decrepit condition of the university buildings, the gloom of its corridors, the soot on its walls, its lack of lights, the dejected appearance of its steps, coat hooks, and benches, in the history of Russian pessimism, occupy one of the first places in the many rows of the diathesis *[prichin predraspolagaiushchikh]*."[57]

Throughout his notes, Nikolai Stepanovich fears that illness may have brought about a change in his view of life. At the end of the novella, however, Nikolai Stepanovich develops a more subtle dialectic on the relationship between mind, body, and society in disease. In these concluding pages, Nikolai Stepanovich no longer seeks to absolve himself of responsibility for his pessimism by appealing to his illness or to his environs. It is not that free will does not exist for Nikolai Stepanovich, but that he himself, Katia, and those around him have not the strength of character to rise above the sway of "external influences." He evokes the possibility of free moral agency—"of a god of the living man" *(bog zhivogo cheloveka)*—only to note its general absence in his life. It is his lack of a "general idea," a lack whose implications are more ethical than psychopathological, that paradoxically provides Nikolai Stepanovich with his final justification for reducing his own thoughts to the level of a mere "symptom."[58]

Melancholia and Insight

As opposed to attributing his pessimism to pathology, Nikolai Stepanovich and Katia both consider the possibility that he has only now attained full insight into the nature of his own existence and of the world around him. In Katia's view, the professor has at last come to see long-standing problems in his family and his career: "You see now what for some reason you did not want to notice before. In my opinion, you must first of all make a final break with your family and leave them. . . . Do they still remember you exist? . . . And the university, too. What do you want it for? . . . You have been lecturing for thirty years, and where are your pupils? Are there many famous scientists among them? . . . You are superfluous."[59] Although Katia and Nikolai Stepanovich ultimately resolve the question of the latter's pessimism in different ways, what remains consistent in their conversations and the professor's monologues is the mutual exclusion of illness and insight. In a letter to Suvorin, Chekhov himself reinforces this mutual exclusion by arguing that Nikolai Stepanovich's opinions should be considered as "things" *(veshchi)*: "For me, as an author, all these opinions do not in themselves have any value. The main thing is not their substance; their substance is interchangeable and not new. The whole thing lies in the nature of these opinions, in their dependence on external influences and such. One should regard them as things, as symptoms, completely in an objective manner, not trying to agree or disagree with them."[60] In *The Skepticism and Belief of Chekhov*, Vladimir Linkov criticizes Chekhov's one-sided interpretation of his own character in this letter. Although Chekhov enumerates many of Nikolai

Stepanovich's flawed personality traits, Linkov argues that the author "is silent about his self-criticism, about his capacity for merciless self-analysis." Rather than falling entirely on the side of either illness or insight, as Nikolai Stepanovich, Katia, Chekhov, and so many literary critics since have done, Linkov proposes that the professor's judgments be divided into two groups whose artistic functions differ. The first type, those in which Nikolai Stepanovich "understands the truth, no matter how terrible it is," represents real, substantial thoughts. The second type, in which he "flees from the truth," reflects "only symptoms of [his] diseased condition."[61]

Linkov's proposal breaks with a long critical tradition of "either-or," but his sorting of the professor's thoughts into groups leaves intact the mutual exclusivity of illness and insight. In contrast to this functional division, I have attempted to argue that within the context of mainstream nineteenth-century psychiatry a pessimism that is symptomatic is by definition devoid of insight. Yet there remains at least one more way to modulate the alternatives of illness and insight in "A Boring Story." Neither Nikolai Stepanovich nor his main interlocutor Katia consider the possibility, so common to the romantic cult of melancholia, that his pessimistic thoughts about himself and the world might be both pathological and insightful. Indeed, the tight and meticulously "realistic" connection between Nikolai Stepanovich's deteriorating body and his deteriorating mind serves throughout the novella as a check to any valorization of his pessimism. His habit of denigrating his own thoughts can nonetheless be seen to sharpen what I would like to call "the paradox of melancholy insight." Nikolai Stepanovich's thoughts become all the more melancholy in that they perpetually erase their own value. Instead of having thoughts that are "as bright and as deep as the sky" *(gluboki, kak nebo, iarki)*,[62] as would be fitting for a man of his station in life, he is overcome by a pessimism that he thoroughly belittles. At the novella's close, nothing has meaning in his life, neither past nor present, not even the insights that could express such an annihilating self-judgment.

While the opposition between illness and insight remains mutually exclusive throughout "A Boring Story," Chekhov does make a connection between nervous disease and nobility of character in an 1899 letter to a young Vsevolod Meierkhol'd about a character in a play: "Now about [this character's] nervousness *[nervnost']*. This nervousness should not be emphasized, or else the neuropathological nature will obscure and overwhelm what is more important, namely, his loneliness, the kind of loneliness experienced only by great and otherwise healthy organisms ('healthy' in the highest sense)."[63] By placing the neuroses of noble organisms beyond the realm of pathology, Chekhov is here echoing a tradition begun by Aristotle, rediscovered by humanists in the Renaissance, and epitomized by Hamlet—namely, the tradition of the melancholy great being. Nikolai Stepanovich's status as a renowned Russian physiologist, one afflicted with pessimism near the end of his life, places him within this humoral tradition. As he tells Katia, "I always felt myself to be a king. . . . But I'm a king no longer" *(ia vsegda chuvstvoval sebia korolem. . . . No teper' uzh ia ne korol')*. The tragic fall of this king of Russian science coincides with the appearance of "evil thoughts" that he considers "tolerable only to slaves" *(prilichno tol'ko rabam)*. Although he once availed himself of the "most sacred right of kings—the right to pardon" *(samoe sviatoe pravo korolei—eto pravo pomilovaniia)*, he has come to react with hate, spite, indignation, exasperation, and fear to all that is wrong around him.[64]

Nikolai Stepanovich's tragic fall occurs before the opening lines of his notes. These notes are not devoted to the events that lead to this fall, however, but to his present experience of loss. While the often tortuous paths of psychoanalysis are foreign in spirit to Chekhov's fictional world, not to mention to the author's views as a physician, Sigmund Freud's understanding of melancholia as loss is relevant to "A Boring Story." In his essay "Mourning and Melancholia," Freud writes that "mourning is regularly the reaction to the loss of a loved person, or to the loss of some abstraction which has taken the place of one, such as fatherland, liberty, an ideal, and so on." Melancholia is "an effect of the same influences," but mourning differs from melancholia in one important way: "the fall in self-esteem is absent in grief."[65] It is not difficult to find instances of loss in Nikolai Stepanovich's life. Not only is he facing death, but he is facing it alone. His family is preoccupied with its own drama—to which he feels entirely indifferent—as his daughter elopes with her fiancé. Even Katia, his "treasure" *(sokrovishche),* leaves him at the end of the story, and likely will not even attend his funeral. In addition to this loneliness, he is afraid that if he were to approach his medical colleagues about his condition he would be advised to give up his work: "And that would deprive me of my last hope."[66] If work is his last hope, however, then it is a bitter one, for he has already lost all the joy he once experienced while lecturing. Nikolai Stepanovich has even become divorced from his illustrious name, which lives its own independent existence in journals and newspapers.[67] This estrangement from his own name epitomizes a general erosion of his former identity. His grief at the approach of death might be considered the work of mourning, but this alteration in his self-image gives rise to a deprecatory self-analysis that is more suggestive of melancholia. If near the beginning of the novella he fears that he is spoiling the end of a life that has otherwise been beautiful and productive, he eventually comes to regard his entire life as having been wasted.

Nikolai Stepanovich has lost not only all sense of the meaning that his life once held for him but also his former nobility of thought. During his trip to Khar'kov he finds himself no longer able to stay above such "external influences" as "family troubles, merciless creditors, the rudeness of the railroad staff, the inconvenience of the passport system, the expensive and unhealthy food in the buffets, the universal ignorance and coarseness in attitudes." Yet the pessimism that has come to supplant his former nobility of thought provides him with insights, however unreliable or pathological they might be, that are self-examining, penetrating, and uncompromising, and that thus partake of a different, yet no less ancient or distinguished, ethos than the Stoicism he would wish to emulate; as he caustically puts it, he has nothing better to do in Khar'kov than to sit on a "strange bed," "[clasp his] knees," and heed the fabled oracle of Delphi: "Know thyself."[68] Freud similarly writes of the insights of the melancholic patient in terms of a greater tendency toward self-analysis: "In certain other self-accusations he also seems to us justified, only that he has a keener eye for the truth than others who are not melancholic . . . for all we know it may be that he has come very near to self-knowledge; we only wonder why a man must become ill before he can discover truth of this kind."[69]

While Nikolai Stepanovich's "boring story" is devoted at least as much to digressions and to the quotidian as to his pessimism and to his failing health, those passages in which he directly confronts his condition illuminate, with short bursts of insight, a crisis of meaning. This crisis follows its own plot development: Nikolai Stepanovich first alludes to his "new thoughts" near the end of the first section; he poses the question of whether he is ill or insightful in the third; and he returns to this question at the end of the fourth. It is only in the sixth and final section of "A Boring Story" that Nikolai Stepanovich at last puts this question to rest. In his final summation of his predicament, he does not climactically resolve the question of whether he is ill or insightful. On the contrary, in an anticlimax permeated in equal measure with pathos and bathos, he dissolves its original meaning. Succumbing to the very pessimism he dismisses, he writes, "in my passion for science, in my desire to live, in my sitting on a foreign bed and my striving to come to know myself, in all these thoughts, feelings, and notions that I form about everything, there is nothing general that might bind them into a single whole." Nikolai Stepanovich concludes that he has lacked a "general idea," not as a result of illness, but all his life, and thus the antithesis between illness and insight no longer preserves the dramatic potential for meaning that it had earlier held for him.[70]

It is this loss of meaning—in the very question from which his crisis of identity arose—that is so characteristic of melancholy insight. Nevertheless, if Nikolai Stepanovich dissolves the original opposition between insight and illness, then his final meditation conceals a self-referential paradox. This paradox of melancholy insight can be expressed in the terms he uses in his argument. If his pessimism is only a symptom of disease, then is his current pessimism about the merit of his life and career likewise only a symptom? If his self-analysis has revealed the absence of a ruling idea in his thoughts, then has not this symptomatic pessimism brought him insight, no matter how bitter, into the true nature of his own existence? Whatever the value of such objections, no further questions along these lines generate conflict in the novella. The paradox in this passage is therefore better articulated in terms of the form of Nikolai Stepanovich's final meditation. Nikolai Stepanovich's writing is never more lyrical than in the very passage where he reduces his thoughts to the level of pathological phenomena. As his own self-analysis becomes more lucid and insightful, as his writing style attains an organic coherence and a sense of conviction that it had previously lacked, he concludes that his view of the world is subject to the whim of external influences, rejects calmly and categorically the value of his long and illustrious life, and perceives, with unflinching clarity, that he has always lacked a ruling idea that might have connected his thoughts and feelings into a meaningful whole. It is the lyrical movement of his self-analysis that seems so discordant with the endpoint to which this self-analysis leads—the dismissal of his thoughts as a symptom.

Notes

Financial support for this project was initially provided by the Hannah Institute for the History of Medicine at the University of Toronto. I presented portions of this article at the annual conference of the Royal College of Physicians and Surgeons, Toronto, 1998, as well as at the annual convention of the American Association for the Advancement of Slavic Studies, Denver, Colorado, 2000. The source for the epigraph is Aristotle, *Problems*, ed. T. E. Page (Cambridge, Mass., 1937), 2:154–155.

1. A. P. Chekhov, "Skuchnaia istoriia (iz zapisok starogo cheloveka)," *Polnoe sobranie sochinenii i pisem v tridtsati tomakh*, ed. N. Bel'chikov et al. (Moscow, 1974–1983), *Sochineniia*, 7:282, 307 (hereafter *Sochineniia*, 1–18, or *Pis'ma*, 1–12).

2. Ibid., 7:282, 291.

3. M. M. Smirnov, "Geroi i avtor v 'Skuchnoi istorii,'" *V tvorcheskoi laboratorii Chekhova* (Moscow, 1974), 219.

4. Carol A. Flath, "The Limits to the Flesh: Searching for the Soul in Chekhov's 'A Boring Story,'" *Slavic and East European Journal* 41, no. 2 (Summer 1997): 279, 281.

5. Lev Shenov, "Anton Chekhov (Creation from the Void)," in Thomas A. Eekman, ed., *Critical Essays on Anton Chekhov* (Boston, 1989), 11; Marina Senderovich, "Chekhov's Existential Trilogy," in Savely Senderovich and Munir Sendich, eds., *Anton Chekhov Rediscovered: A Collection of New Studies with a Comprehensive Bibliography* (East Lansing, Mich., 1987), 84.

6. Leonid Gromov, *Realizm A. P. Chekhova vtoroi poloviny 80-kh godov* (Rostov-on-Don, 1958), 186. In contrast to these two main lines of interpreting Nikolai Stepanovich's pessimism, several critics have transferred the novella's emphasis on lack and deficiency from his thoughts themselves to character flaws that his self-analysis fails to address. Beverly Hahn, for example, commenting on Nikolai Stepanovich's indifference toward a despondent Katia in her own home, argues that he "fulfills the pattern of unconscious compromise, of which, one way or

another, he has been guilty throughout his adult life." See Hahn's *Chekhov: A Study of the Major Stories and Plays* (Cambridge, Eng., 1977), 164.

7. See E. Meve, *Meditsina v tvorchestve i zhizni A. P Chekhova* (Kiev, 1989), 92–103.

8. *Sochineniia*, 7:257.

9. Such an exercise in differential diagnosis is not foreign to Chekhov's own scholarly endeavors. Having studied forensic medicine in his fourth year of medical school, he assisted forensic experts several times during autopsies in criminal investigations. Furthermore, during his preparation for an eventually abandoned dissertation on the history of medicine in Russia, Chekhov argued that it was theoretically possible, as the official tsarist version attested, that the tsarevich Dmitrii killed himself with a knife during an epileptic fit in 1591. His investigation of whether the False Dmitrii ever suffered seizures similarly led him to conclude "that the pretender was in fact a pretender, because he did not have epilepsy." See A. V. Maslov, A. P. Chekhov—sudebno-meditsinskii ekspert," *Sudebnomeditsinskaia ekspertiza* 34, no. 4 (1991): 59–60. Commenting on *War and Peace,* moreover, Chekhov writes that it is "strange that the wound of Prince [Andrei] . . . gave off a cadaverous odor . . . if I had been nearby, I would have cured Prince Andrei." See his letter to A. S. Suvorin, 25 October 1891, *Pis'ma,* 4:291. As Leonid Grossman suggests, "even in letters to young writers, as he indulgently and gently examines their purely artistic shortcomings, Chekhov mercilessly chides them for the slightest defect in medical matters in their stories." See Grossman's "The Naturalism of Chekhov," in Robert Louis Jackson, ed., *Chekhov: A Collection of Critical Essays* (Englewood Cliffs, N.J., 1967), 33.

10. Indeed, such a reductionism, has at times occurred in Russian criticism on Chekhov. Meve, for example, in his highly informative study *Meditsina v tvorchestve I zhizni A. P. Chekhova,* diagnoses the character Kovrin in "Chernyi monakh" (The black monk) with dysnoia or, "in the modern understanding," schizophrenia. Dysnoia is a diagnosis with which Chekhov would likely have been familiar from his copy of S. S. Korsakov's 1893 *Kurs psikhiatrii.* Meve suggests that it was not Chekhov's intention to use the "mystical and decadent ideas of [Fedor] Dostoevskii . . . to uncover the theme of the story" but precisely to "condemn" these ideas (162). Nevertheless, if mysticism falls under Chekhov's pervasive critical gaze, then this is no less true of psychiatry. When Kovrin is treated for "megalomania" (*maniia velichiia, Sochineniia,* 8:251), partly against his will, his academic career decidedly suffers. If he is not a divinely chosen one, as the black monk suggests, then is he not, as he himself argues during a period of remission, a greater man when he is manic? Meve's diagnosis of dysnoia does not resolve this philosophical question on the relationship between genius and mania. Moreover, this question itself extends to the problem of differential diagnosis. Korsakov writes that it "is often difficult" to distinguish between pure mania and the "maniacal form of dysnoia." The criteria for distinguishing mania from dysnoia include the manic's "accelerated flow of representations" and "ease of associations," two characteristics that might arguably have facilitated Kovrin's academic work. See Korsakov's *Kurs psikhiatrii,* 2d ed. (Moscow, 1901), 2:826, 909. Even when drawing on a contemporary psychiatric text, it is not possible to determine categorically the full implications of Kovrin's mental illness in "The Black Monk." Korsakov's diagnostic dilemma between dysnoia and mania could even be considered a restatement of the story's central philosophical question.

11. A. P. Chudakov, *Chekhov's Poetics*, trans. Edwina Jannie Cruise and Donald Dragt (Ann Arbor, Mich., 1983), 141.

12. *Sochineniia*, 7:252.

13. Ibid., 7:252, 305.

14. Ibid., 7:252.

15. Ibid., 7:252, 282.

16. Ibid., 7:263.

17. Ibid., 7:301.

18. Ibid., 7:290.

19. Ibid., 7:306.

20. Korsakov, *Kurs psikhiatrii*, 1:1.

21. For example, Chekhov's "Ivanov" opens a little less than a year after the play's eponymous protagonist first begins to struggle with "psychopathy" (*psikhopatiia*, *Sochineniia*, 12:58), and in the first paragraph of "The Black Monk," Kovrin, already unwell, is advised by a "physician friend" to retire to the countryside for the spring and summer (*Sochineniia*, 8:226).

22. *Sochineniia*, 7:284.

23. Ibid., 7:290.

24. In the history of medicine, this conceptual distinction between "disease" and "illness," at least in English, belongs to the nineteenth century. See Stanley W. Jackson, *Melancholia and Depression: From Hippocratic Times to Modern Times* (New Haven, 1986), 12, 13. In a related manner, Chekhov's former classmate, the neurologist Grigorii Rossolimo, records the author as having said, "If I were an instructor, I would try as much as possible to involve students in the domain of the patient's subjective experience." See G. I. Rossolimo, "Vospominaniia o Chekhove," in A. K. Kotov, ed., *A. P. Chekhov v vospominaniiakh sovremennikov* (Moscow, 1960), 670.

25. *Sochineniia*, 7:282.

26. Claude Bernard, *Leçons sur le diabète et la glycogenèse animale* (Paris, 1877), 70–72.

27. W. Howship Dickinson, *Diabetes* (London, 1877), 64.

28. Ibid., 95.

29. Pierre Alexandre Costes, *Des terminaisons du diabète sucré* (Paris, 1872), 8, 9.

30. Flath, "Limits to the Flesh," 273; Meve, *Meditsina v tvorchestve i zhizni A. P. Chekhova*, 93. Focusing on this episode, Meve draws a suggestive clinical parallel between Nikolai Stepanovich's condition and that of one of his acknowledged prototypes, the embryologist A. I. Babukhin: "In the last years of his life A. I. Babukhin suffered terribly from angina pectoris or, in modern terms, stenocardia. His sufferings and those of the hero of 'A Boring Story' were extremely similar." Unfortunately, Meve does not develop this clinical parallel, nor does he address symptoms beyond those that appear in the "sparrow's night" episode.

31. *Sochineniia*, 7:301.

32. See Jean-Jacques Peumery, *Histoire illustrée du diabète: De l'antiquité à nos jours* (Paris, 1987), 109.

33. Bernard, "Leçons sur le diabète," *Leçons de pathologie expérimentale* (Paris, 1872), 338.

34. J. Thiroloix, *Le Diabète pancréatique: Expérimentation, clinique, anatomie pathologique* (Paris, 1892), 5.

35. Horst and Joseph Schumacher, "Then and Now: 100 Years of Diabetes Mellitus," in Dietrich von Engelhardt, ed., *Diabetes: Its Medical and Cultural History* (Berlin, 1989), 251 (my emphasis).

36. Francis E. Anstie, *Neuralgia and the Diseases That Resemble It* (New York, 1882), 31.

37. *Sochineniia,* 7:280, 302.

38. Costes, *Des terminaisons du diabète sucré,* 9, 10. Compare, for instance, Nikolai Stepanovich's description of his condition during his stay in a hotel in Khar'kov in the final section: "I felt sick on the train, chilled by the drafts passing through, and now I'm sitting on the bed. . . . I should really go to see some fellow professors today, but there's no strength or desire" (*Sochineniia,* 7:304).

39. William Osler, *The Principles and Practice of Medicine: Designed for the Use of Practitioners and Students of Medicine* (New York, 1892), 295.

40. Dickinson, *Diabetes,* 2, 20, 75.

41. Bernard, *Leçons sur le diabète et la glycogenèse animale,* 46, 475.

42. *Sochineniia,* 7:282.

43. Claude Bernard, *An Introduction to the Study of Experimental Medicine,* trans. Henry Copley Greene (New York, 1927), 198–199. In an article on Chekhov's realism, the literary critic Aleksandr Roskin draws an intriguing parallel between the author's aesthetic of "accidentalness" *(sluchainost')* and Bernard's emphasis on the importance of the accidental in medical observation. See A. Roskin, *A. P. Chekhov: Stat'i i ocherki* (Moscow, 1959), 193–201.

44. Nikolai Stepanovich is here quoting a maxim of one of Chekhov's own teachers, G. A. Zakhar'in, who sought to impart to his students a patient-oriented clinical methodology. For a discussion of Chekhov's relationship to the "school of Zakhar'in;" see Vladimir B. Kataev, "Ob'iasnit' kazhdyi sluchai v otdel'nosti," *Proza Chekhova: Problemy interpretatsii* (Moscow, 1979), 87–97.

45. In Émile Littré's *Dictionnaire de la langue française* (Paris, 1873–1874), 4:1889, "sémiologie" is defined as: "Terme de médecine. Partie de la médecine qui traite des signs des maladies."

46. Quoted in Gerlof Verwey, *Psychiatry in an Anthropological and Biomedical Context* (Dordrecht, 1985), 27.

47. Wilhelm Griesinger, *Mental Pathology and Therapeutics* (New York, 1965), 9.

48. *Sochineniia,* 7:307.

49. I. M. Sechenov, "Refleksy golovnogo mozga," in M. G. Iaroshevskii, ed., *Psikhologiia povedeniia: Izbrannye psikhologicheskie trudy* (Moscow, 1995), 107 (emphasis in the original). It is interesting to note that Nikolai Stepanovich's eclectic list of "famous friends" (*Sochineniia,* 7:251) includes the historian and psychologist Konstantin Kavelin, who defended the duality of body and soul in a public polemic with Sechenov during the 1870s.

50. *Sochineniia,* 7:307.

51. Ibid., 7:264, 291.

52. George M. Beard, *American Nervousness, Its Causes and Consequences* (New York, 1881), vi.

53. Edward Shorter, *From Paralysis to Fatigue: A History of Psychosomatic Illness in the Modern Era* (New York, 1992), 221. Daniel Gillès has suggested that Chekhov's first encounter with neurasthenia occurred in 1885, when his acquaintance, the artist Isaak Levitan, happened to be diagnosed with the new

disease. See Daniel Gillès, *Chekhov: Observer without Illusion,* trans. Charles Lam Markmann (New York, 1968), 70.

54. The term *neurasthenic (nevrastenik)* appears, for instance, in "Duel'" (The duel), which Chekhov began writing before the completion of "A Boring Story" (*Sochineniia,* 7: 374). Ivanov, in the play of the same name, complains about his "weakness" *(slabost')* and "nerves" *(nervy, Sochineniia,* 12:53). And in "Pripadok" (An attack of the nerves), the doctor's use of the catchword *exhaustion (pereutomlenie)* during his examination of Vasil'ev, as well as his testing of reflexes *(reflexsy)* and skin sensitivity *(chuvstvitel'nost' ego kozhi),* all suggest that he fears his patient may be suffering from neurasthenia (*Sochineniia,* 7:220, 221). "The Black Monk" focuses mostly on Kovrin's megalomania, but the narrator opens the story with a clear, and lightly parodic, allusion to neurasthenia: "Andrei Vasil'ich Kovrin, Master [of Sciences], became exhausted and upset his nerves *[utomilsia i rasstroil sebe nervy]*" (*Sochineniia,* 8:226). Kovrin's progression from neurasthenia to megalomania follows a pattern outlined by Korsakov in *Kurs psikhiatrii,* 2:1015.

55. George M. Beard. *A Practical Treatise on Nervous Exhaustion (Neurasthenia), Its Symptoms, Nature, Sequences, Treatment* (New York, 1880), 3. In a popular tract on neurasthenia, Bernard goes so far as to suggest that the five major precipitating causes of neurasthenia are steam power, the periodical press, the telegraph, the sciences, and the mental activity of women: "when civilization, plus these five factors, invades any nation, it must carry nervousness and nervous disease along with it." See Beard, *American Nervousness: Its Causes and Consequences,* 96.

56. Letter to Suvorin, 29 March 1890, *Pis'ma,* 4:50. Regarding Chekhov's interest in the new discipline of social pathology, see G. V. Arkhangel'skii, "A. P. Chekhov i zemskie vrachi," *Sovetskoe zdravookhranenie,* 1986, no. 3:61–64.

57. *Sochineniia,* 7:257, 258.

58. Ibid., 7:307.

59. Ibid., 7:282, 283.

60. Letter to Suvorin, 17 October 1889, *Pis'ma,* 3:266.

61. V. Ia. Linkov, *Skeptitsizm i vera Chekhova* (Moscow, 1995), 50.

62. *Sochineniia,* 7:291.

63. Letter to V. E. Meierkhol'd, October 1899, *Pis'ma,* 8:274.

64. *Sochineniia,* 7:281, 282.

65. Sigmund Freud, "Mourning and Melancholia," in Philip Rieff, ed., *General Psychological Theory* (New York, 1997), 164, 165.

66. *Sochineniia,* 7:290, 310.

67. Ibid., 7:251, 305, 306.

68. Ibid., 7:305, 506.

69. Freud, "Mourning and Melancholia," 167.

70. *Sochineniia,* 7:307.

KERRY McSWEENY

Chekhov's Stories:
Effects or Subtexts?

1

In adult life, Chekhov professed to have "no religion" and to be "not a believer." Yet during childhood, as he remarks in a letter, "I received a religious education and . . . upbringing—choir singing, reading the epistles and psalms in church, regular attendance at matins, altar boy and bell-ringing duty" (*Letters* 217, 374). His prose fiction gives ample evidence of Chekhov's deep knowledge of the rituals, liturgy, and customs of Russian Orthodox Christianity, and the presence of these elements in his work has long been noted by commentators. But only recently has an American trend in criticism led to "the serious study of this religious subtext in Chekhov's work," which according to Robert Louis Jackson, writing in 1993, "certainly is one of the major tasks of Chekhov criticism." When Chekhov "left the Church," Jackson asserts, "he did not step out of the Judeo-Christian world or divest himself of the culture and traditions of Russian Orthodoxy that he imbibed as a child and lived with all his life . . . biblical and liturgical vision, imagery, and allusion permeate his art" (*Reading* 8–9). Julie de Sherbinin agrees. In "Chekhov and Christianity: The Critical Evolution," she writes that "Chekhov has left us with a body of texts saturated with allusions to Christian scripture, liturgy, iconography, holidays, and saints that serve as signposts pointing to layers of meaning not immediately accessible on the surface. . .

Modern Language Studies, Volume 34, Numbers 1–2 (Spring–Fall 2004): pp. 42–51. Copyright © 2004 Kerry McSweeny.

[These] represent unturned stones that may potentially yield interpretations of great interest" (286, 294).

In my view, the principal results of this critical stone-turning have been bad readings of marvelous stories. In what follows, I offer a critique of the methodology of recent religious interpretations of Chekhov's stories and exemplifications of how his stories, even ones saturated with Christian allusions, are better read in terms of their aesthetic effects than their alleged subtexts.

2

Let us begin by examining the concept of a *subtext*—the *sine qua non* of the critical discourse of Jackson, de Sherbinin, and the other recent commentators offering religious readings of Chekhov's stories. In Savely Senderovich's formulation in his "Towards Chekhov's Deeper Reaches," his works "possess a dimension of depth; there are in his texts layers of meaning not immediately apparent to an unaccustomed eye which constitute a second plane of meaning different from the surface and symbolic in nature" (2). Before this assumption can become a useful critical tool, a number of matters need to be clarified. Is a subtext intentionally encoded in the text by the author, as some critics assume? If so, in the case of religious layering, is the intention to promote or demote Christian beliefs? The answer is not necessarily the former. Edward Wasiolek, for example, argues that the effect of the Christian references in Tolstoy's *Master and Man* is ultimately to suggest that "it is not Christian principles or faith that moves men to give themselves for others, but instincts of another sort" (188). Or should a subtext rather be considered, as it is by deconstructive critics, "a subversive or repressed text which is not consistent with the explicit text" and of which the author is "not wholly in control" (Rajan 21n)? Or should religious subtexts in Chekhov be considered a matter of cultural saturation—that is, in a phrase from Northrop Frye's *The Great Code: The Bible and Literature* quoted with approbation by Jackson, a kind of "imaginative framework—a mythological universe" (*Reading* 8) that, so to speak, chose Chekhov's stories as host and embedded itself in them?

These questions cannot be easily decided. On the one hand, it would be difficult to argue convincingly that Chekhov had as little creative control over his texts as the second and third possibilities presuppose. On the other, determination of intention is always a problematic undertaking. Take, for example, this attempt of de Sherbinin to resolve the question in the introduction to her *Chekhov and Russian Religious Culture: The Poetics of the Marian Paradigm*: "If Chekhov's citation of Christian scripture and allusions to Christian images are taken for something akin to the 'real coin,' as they have been in several recent studies, then the question of intention is resolved by stating or intimating that these references reveal authorial sympathies in accord with the values of the sacred, of moral betterment, redemption and/or salvation" (7).

But "these studies," like the ones offered in her book, presuppose the presence of the very same values she goes on to state. This means that her reasoning is circular and that nothing is resolved.

A key feature of these varieties of subtext is that they all have the same two premises. One is that a subtext is an empirical substrate of a literary work rather than a critical construction. The other is that the central critical task is the discovery and articulation of meaning through interpretative methods involving recuperation and decoding. But just because such exegetical operations can be performed on an author's works does not mean that it is good for them to be so treated. Consider, for example, the short stories in James Joyce's *Dubliners*. Joyce had as religious an upbringing as Chekhov, and his short fiction is every bit as saturated with the paraphernalia of Roman-Catholic Christianity as Chekhov's are with that of Russian-Orthodox Christianity. If one operated on the assumption that the Roman-Catholic elements in Joyce's stories were subtextual reading keys symbolizing transcendent beliefs, one could without difficulty produce religious interpretations of the stories. But doing so would presuppose ignoring the essentials of Joyce's creative method —particularly the concept of epiphany. This is the sudden realization by character or reader of the unique particularity of an object, event, or person, and not its conceptual transference into a symbol of something else.

Much of the critical writing on Chekhov attests to his stories involving the communication of a mood, feeling, attitude, or emotion rather than the communication of ideas or beliefs. And other readers have given similar witness—for example, the distinguished American short-story writer Raymond Carver: "When I read and am moved by a story of Chekhov it's similar to listening to a piece of music by Mozart and being moved by that, or being emotionally moved by something by Edith Piaf" (Gentry 143). Prima facie, it would follow that the kind of critical attention Chekhov's stories invites is not exclusively or even primarily interpretative. Inter alia, such attention would be sensitive to how literary allusion works in a text. This device is the explicit or implicit reference to another literary text that is "sufficiently overt" to be recognized and understood by competent readers (Perri 290). It contains what Ziva Ben-Porat calls a "built-in directional signal" or "marker" that is "identifiable as an element or pattern belonging to another independent text." But I disagree with this critic when she asserts that in a literary allusion the "simultaneous activation of the two texts thus connected results in the formation of intertextual patterns whose nature cannot be predetermined" (108). Good writers exercise a large measure of control over the results of the activation. They do so by choosing one marker rather than another, by positioning the marker in one place rather than another, by the degree of explicitness of the allusion, by its proximity to other features of the text, and by the generic context. It is the critic's task not merely to identify an allusion but also to determine how the intertextual possibilities signalled by the marker should be activated. Is it a relationship of part to part, part to whole, whole to part, or whole to whole? Is the allusion a ping or a thud?

This is part of a larger consideration. Pascal observed that in reading the Bible there were two kinds of error: to interpret everything literally and to interpret everything in a spiritual sense. Something similar might be said of literary works. How is the critic to decide when to read one way and when to read the other? In the case of Christian allusions in nineteenth-century works, another distinction is also necessary: that between denotation and connotation. Near the end of "Tintern Abbey," for example, Wordsworth speaks directly to his sister Dorothy, saying that he can accept the diminished present and face the uncertain future

> For thou art with me here upon the banks
> Of this fair river, thou my dearest Friend,
> My dear, dear Friend.

"For thou art with me" are the very words the speaker of the twenty-third Psalm (in the King James version of the Bible) uses to explain why, "though I walk through the valley of the shadow of death, I will fear no evil." In Wordsworth's patent allusion to the psalmist's affirmation, the denotation is changed—a human bond replaces a supernatural one—but the connotations of a fortifying and saving power are retained. And, to cite only one other example, some commentators have found comparable denotative-connotative dynamics in the allusions to the Passion and the Resurrection at the end of Tolstoy's *Death of Ivan Ilich* (see Jahn and Gutsche).

Such determinations are part of the task of the aesthetic critic, which is to offer as inclusive, nuanced, and balanced an account of the artwork as he/she can. This involves considering the status of any particular of the work in relation to the ensemble of details, motifs, figures, themes, and technical and presentational features of which it is part. That is to say, an explication of any one feature of a Chekhov story should be well-tempered in relation to its other distinguishing features.

With this in mind, let us now consider Chekhov's story "Ionych."[1] Its opening pages foreground *poshlost* (stifling mediocrity) in a provincial town, epitomized by the Turkin family and focused by the title character, a callow young doctor new to the town. When the story concludes some years later, Ionych has become obese, crass, obsessed with material values, and terminally unfulfilled emotionally. In the story's second section, he goes to the town's cemetery at night for what he thinks will be a romantic rendezvous with Yekaterina, the Turkins' daughter, at the tomb of Denetti—a female singer in a touring Italian opera company who had died in the town years before. As he approaches the cemetery,

> its white stone wall appeared and a gate. In the moonlight the inscription over the gate could be read: "Behold the hour is at hand." [Ionych] went through the wicker gate, and the first thing he saw was a wide avenue lined with poplars, and white crosses and monuments on either side of it, all of them casting black shadows: all around and stretching far into the distance only black and white was visible, and the drowsy trees spread their branches over the white monuments.

What is one to make of the inscription over the gate? How is it to be read? There are several possibilities. It could be considered simply as one of those inconsequential details in a realist text that give verisimilitude. But this particular detail is not like those in other Chekhov stories that Vladimir Nabokov describes as "trifles [that] are meaningless" in themselves but "all-important" in creating a "real atmosphere" (263). The inscription is more portentous than trifling, and it would be incurious of a reader not to consider what it suggests or signifies. At the referential level, there is clearly a meaning intended by those who affixed the inscription: the gate is a liminal space between ordinary human life and the mysteries of human existence. Indeed, in the solemn black-and-white spaces inside the cemetery, Ionych has an extraordinary psychological experience. The scene seems to offer "the promise of a quiet, beautiful, and everlasting life . . . forgiveness, sorrow, and peace." But a moment later it seems to be offering instead "the dull anguish of non-existence." Then, while waiting at the appointed tomb, Ionych's imaginings become sexualized. Experiencing the "agony of unfulfilled desire," he begins to imagine kisses and embraces and to see erotic marbled bodies and warm shapes in the shadows.

One need not end consideration of the inscription at this point, however, for what is inscribed over the gate is a literary allusion to the New Testament. Thus, at the textual rather than the referential level there is the possibility of another layer of signification. The reference is to John 5:28 and refers to Christ's prophecy of the resurrection of the dead on Judgment Day. If this allusion must be activated, I would allow myself to hear only a figural ping. The vehicle or denotation is the Christian promise of eternal life triumphing over the grave; its tenor or connotation is the promise of sexual love as a way out of the death-in-life of *poshlost*. In this reading, given the demoralizing ending of the story, the inscription becomes a comic/ironic foreshadowing of the non-appearance of the skittish and immature Yekaterina, and ultimately of the doctor's loveless non-fulfillment in life.

For Alexander Mihailovic, however, in an article in *Reading Chekhov's Text* entitled "Eschatology and Entombment in 'Ionych,'" the allusion is a resounding thud. It is nothing less than the center of "a network of Christological associations and references." Ultimately expressed in "eschatological terms" by the inscription is the potentially saving "revelation that salvation and life are a matter of choice and not the passive and cyclical inevitability of nature" (104, 113). This reading seems to me to attach far too much symbolic weight to a detail that is not the only potential signifier in the cemetery scene. More conspicuous is the tomb of the Italian opera singer, a description of which is prominently placed in the middle of Ionych's imaginings and is the hinge of the turn in his thoughts from death to sex.

Demetti's tomb, I would argue, invites one to regard Ionych's imaginings as operatic in the pejorative sense—as stagy, excessive embellishments of mortal and sexual feelings and thoughts. This suggests that as a performer, Ionych is on a par with Mr. Turkin, a tedious, boorish raconteur; with Mrs. Turkin, who loves to read aloud from her unpublished romance novels that have nothing to do with real life; with the Turkins' servant, whose one theatrical gig is a burlesque of tragic stage postures ("Die, unhappy woman"); and with Yekaterina, whose "noisy and tiresome" piano playing gives one the feeling that "she would go on hitting the keys till she had driven them into the piano." This reading is bolstered by the abrupt ending of the cemetery scene: the moon disappears behind a cloud "as though a curtain had been lowered." Once off-stage, when Ionych enters his carriage to return home, his only thought is that he has been putting on too much weight. When he proposes to Yekaterina the next day, her refusal comes in the form of a stagy declamation: "You know that I love art more than anything in the world; I love music madly, I adore it . . . A human being must aspire to some lofty, brilliant goal and family life would bind me forever." Ionych can hardly believe that his romantic aspirations have "petered out so stupidly, an ending worthy of a silly little play performed by some amateur company." The implication is that Ionych is not a creature of free will in a redemptive drama but rather a player in a provincial melodrama with a hardwired predisposition to *poshlost*.

How is one to adjudicate the differing meanings of the inscription and to decide on its relative weight in relation to the competing signifier of the tomb? Not by asking which meaning is correct by reference to some outside-the-story criterion or to the presence of a subtext revealed by critical excavation; but rather by reference to which meaning(s) are best for the story —which make the story stronger, more richly textured and cohesive, with greater cumulative impact? The answer seems to me clear: the secular pings are better than the religious thud because they are compatible with each other and in aggregate make for a powerful impression. The inferior interpretation of "Ionych" is the doctrinal one because it is totalizing and smothers the other meanings. It reduces a socially and psychologically penetrating story of a failed life to a Christian cautionary tale.

3

Several of Chekhov's stories contain features that while explicable as part of the narrative can also be read as commenting reflexively on the story and containing suggestions concerning how it should be read. There is nothing unusual about nineteenth-century realist writers embedding such features in their work. In chapter 16 of George Eliot's *Middlemarch,* for example, the narrator's description of Lydgate's scientific method of medical research is at the same time a description and celebration of the creative method of the author in her anatomy of provincial society and investigation into the cause of moral disease in her characters. And in the fifth part of Tolstoy's *Anna Karenina,* the scenes in Italy involving the painter Mihailov work perfectly at the diegetic level and at the same time contain an extra-diegetic or meta-poetical level of implication. In describing Mihailov's art, particularly his portrait of Anna Karenina, Tolstoy simultaneously calls attention to his own narrative method in *Anna Karenina.*

When found in Chekhov's stories, such features can be of considerable help in choosing between competing readings. As it happens, "Easter Night" and "The Student," both of which contain conspicuous reflexive elements, are also stories supersaturated with Christian motifs. Not surprisingly, both stories have recently been interpreted in the light of religious subtexts. In the former story, a first-person narrator, resembling the genteel narrator of Turgenev's *Sketches from a Hunter's Album,* recounts an incident involving socially inferior provincial persons. The story opens on a magnificent starry spring night with the narrator's account of taking a cable ferry across an expanse of swollen river to attend the midnight Easter celebrations at a monastery. The ferryman is a lay brother of the monastery named Ieronym. In conversation with him during the crossing, the narrator learns that Ieronym is deeply grieving the death that very day of his dearest friend and mentor, the deacon Nicolai, a "kind and merciful soul" whose sweetness of being is epitomized by his gift for composing akathists (special canticles sung in honor of Christ, his mother, or a saint). By the time they reach the monastery, the celebrations, including special illuminations, have begun. These are described in some detail. Dawn is breaking when the celebrations end and the narrator returns with others on the ferry, which is still being operated by the sad and weary Ieronym.

In Willa Chamberlain Axelrod's reading, the surface of "Easter Night" is ruthlessly decoded and a symbolic religious meaning laid bare. The initial crossing of the river, she asserts, "represents the Church's liturgical passage from Lent to Easter" and is thus "a metaphor for spiritual transition." Through Ieronym's account of Nicolai, "who is a Christ figure, [the narrator] is exposed to death and resurrection." The stop at the monastery "signifies the harrowing of hell, commemorated on Great Saturday," During the return crossing, the dew on Ieronym's face signifies that he "has passed over from a Lenten to a paschal disposition," while the dew on the ferry's cable transforms what the cable signifies (the Cross) "from a sign of death to a sign of resurrection." In the final paragraph, Ieronym "knows to look for Nicolai among the living, in the young woman with the rosy cheeks, the only passenger who specifically is wrapped in the white robe of fog." Previously a symbol of "the shroud of burial," the fog now, "in the context of the dew and resurrection . . . represents the white garments of Easter" (96–102).

What is wrong with this reading? In my view, everything. It is an act of interpretative totalitarianism in which every particular of the surface of Chekhov's story becomes grist to a symbolic mill. In the reading I shall offer, the focal point of "Easter Night" is found not in a subtext but in the activation of the sympathetic imagination of the narrator, which invites the sympathetic emotional participation of the reader. That is to say, "Easter Night" is designed not to communicate religious meanings but to produce an intense effect. Readers will have to determine for themselves which account of "Easter Night" is stronger. But decide they must. One cannot have both readings because Axelrod's reading involves repeated acts of conceptual transference, and the more this is done the more cerebral and the less affecting one's response to the story necessarily becomes.

At the reflexive level, the correctness of an aesthetic rather than an interpretative engagement is suggested by the implicit invitation in the text to consider similarities between the qualities of Nicolai's akathists as described by Ieronym and the qualities of Chekhov's "Easter Night." Nicolai possesses an extraordinary gift:

> Monks who don't understand about it reckon you only need to know the life of the saint you're writing to, and then follow the other akathists . . . but the main thing is not in the life, not in the correspondence with the others, but in the beauty and the sweetness. It all has to be shapely, brief, and thorough . . . It has to be written so that the one who is praying will rejoice and weep in his heart, but shake and be in awe in his mind.

At the center of the story is the loving relationship between Ieronym and Nicolai. The quality of being of the lost loved one and of their relationship is expressed through what Ieronym tells the narrator and through other features of the story that analogously suggest qualities of the monks' relationship. In the private space of their friendship, "he embraced me, stroked my head, called me tender words as if I were a little child." But now Ieronym is "like an orphan or a widow" in a hostile environment: "in our monastery the people are all good, kind, pious, but . . . there's no softness and delicacy in any of them." The description of the "veritable chaos" of the public Easter celebration at the monastery—it is "filled with suffocating smoke, sputtering lamps, and tumult"—is a writing large of the absence in monastery life of the softness and delicacy associated with the being of Nicolai. Similarly, the pyrotechnical visual aspects of the monastery's Easter celebration contrast with the silent illumination of the stars and their reflection in the water that are the natural visual equivalents of the beauty of the akathists.

The akathists are part of the ritual and liturgical details of the Easter celebration of the central Christian belief in Christ's resurrection from the dead and the consequent salvation of the human race. Chekhov's story is full of these elements and there is no question that the religious connotations add greatly to the richness and resonance of the work and that, as Donald Rayfield notes, they foster a "strange magical atmosphere of regeneration and elegy" (44). But the key progression in "Easter Night" is not from death to eternal life. It is from ordinary consciousness to expanded, sensitized consciousness—both for the narrator and the reader.

A first-person dramatized narrator helps to link the story's two settings—the ferry and the monastery. But the more important function of the narrator is to serve as the reader's surrogate and show him or her how to respond to the story of Ieronym and Nicolai. The narrator's initial response to hearing the former speak of his grief is dismissive. He thinks it is "an invitation to one of those 'longanimous' soul-saving conversations that idle and bored monks love so much." And after listening to the monk's description of the beauty of Nicolai's akathists, his reaction is brusque and patronizing: "In that case, it's a pity he died . . . however, my good man, let's get moving, otherwise we'll be late." But when the narrator merges with the worshippers at the monastery, he becomes "infected with the general joyous excitement," finds that he feels "unbearably pained for Ieronym," and vividly imagines how Ieronym would be feeling were he present.

Just after this, in the magical atmosphere of the Easter celebration an image of Nicolai himself arises in the narrator's imagination:

God knows, perhaps if I had seen him I would have lost the image my imagination now paints for me. This sympathetic, poetic man, who came at night to call out to Ieronym and who strewed his akathists with flowers, stars, and rays of sunlight, lonely and not understood, I picture to myself as timid, pale, with gentle, meek, and sad features. In his eyes, alongside intelligence, tenderness would shine, and that barely restrained, childlike exaltation I could hear in Ieronym's voice when he quoted the akathists to me.

This "now" is the climactic moment of "Easter Night": the shift from the past tense to the present signals a moment of expanded consciousness in which the dead Nicolai is raised to life in the imagination of the narrator—and of the reader. The raising is made possible for the narrator by an act of sympathetic imagination and for the reader by intense engagement in Chekhov's text.

In the story's final scene, we are once again on the ferry but it is now dawn. All that remains of the monastery's luminations are heaps of black ashes. Nature seems tired and sleepy, as does the "extraordinarily sad and weary" Ieronym. What remains vivid is suggestive not of religious sublimity but of human pathos—not resurrection but human love, loss, and longing. It is the "prolonged gaze" of Ieronym seeking in a young woman's face "the soft and tender features of his deceased friend."

4

"The Student" also has a paschal setting. This four-page story opens at sundown on Good Friday with a seminary student returning from a day's hunting to his impoverished family home. The weather has turned inhospitable and he is painfully hungry. It "seem[s] to him that the sudden onset of cold violated the order and harmony of everything." Recalling the miserable living conditions of his parents and "hunching up from the cold," he begins to think "how exactly the same wind had blown" centuries before in Russia and how "there had been the same savage poverty and hunger . . . ignorance and anguish, the same surrounding emptiness and darkness, the sense of oppression." The student is drawn by the light of an outdoor fire to where two peasant women are washing up after supper. As he warms his hands at the fire, he is reminded of a gospel reading from Holy Week, also known to the women, of how on a cold night Peter had warmed his hands by a fire in a courtyard. This prompts him to recount to the women the story of how on that occasion Peter denied three times that he knew Christ, and after the cock crowed went out and wept bitterly.

The women are strongly affected—tears roll down the cheeks of one, and the other gazes fixedly at the student with the look of "someone who is trying to suppress intense pain." Their reaction leads the student to reflect that if the woman wept then "everything that had happened with Peter on that dreadful night had some relation to her . . . something that had taken place nineteen centuries ago had a relation to the present." At the realization, "joy suddenly stirred in his soul . . . The past, he thought, is connected with the present in an unbroken chain of events flowing one out of the other." As he leaves the women to cross a river by ferry and walk uphill to his village, he keeps thinking how "the truth and beauty that had guided human life" in the garden where Jesus prayed and the courtyard where Peter denied him "went on unbroken to this day." The story ends with the student feeling "an inexpressibly sweet anticipation of happiness, an unknown, mysterious happiness ... life seemed to him delightful, wondrous, and filled with lofty meaning."

In an article on "The Student," Jackson immediately locates himself "on the symbolic plane of the story [where] one moves from Good Friday, the day on which Christ is crucified, to the 'feast of faith' of Easter Day." Like "Dante's confused traveler," the student is said to find himself in "a dark and threatening woods." His "paschal revelation" is signalled in the description of what he sees when he looks back upon leaving the women: "The solitary fire flickered peacefully in the darkness"—a sentence that according to Jackson "evokes John 1:5: 'And the light shineth in darkness; and the darkness comprehended it not'." For Jackson, "the message is clear": "The passage from forest to mount, from momentary despair through communion with [the women] to a moment of spiritual transfiguration, defines the journey of both student and story." The student's walking uphill at the close of the story alludes "not only to Jesus' ascent to the mount" but also to Moses on Mount Nebo: "Like Moses, [the student] will not see the promised land on earth; like Peter, he, too, will surely experience new trials and tribulations. What is important, though, is his sustaining vision, a profoundly ethical one, of 'truth and beauty'" (127–132).

As these excerpts indicate, in Jackson's reading a religious subtext becomes a platform from which an ethical-religious message is promulgated. But Jackson misses the delicate qualifications in the story's closing sentences: that the student "was only twenty-two" and that "life seemed to him [but not necessarily to the narrator] delightful." Nor does he consider the similar implications of the story's title (changed by Chekhov from "In the Evening" after the story's first appearance in print), which emphasizes the central character's youth and inexperience. The effect of these qualifications is not to undercut the affirmations of the story's concluding paragraphs but to keep the reader aware that they are a rendering of powerful subjective feelings in the consciousness of a impressionable young person of religious predisposition, and not tapping out in code a saving religious message.

It is also telling that Jackson fails to consider an essential feature of "The Student"—its reflexive element. It is a story about the telling of a story and its effect on its auditors and its teller. As such, one might expect that any close reading of "The Student" will consider fully this reflexive dimension. Exemplary in this regard is the reading of L. M. O'Toole (unmentioned by Jackson). This critic argues that the theme of "The Student" is aesthetic rather than ethical: it is "the power of tragedy to move and inspire" through catharsis. "The choice of a Christian myth ... is certainly vital to the story, but more in terms of setting and character than for the essential theme," which is "not the power of faith, but the power of tragedy"—the human tragedy of Peter's betrayal (46–47).

But O'Toole's structuralist "deep study of the work itself" (67) does not consider the reader's reception of the text. Is the effect of "The Student" on the reader the same as or different from the effect on the student of telling the story of Peter's betrayal to the two women and noting its effect on them? I would say the difference is that the "joy" and the sense of "truth and beauty" spoken of at the close of the story are felt experientially by the student and aesthetically by the reader. In different ways both student and reader have come into contact with one end of "an unbroken chain of events" that has been extended in one case by the student's retelling of the gospel story and in the other by Chekhov's evocative representation of the student's experience. In this sense, what happens to the characters in the story happens to its readers. And the student's exhilaration at the end of the story is similar in kind to the reader's. How long will the student's exhilaration last? How long will the reader's? These questions are peripheral. Concerning the former, there are several suggestions that it will be shorter-lived than he thinks it will be. Concerning the latter, all one can say is that, as with any intense experience, duration is a function of intensity. What is central is the continuing power of Chekhov's artwork to establish connections—to forge new links in a living chain that is not vertical, timeless, and sacred but horizontal, temporal and secular.

5

In a letter to an American professor of literature concerning one of her short stories, Flannery O'Connor included a stern rebuke:

> The meaning of a story should go on expanding for the reader the more he thinks about it, but meaning cannot be captured in an interpretation. If teachers are in the habit of approaching a story as if it were a research problem for which any answer is believable so long as it is not obvious, then I think students will never learn to enjoy fiction. Too much interpretation is certainly worse than too little, and where feeling for a story is absent, theory will not supply it. (*Habit* 437)

In another place, O'Connor speculated on the reason for the prevalence of this bad critical habit. While the novel works by a slow accumulation of detail, "the short story requires more drastic procedures . . . because more has to be accomplished in less space. The details have to carry more immediate weight. In good fiction, certain of the details will tend to accumulate meaning from the story itself, and when this happens, they become symbolic in their action." The problem was that many readers misunderstood how symbols function in verisimilar short fiction: "They seem to think that it is a way of saying something that [the writer is not] actually saying, and so . . . they approach it as if it were a problem in algebra. Find x. And when they do find or think they find this abstraction, x, they go off with an elaborate sense of satisfaction and the notion that they have 'understood' the story" (*Mystery* 70–71).

The procedures of the Christian exegetes of Chekhov's stories might be described in similar terms for similar reasons. Meaning in these stories is not something to be extracted by some interpretative act involving subtexts, decoding, and conceptual transference. It is rather to be found in the sum of the reader's sympathetic engagement with the story (his or her "feeling" for the story) and his or her reflective inquiry (thinking about the story). An essential presupposition of this process is determination of what kind of story one is reading and what kind of critical treatment is best for it. Some short stories invite interpretation in the sense of conceptual transference or decoding—for example, Hawthorne's allegorical tales and Nabokov's "The Vane Sisters," which requires the reader to recognize that there is an embedded acrostic in the final paragraph and to decipher it. Chekhov's stories invite a different kind of critical attention—not interpretative problem-solving but correct construal and an articulate aesthetic response.[2]

Notes

1. Quotations from "Ionych" are from David Margarshack's translation. For "Easter Night" and "The Student" I have used the translations of Richard Pevear and Larissa Volokhonsky.

2. For their excellent suggestions, I am most grateful to MLS's anonymous reader, and to Lyudmila Parts of the McGill University Department of Russian Studies.

Works Cited

Axelrod, Willa Chamberlain. "Passage from Holy Saturday to Easter Day in 'Holy Night'." *Reading Chekhov's Text*. Ed. Robert Louis Jackson. Evanston, IL: Northwestern University Press, 1993. 96–102.

Ben-Porat, Ziva. "The Poetics of Literary Allusion." *PTL: A Journal for Descriptive Poetics and Theory of Literature* 1 (1976): 5–28.

Chekhov, Anton. "Ionych." *Lady with Lapdog and Other Stories*. Trans. David Margarshack. London: Penguin, 1964.

———. *Letters of Anton Chekhov*. Trans. Michael Henry Heim. Ed. Simon Karlinsky. New York: Harper, 1973.

———. *Stories*. Trans. Richard Pevear and Larissa Volokhonsky. New York: Bantam, 2000.

Gentry, Marshall Bruce and William L. Stull, eds. *Conversations with Raymond Carver*. Jackson: University Press of Mississippi, 1990.

Gutsche, George P. "Moral Fiction: Tolstoy's *Death of Ivan Il'ich.*" *Tolstoy's "The Death of Ivan Il'ich": A Critical Companion.* Ed. Gary P. Jahn. Evanston, IL: Northwestern University Press, 1999. 55–101.

Jackson, Robert Louis. "Chekhov's 'The Student.'" *Reading Chekhov's Text.* Ed. Robert Louis Jackson. Evanston, IL: Northwestern University Press, 1993. 127–133.

——, Ed. *Reading Chekhov's Text.* Evanston, IL: Northwestern University Press, 1993.

Jahn, Gary P. "A Note on Miracle Motifs in the Later Works of Lev Tolstoi." *Tolstoy's Short Fiction.* Ed. Michael Katz. New York: Norton, 1991. 481–487.

Mihailovic, Alexander. "Eschatology and Entombment in 'Ionych.'" *Reading Chekhov's Text.* Ed. Robert Louis Jackson. Evanston, IL: Northwestern University Press, 1993. 103–114.

Nabokov, Vladimir. *Lectures on Russian Literature.* Ed. Fredson Bowers. New York: Harcourt Brace, 1981.

O'Connor, Flannery. *Mystery and Manners: Occasional Prose.* Ed. Sally and Robert Fitzgerald. New York: Farrar, 1969.

——. *The Habit of Being: Letters.* Ed. Sally Fitzgerald. New York: Farrar, 1979.

O'Toole, L. M. "Structure and Style in the Short Story: Chekhov's 'The Student.'" *Slavic and East European Review* 49 (1971): 45–67.

Perri, Carmela. "On Alluding." *Poetics* 7 (1978): 289–307.

Rajan, Tilottama. *Dark Interpreter: The Discourse of Romanticism.* Ithaca, NY: Cornell University Press, 1981.

Rayfied, Donald. *Understanding Chekhov: A Critical Study of Chekhov's Prose and Drama.* Madison, WI: University of Wisconsin Press, 1999.

Senderovich, Savely, and Munir Sendich, eds. *Anton Chekhov Rediscovered: A Collection of New Studies with a Comprehensive Bibliography.* East Lansing: Russian Language Journal, 1987.

——. "Towards Chekhov's Deeper Reaches." *Anton Chekhov Rediscovered: A Collection of New Studies with a Comprehensive Bibliography.* Eds. Savely Senderovich and Munir Sendish. East Lansing: Russian Language Journal, 1987. 1–8.

Sherbinin, Julie de. "Chekhov and Christianity: The Critical Evolution." *Chekhov Then and Now.* Ed. J. Douglas Clayton. New York: Peter Lang, 1997. 285–299.

——. *Chekhov and Russian Religious Culture: The Poetics of the Marian Paradigm.* Evanston, IL: Northwestern University Press, 1997.

Wasiolek, Edward. *Tolstoy's Major Fiction.* Chicago: University of Chicago Press, 1978.

Wordsworth, William. *Poetical Works.* 5 vols. Ed. E. de Selincourt and Helen Darbishire. Oxford: Clarendon, 1940–1949.

KJELD BJØRNAGER

The Masculine Triangle
in Uncle Vania

In Chekhov's *Uncle Vania* Serebriakov, Voinitskii and Astrov form a tense masculine triangle. And, as most often in Chekhov's works, the essence of these characters is not revealed in any simple or straightforward manner and the interaction between the characters is not openly motivated.

In this essay I shall present my own reading of Chekhov's text supplemented by the views of contemporary directors who have offered interpretations of these characters, two of them via both writing and production and two of them via production alone. The first two are Mark Rozovskii, who staged *Uncle Vania* in his own Moscow theatre, U nikitskikh vorot, in 1993 and Leonid Heifetz who staged the play in the Central Soviet Army Theatre in Moscow in 1969 and again in Turkey in 1991. Finally I include my comments on a Czech staging at the famous small theatre Na Zábradli in Prague in 1999 by Petr Lebl and some impressions of Lev Dodin's production at his Maly Drama Theatre in Petersburg in 2003.

Voinitskii is the title character of the play, by dint of his relationship to his sister's daughter. This in itself is somewhat curious: it underlines the play's lack of a main character. Voinitskii does not have a central or dominant role in the play. Many commentators have noted that the real central character in the play is Elena, around whom the three main male characters develop their interaction. But *Elena* was never an alternative title for the play. An

In *Chekhov 2004: Chekhov Special Issues in Two Volumes, Vol. 1: Aspects of Chekhov. Essays in Poetics: The Journal of the British Neo-Formalist Circle*, Volume 30. Eds. Joe Andrew and Robert Reid (ed. and preface). (Keele, England: Keele University Students Union, 2005): pp. 45–52.

91

earlier work that provided material for *Uncle Vania* was entitled *The Wood Demon*—pointing towards the importance of Dr Astrov in his association with forestry and as a protector of nature. So even if Elena is at the centre of the emotional storms of the play, she was never considered as a candidate for its title. Sonia, Voinitskii's niece, who, in a sense, is present in the title, is one of the main characters of the play, but not *the* main character. Like the three men she too becomes fascinated by Elena and expresses the growing and general feeling that everything in the house is centered around Elena: 'You must be a witch' (p. 218) as Sonia puts it in act three.[1]

Uncle Vania has recently suffered the shock of his life: he has come to the conclusion that the life he has lived thus far has been based on a lie. For the whole of his adult life he has admired Professor Serebriakov, but now he has realized that there was no reason for this admiration. The Professor is now worthless in Uncle Vania's eyes, but until a year or so ago he was an idol. This revelation came to Uncle Vania either before or after he realized that he was deeply and hopelessly in love with Elena, the Professor's wife. Now the puzzling question is: what is the relationship between his disappointment with Serebriakov's professional competence and the onset of his love for Elena? Is there a causal link between these two dominating sentiments in Uncle Vania's present life? This question is not answered directly in the play, but it seems to me that it has to be addressed by any actor playing the role. Time is an important factor here. Uncle Vania's mother says that he has 'changed so much over the last year' (p. 194)—that is that he has begun to express disagreement with the Professor's work. Now it seems that Elena and the Professor came to live permanently on the estate only a few months before the start of the play. It is mentioned three times during the play that Astrov comes to the estate once a month, not more often, and both Uncle Vania and Marina explain in detail how the Professor has changed the lifestyle on the estate as if they have not told Astrov of this before. Now Astrov has, according to Elena's words to Uncle Vania by the end of act one, been to the estate three times since her arrival. If we assume that Uncle Vania realized his deep feelings for Elena only when meeting her again—i.e. when she came to the estate to stay—it would indicate that Uncle Vania grew disillusioned with the Professor first and then, on subsequently meeting Elena, experienced a new kind of feeling for her. In other words only having liberated himself from admiration for the Professor, was he able to give free rein to his feelings for Elena. This is within the bounds of the probable. It is possible too that he fell in love with Elena during her stay the previous summer—assuming that till then the Professor and his wife only came to the estate to spend their summers. But in reading Chekhov we cannot limit ourselves to what we can conclude from the printed text; we must go between the lines and behind them and include what is possible, but not explicitly expressed.

Astrov is disillusioned, but in a different way from Uncle Vania. The greyness of daily existence is sapping his life. The one thing that is still able to call his emotions to life is the forest and—as it transpires in the course of the play—Elena. She draws his attention away from the forest with her beauty even if he condemns her life style. Beauty should be useful. Astrov is attracted to Elena during the play and she is attracted to him. He is ready to seduce her, in disregard for his friendship with Uncle Vania, and in full awareness of Uncle Vania's feelings for Elena. A remarkable thing in Astrov's development is his relationship to Sonia. He admits that if he had been told of Sonia's deep love for him before meeting Elena, he would have considered her as a fellow companion in life, but now it is impossible. This declaration in act three says something about the nature of his new and growing feelings for Elena. It is has an impact on his life, as evinced in his final remark to her: 'Finita la comedia!' (p. 240) As with Uncle Vania we must ask ourselves: is Astrov's attitude toward Serebriakov influenced by his feelings for Elena? At the beginning of the play Astrov has arrived in response to a call from the estate—the Professor was ill the previous evening and the doctor was called. But now in the morning he is well again and out walking in the countryside, enjoying the fine weather with his wife and daughter. Astrov is waiting to attend him but as soon as he enters (and this includes 'as soon as he sees Astrov') Serebriakov runs off to his own room in order to work. Is he embarrassed because he knows that the doctor has been called in vain? He doesn't make any apology to the doctor, neither does Elena, who apparently was the one who called the doctor. It has been suggested that this is an early expression of a kind of jealousy—that Serebriakov is aware that feelings are developing between Elena and Astrov. This is apparently the meaning of Leonid Heifetz who writes 'It is hard for her to conceal her growing passion for Astrov, for whom, from the moment they meet, she has been burning with desire and love'.[2] Mark Rozovskii has no doubt about this either. He develops his detailed understanding of act one based on an assumption that Astrov and Elena are both aware that they are very much attracted to one another, that Sonia sees it and that even the nanny Marina's reactions are based on this.[3] It does not seem very plausible to me. In act one Astrov and Elena hardly know one another. Elena says that she has so far not spoken to him, and Astrov does not speak to Elena as if they have known one another before. In Dodin's staging there is little doubt that from act one Serebriakov considers Astrov the competitor, not Uncle Vania. When Serebriakov enters in act one and sees Astrov he is especially careful to take Elena with him when leaving the stage. He grabs her hand and drags her off stage.

I think it reasonable to keep in mind that Astrov has been called out to Serebriakov for no purpose and that he is annoyed at having wasted his time. Serebriakov has met with Astrov a few times and already made up his mind that he doesn't agree with Astrov's medical diagnosis, as we hear at the beginning of act two where Astrov has again been called to the sick Serebriakov. In this instance Serebriakov does not even speak to Astrov. I would say that during act one the bad feelings between Serebriakov and Astrov are most likely based on disagreement about Serebriakov's illness. Astrov makes a diagnosis of gout and Serebriakov does not agree: he is sure it is rheumatism. They are close in symptoms but need different treatment. With gout the patient is recommended to lie down, with rheumatism to sit. And at the beginning of act two Serebriakov has been SITTING in pain for two nights. Even when Marina has taken him to bed, Elena returns and to Sonia's question, 'Has papa gone to bed?' answers 'No, he is sitting in the drawing room' (p. 213). Serebriakov is afraid of the bed.

The reason that Serebriakov does not want to follow doctor's orders and plainly states that Astrov is incompetent, lies in his fear of death, expressed in Serebriakov's reference to Turgenev, who died from pneumonia—angina pectoris—developed from gout. Accepting the bed instead of the chair would mean accepting gout and the nearness of a death like Turgenev's. Significantly Serebriakov does not refer to other doctors giving an alternative diagnosis to Astrov's. It is an interesting detail, too, that for Uncle Vania it is a matter of indifference which illness it is, whereas Sonia speaks directly to her father about his gout as a proven fact.

Do Astrov and Serebriakov speak to one another at all during the play? Not in act one; they just meet without words. In acts two and three they are not on stage together. But in the farewell scene in act four Serebriakov suddenly speaks to Astrov: 'Thank you for the pleasure of your society. I respect your attitude of mind, your enthusiasms, your spontaneity, but permit an old man to add one thing to his farewell greetings: you must try to do real work, yes, real work!' (p. 241) Now it seems that Serebriakov is not talking to Astrov as a doctor at all here! He is talking, presumably, about Astrov's fight to protect the forest. And he does not consider it real work! Serebriakov's total disregard for Astrov as a doctor is significant, but something more is hidden in these lines: Serebriakov openly admits that he is aware of Astrov's enthusiasm and spontaneity—precisely the qualities of character which have attracted Serebriakov's wife to him from the start. Maybe Astrov, when he is not feeling old, tired and disillusioned, but is talking about his beloved forest and defending it against destruction, is showing the same qualities that used to be professor Serebriakov's when he was younger and not so often martyred by his illness—namely enthusiasm and spontaneity, the qualities that made beautiful women fall in love with him—Sonia's mother and later Elena. In other words Serebriakov expresses, in these his only words in the play addressed directly to Astrov, that he has been fully aware that Astrov has been a danger to his marriage. But now, when they are about to leave forever, he can express this to Astrov and be very patronizing at the same time because he—Serebriakov—is taking Elena away. In Dodin's staging this is shown explicitly by Serebriakov's being allowed, against Chekhov's stage directions, to enter the stage while Elena and Astrov are kissing. Serebriakov's words, and especially the word 'spontaneity', refer to the act of kissing, thus stressing that he is not talking about Astrov the doctor, but Astrov the man. If one interprets his final words to Astrov in this way, one can also understand why Serebriakov tells Astrov: 'You must try to do real work!' To say that to *Doctor* Astrov would be meaningless since he works in that capacity day and night. (In Dodin's staging Astrov expresses his disbelief at Serebriakov's 'You must do real work' by bending forward as if he does not believe his ears!) On the other hand Serebriakov could, with some justification, say this to a man who has spent all his time at the estate for the last month or so just talking about his ideas about conserving nature, but not doing much (Astrov in act three to Elena: 'I've done nothing for a whole month' [p. 240]). It makes sense. Serebriakov is talking from the tradition of the men of the 1860s, criticizing intellectuals for just being men of words and more words and no action.

I'm not sure when Elena becomes aware of the seriousness of her feelings for Astrov, but she shows interest in him—in his enthusiasm—as early as the first act. This may be based on what she has heard from Uncle Vania or Sonia, which is most likely, because Elena also says in act one that she has as yet hardly spoken to Astrov herself. And Astrov does not seem to be very familiar with her at this time. During act two there is little doubt that they both feel attracted to one another. But the directors Heifetz, Rozovskii and Dodin seem to agree that the attraction between Astrov and Elena is already a dominant fact at the beginning of the play. As I mentioned earlier, I think that Serebriakov had his reasons for disliking Astrov the doctor even before he was given reason to dislike Astrov the man.

Let us now turn to Serebriakov himself. Most directors have seen him as a dreadful person in all respects. In the Prague staging by Petr Lebl he is a very old man showing sign of previous strokes in the way that his speaking abilities are disturbed: he mispronounces words and speaks with difficulty. In fact he shows no sign of ever having been the man who was admired by students, and loved by all women, as Uncle Vania puts it in his envy of him. He is just a disgusting, and, in his manner of speaking, even ridiculous old man. The scene at the beginning of act two underlines this and, in the scenes between him and Elena, she does not (and for the Prague audience this was made quite explicit) show any sign of love ever having existed between them. Therefore this interpretation gives a ring of falseness to her words to Sonia, just following that scene. She says that she married him for love even if she realized later on that it was not real love. Dodin's interpretation of this scene gave, in my opinion, a very well balanced impression of intimacy between Serebriakov and Elena but also of the reluctance in Elena's feelings towards him.

Heifetz tries to be more just to Serebriakov: 'It is unfair to think of Serebriakov as a monster, an evil creature and the *only* source of the conflict that strikes the family'. He continues 'I would be bored to see a play in which the Professor is presented only as a talentless fraud'.[4] Meaning that Serebriakov should be presented in a way that gives understanding of what qualities the man must have had in his former life. That is what I found in Dodin's staging of the play. But I find it remarkable that so many directors and Chekhov scholars have been so rude in their attitude to Serebriakov. Magarshack's *Chekhov the Dramatist*, which received so much attention all over the theatrical world in the early 1950s, is perhaps the principal source for this impolite attitude towards the Professor.[5] It seems to me that Uncle Vania's description of Serebriakov in act one has been generally taken for granted without noticing a few very Chekhovian hints hidden in his negative words. If we read Uncle Vania's words and deduct some of their negative intonation, we find that Serebriakov is a self-made man, who has been given nothing by way of heritage or by rich relatives. That means that he has created his impressive academic career by his own talent and work. His writing has dealt with—in Uncle Vania's words—'realism' and 'naturalism' in art and, as the person who for more than twenty-five years has been copying Serebriakov's manuscripts for him, Uncle Vania is likely to be quoting terms frequently met with in Serebriakov's works. Now who would write about 'realism' and 'naturalism' in art in the period of twenty-five years up to the time of *Uncle Vania* (that is from the 1860s onwards)? It is hard to believe that these words were frequent in writing about antique art from the time of ancient Greece and Rome. They would most likely be found in writing on contemporary Russian art. This was the period of new realist art, when painting became a field of social struggle and intense social debate. Art exhibitions became a place where the problems of society were debated in front of paintings that were sometimes considered dangerous to the security of the state. Art students of those days were often very active participants in the social debate. This again gives a link to the admiration that Uncle Vania's mother, Mariia Vasilevna, still holds for the Professor. She has been reading brochures for fifty years, but what kind of brochures? About emancipation. She is not fascinated by Serebriakov because of his profound knowledge of ancient art, but because he stands for her progressive social ideas!

Now this portrait of Professor Serebriakov, hidden behind Uncle Vania's very critical words, corresponds more, to Serebriakov's own remarks at the beginning of act two, where he complains about his life in the countryside in comparison with life in Petersburg or Moscow: 'I love success, I like being a well-known figure, I like creating a stir . . .' (p. 203). This is not what you would connect with an academic life devoted to the study of Greek and Roman art, but if—as I assume—Serebriakov was from time to time at the centre of public debate and agitated discussions about 'realism' and 'naturalism' where he attracted the attention of colleagues, students and even the public, then there is much more foundation to his words and to his bitterness and disappointment with a life in the countryside, not wished for by himself, but forced upon him by the poor pensions given to retired academics.

One might say that Chekhov has not given Serebriakov scenes in the play in which he could show the more positive sides of himself but, as we know, Chekhov was counting on his readers' (including the director's) capability of reading and understanding not only the lines themselves but what is to be inferred between and behind them. So maybe we should be more polite to Professor Serebriakov?[6]

Notes

1. Quotations from *Uncle Vania* are from Anton Chekhov, *Plays*, translated by Elisaveta Fen, Penguin Books, Harmondsworth, 1972 (first published 1954).

2. Leonid Heifetz, 'Notes from a Director: *Uncle Vanya*' in Vera Gottlieb and Paul Allan, eds, *The Cambridge Companion to Chekhov*, Cambridge University Press, Cambridge, 2000, pp. 91–100 (99).

3. M. G. Rozovskii, 'Chitaem *Diadiu Vaniu*' in *Chekhoviana. Melikhovskie trudy i dni*, Nauka, Moscow, 1995, pp. 169–201; also included in his book: *K Chekhovu. . .*, Moskovskii gumanitarnyi universitet, Moscow, 2003.

4. Heifetz, op. cit., p. 98.

5. David Magarshack, *Chekhov the Dramatist*, John Lehmann, London, 1952. Magarshack expresses his opinion on Serebriakov mainly on pages 205 to 208.

6. This article is a revised version on my paper on the conference, arranged by the Neo-Formalist Circle to mark 100 years since the death of Anton Chekhov in September, 2004. It is based on my book (published in Danish) *Tjekhovs teater*, Drama, Gråsten, 2003.

CYNTHIA MARSH

Two-timing Time
in Three Sisters

In a recent analysis of the effects of quotation in *Three Sisters* in performance[1] I reached the conclusion that quotation far from being merely referential can have a subversive and even destabilizing effect. This effect arises
from the repetition of quotation as a device, for example, the repetition of
Masha's lines from Pushkin throughout the play. Applying Derrida's understanding of repetition, iteration, where no two repetitions can ever be identical,[2] I reached the conclusion that *Three Sisters* argues that memory is fallible
and deceives. The central image of the play contains this notion. The sisters'
desire to return to Moscow is based on childhood recollection, which every
single member of the contemporary theatre audience sitting in the Moscow
of the sisters' adulthood could measure to be deceptive. Equally implied in
this argument and equally deceptive is the play's treatment of time.

Much of the existing discussion of time in *Three Sisters* focuses on references to time in the text.[3] It has shown how these references create the play's
narrative world, has examined the devices built into the text which indicate
that time passes, has examined the response of Chekhov's characters to time
and has traced the historical links between Chekhov's plays and his own period. I wish to consider here whether the time aspect of the play goes deeper
than these fictional and functional levels to express perhaps not a philosophy
of time, but at least a critique of existing concepts.

In *Chekhov 2004: Chekhov Special Issues in Two Volumes, Volume 1: Aspects of Chekhov. Essays
in Poetics: The Journal of the British Neo-Formalist Circle,* Volume 30. Eds. Joe Andrew and
Robert Reid. (Keele, England: Keele University Students Union, 2005): pp. 104–115.
Copyright © 2005 Cynthia Marsh.

I rely on Chekhov's irony, a factor which is so often missed in interpretations of his works. Take the opening to *Three Sisters*. Is not Chekhov
emphasizing a point about time in the opening lines? For someone as sensitive as Chekhov to the demands of the theatrical medium, to insert a clock
striking twelve into the opening lines of the play is surely to exaggerate, in
fact to be implying things other than that it is simply midday'? His text an-
ticipates some of his intended potential with a spoken reference to the clock
striking at the time of the sisters' father's funeral. There are also connotations
of the fateful hour of twelve, ironically midday here and not the midnight of
fairy tale lore. The practical issues created for performance by this striking
clock are rarely discussed. Twelve strikes of a clock (not including the ding
dong chimes signalling the full hour which precede the twelve beats) is extraordinarily long in stage time. In my experience rarely is the clock allowed
its full quota of strikes, even given the pause Chekhov has also inserted into
the text. It is a knowing and conscious exaggeration. Then, we can add in the
other references to time in Olga's opening speech: the already implied first
anniversary of the father's death; 5 May; the name day; 'тогда' (then), the use
of a verb with a time implication, 'переживу' (to survive, get through); time
passing in the intervening year ('прошел год'), the verb 'воспоминать' (to
remember), the adverb 'уже' (already). It is a text which has time references
packed into its spoken lines, as if Chekhov is signalling to the audience to be
doubly aware of time.

My argument about time in this play rests on the interaction between
the references to time in the text on the page and aspects of the performance
text, or more precisely here, the text as realized in the particular temporal
conditions of the theatre auditorium.[4] There are many implied devices in this
text which together weave a discourse on time which is quite distinct from
the references to time which create the fictional world of the play. The first
of these is the striking clock. Others include the verbal device of quotation;
the gifts given to Irina for her name day; photography; and a clock smashed
on stage and several more. This extra-textual discourse on time counterpoints
the discourse on time woven into the fictional world of the play: that night
follows day, as spring follows winter and is itself followed by summer and
autumn; people change and age, and discuss the past and the future; children
are born; trees bud and shed their leaves to mark the passing of the year;
birds migrate and return. These references to the fictional world are also the
functional means by which the passing of time is registered, implying the
commonly held notion of time as a linear, flowing entity. The first hints that
Chekhov is building in a discourse on time in relation to the performance
environment come in the surprises that initial analysis of this temporal reference reveals. These are well known. For example, it is easy to be seduced into
thinking that the play takes place over a twenty four hour cycle. Act one is

at midday, act two is in the evening, act three is the middle of the night and act four is at again at midday. This patterning is counterpointed to a four year cycle. The structure of a clock mechanism comes to mind: the smaller cog of the twenty-four hour structure turns the greater wheel of the seasonal and yearly cycles.

This surprise element is tuned to collapse the at best sentimental, and at worst unthinking, relation to time that most of us as well as the play's characters display. This extra-textual discourse is crucially created in that notional space where the performance on stage interacts with the sensitive mechanism that is theatre. Let me remind you of the concepts of time in a theatre performance as exemplified in *Three Sisters:* the fictional time of the play (1900); duration (approximately four years); seasonal setting (spring, winter [Lent]; summer; autumn); the past of the characters; the sisters' childhood in Moscow; the remote past (different periods even here: the remote fairy tale past and the decades old world glimpsed in quotation from Krylov, Pushkin, Lermontov and Gogol); one year ago; the present (changing within the four year span); the immediate future (again many indices here: Natasha's future [marriage; babies; achievement of ousting of the sisters]; Irina's future [marriage; career as a teacher etc.]); and the remote future discussed by Vershinin and Tuzenbakh in act two (variously two or three hundred years, or a thousand years, even a million).

Side by side with this narrative world are the actual historical times of the performance, (1901, 2004 or whenever); the time of day (in Britain the sacred hour of 7:30 pm); the duration (between two and three or so hours), sectioned by an interval. In addition, there are concepts such as pace involving dilation (slowing down) and acceleration (speeding up). These effects amount to the concept often referred to as 'stage time', which cannot tolerate the actual pace of real life. There is also the important insertion of real time elements, or points in the text where actions cannot be subjected to this extension or contraction frequent in dramatization. Examples are to be found in the real time performance of the musicians in act four, Masha's performance of her quotations, the posing and taking of photographs and the demonstration of the spinning top.

Another level is to be found in the period implications of the theatre building; the stage shape (e.g. proscenium arch or apron stage); and production decisions such as in-the-round staging, period or modern dress, and performance style. And yet another experience of time is felt in the ephemeral nature of theatre performance itself. Live performance is transitory, fleeting, and most frequently only recorded in the memory of the spectators and performers.

It is also important that *Three Sisters* was written almost exactly at the turn of the nineteenth to the twentieth century. At these centennial moments, the significance and nature of time are matters of public attention. Awareness of time for Chekhov came also from the theatre genres of his own period as focus shifted from realism to naturalism. As well as many other things, naturalism signalled an awareness and utilization of time which could be very different from that of realism. Steps were taken in the naturalist performance to replicate experience of real life: plots tended to disappear; characters engaged in ordinary conversation reflective of their social milieu, which could seem inconsequential, uncharted, and was often accused of being inartistic, even boring; historic and future time became fudged and of less consequence; and in naturalistic plays all that counted was the present. References to time tended to be suppressed. There was also often a complementary suppression of theatricality, a masking of the fact that this was theatre and not actual.

To a great extent *Three Sisters* exemplifies the opposite to naturalism. Historic time is recaptured through memory; there is discussion of the future; there is precise reference to ages and dates, anniversaries and obvious points are made about time passing. However, Chekhov is making his own counter point: memory is shown to be fallible, discussions about the future are futile. In its last line the play repeats the idea that we cannot know the future: 'If only we knew, if only we knew!' All we are left with is the present.[5]

Chekhov has not been alone in this sensitivity to time: many great artists have been compelled to dwell on this dilemma. What I find new and distinctive in Chekhov is his demonstration of the instability, and ever-changing nature of the present. He achieves this by matching the characters' experience of the present to the ephemeral quality of theatre. He also emphasizes this ephemerality ironically by frequently allowing the characters to dwell in the past or future of their fictional worlds. At the very least this mechanism encourages the audience to pity them. At deeper levels Chekhov is making a profound point about the fallibility of our recourse to time to structure and explain our world.

Derrida's 'iteration' gives a key to this approach. His concept of the present is as an endless series of repetitions, but these are repetitions which are never identical. Applying this idea to the verbal text when it is live in performance brings out a different understanding of Chekhov's dealings with time. By leaning on the theatrical structures which surround the play, in the very liveness[6] of performance, Chekhov indicated where we might find a true sense of existence: in those repeating but fleeting moments of stasis which are ever-changing, elusive and totally at odds with our desired experience.[7] Each moment is separate, to be experienced of and for itself and not as a continuum. The essence of the theatrical performance is repetition, and also a repetition that is never quite the same, and is therefore a continual experience of the present tense.

Live performance is quintessentially present tense so a live performance depends upon an ever self-regenerating concept of the present. It can disrupt a linear concept of time. For the audience looking at this performance, the fact that there are historical performances and future performances is irrelevant. In Chekhov's play this experience of existence comes not so much from the verbal text (itself a linear construct) but from the non-verbal: from props and the moments of stasis they introduce which engage the whole mechanism that is theatre in the audience's awareness. The props include the gifts brought to Irina's name day celebration. The moments of stasis embrace them and the use of photography, the breaking of the clock and the final tableau-esque moment of the play. There are others, but space and time permit me to discuss only these.[8] The use of these aspects enables Chekhov to engage in his critique of the conventional modes of thinking about time. Taken together they create a discourse which interlocks with the theatrical experience. In other words the play presents us with two quite different time mechanisms within the same theatrical event.

In act one Irina receives several gifts: a cake, a samovar, a history of her brother-in-law's school, a wooden picture frame, flowers and a spinning top.[9] There is a strongly ironic implication here of the fairy tale, where a beautiful, young girl is presented with gifts some of which have a sinister or loaded purpose. The time connotations and stage functions of the gifts have not been fully explored. The cake and the samovar arrive first. A cake is a temporary, present-time object: it will be consumed immediately (Ferapont is offered a piece almost straight away). As well as other significations, the cake's giver, Protopopov, is also a being very much of the present tense of the play. In contrast, the silver samovar is more solid, and the audience knows it is a gift associated with the celebration of a substantial anniversary, thus recalling the past. And Chebutykin is a character very much associated with the past tense of the play. Both gifts cause some embarrassment: the implications of a beautiful, young girl receiving a cake from the local councillor need not be spelled out, but the emphasis on blandishment and consumption are recognizable. This is acknowledged in Masha's comment and Irina's protesting reply:

Masha: I do not like Protopopov. What's his name, Mikhail Potapych? Or is it Ivanych. He ought not to be invited.

Irina: I haven't invited him.

Masha: Good.[10]

The samovar is embarrassingly inappropriate, for its cost and its association with a wedding anniversary rather than young girl's name-day (which as we know develops a thread of its own in the relationship between Irina and

Chebutykin in the course of the play). Both cake and samovar are quickly removed. These two items not only contrast the present and the past, but also momentarily stop the action of the play. The act of presentation is a ritualistic moment, and in both cases the presentation is formalized by the presence of messengers or functionaries: Ferapont with the cake, and the soldier with the samovar.

Kulygin is a precise and limited teacher ruled by time (the clock, he tells us, is seven minutes fast).[11] He brings a history of the last fifty years of his school. The listing of all the graduates is comic when seen, within the context of Kulygin's personal limitations, as a futile attempt at nailing down and capturing time through the accumulation of facts. The picture frame for a portrait made by Andrei has the same function: the capturing of one moment in the life of the subject. Feodotik and Rode arrive with flowers (fragile and present tense), presented by Rode, while Feodotik has brought his camera and takes three photographs. Forcing the company to pose, Feodotik stops the action of the play to take his three photographs. The photographs are another attempt to capture the moment. Immediately they are followed by the presentation of a spinning top to Irina. There is no stage instruction that the top is demonstrated, but the broken speech and reference to the noise suggest it is. Again the action stops as all listen. Masha then repeats her quotation from Pushkin, also by this point in the play an action-stopper.[12]

Let us look more closely at these moments of stasis provided by the gifts, the photographs, the spinning top and the quotation. The presentation of the first was marked by ritual which has the effect of focusing all attention upon itself, and pausing the action. Photographs capture one moment, implicitly deceiving about the past and the future. They are also utilizing real time within the artificial flow of stage time. Quotation is by its very nature a performed repetition, which replicates a real time action in real life. It too, however, deceives: it is never exact repetition. Masha's increasingly muddled repetition of this quotation in the course of the play indicates on one level that memory is fallible. This is the second instance of the quotation. Masha immediately questions why it is still on her mind, recalling her earlier rendition for the audience.

A spinning top is both movement and noise. Its circular motion is almost a perfect epitome of repetition, but matches Derrida's definition of iteration in that it is accompanied by an element of change: a humming noise which rises to a crescendo and then falls back. Technically each circular movement is accompanied by a minutely different level of sound. Beyond that, the spinning top in motion is a simulacrum of the world with its spinning planets which encapsulates as far as humanity, grounded in its own temporality, is able to perceive, a sense of timelessness. Together these moments of stasis provide a chain of repetitions, which are each further characterized by being played out in real time. The presence of this span of real time actions both foregrounds and destabilizes the theatrical illusion. They provide moments of actuality within the 'liveness' of performance.

Each of these devices creates a performance-within-a-performance, and consequently an on-stage audience. The samovar and the cake are given a general response. Posing for the photographs implies the many audiences they will have; the top and the quotation create a silent listening audience among all the characters on stage. The consequence is to unite on-stage and auditorium audiences. An objection may be that these moments of stasis are very short-lived, but when seen in conjunction with the many other similar moments in the play they begin to form a strong discourse. Two further key moments to be discussed here are the smashing of the clock in act three and the tableau-like ending to the play.[13] The incident in act three has strong echoes of the striking clock which opens the play, and Chebutykin's demonstration of his pocket watch which strikes the hour in the closing act. The act three incident creates an on-stage audience as the clock is dropped and breaks to pieces. Similarly the pocket watch striking in act four stops the action as the striking clock does at the beginning of the play. The clock is dropped at the moment that Chebutykin hears the brigade is leaving, providing a turning point to his own life and a connecting link to the actual departure of the soldiers at the end of the play. In acts three and four Chebutykin accompanies his actions related to time with his 'philosophy' that perhaps we do not exist, but only think we do. The breaking of a time piece has an appropriate symbolism for our theme. Clocks and watches are the most obvious ways for registering the human construct of time as a means of imposing order on the universe. If, however, we do not exist that implies that our human construct of time is a nonsense.

In their uniting of auditorium and stage audiences, these action-stopping moments reinforce to the audience the presence of theatrical illusion. This discourse utilizing real time also suggests that human constructs of time are as false as the theatrical illusion. The world the theatre falsely creates for the three sisters, regulated by the seasons, by clocks and watches is comfortable and tangible, but in the end unreal. The play shows there is another implacable, inevitable truth in the growing presence of Natasha in the most intimate and comfortable place inhabited by the sisters, their home.

The ending to the play intensifies this discourse on the deceptive comfort of time. I need hardly recall the stage directions to the end of the play which turn the sisters into a statuesque stillness, as they recognize the discomfort of the human situation. This ending provides a posed moment of stasis to crown all the other moments of stasis in the foregoing play. All the while ironically matched to the linear, onward, temporally driven movement of the music in the military march signalling the departing brigade, their immobility and words suggest that there is a horrifying bleakness, invulnerable to time, at the heart of human life. Their admission of ignorance of the truths of existence is an admission of the inability of the human construct of time to provide any real answers. In the context of live performance, it is important that this understanding comes at the end of the play. The ending of a theatrical performance is a point where the structures of the two time worlds, the narrative of the play and the time registers of the theatrical world, are simultaneously present as the audience members ready themselves to re-enter their own real worlds. Chekhov utilized his instinctive knowledge of this process, not only here but in the endings to his other major plays.

I wish to argue that through this constructed interaction between different concepts of time the audience of *Three Sisters* can reach to the meta-field of this text in live performance. On one level there is the circumscribed world of the play, its narrative level set in 1900 or thereabouts in Russia. On another is the world of temporal illusion engaged every time the play is in live performance. Here lies the two-timing of time referred to in my title. Both aspects are simultaneously courted, making the undeniable historical narrative, lodged in the play's references to time, a deception. So equally the function of these time references is not pedantry or exaggeration, for precisely by these continual and repeating time references, the sense of deception is constantly engaged. Full appreciation of these references comes from the knowledge of the interaction of the two aspects of time. Subtle touches, such as the fate of the clock, the echoing striking of clocks and watches, or Feodotik's loss of his camera in the time-denying raging of the fire in act three; or obvious developments such as Masha's confusion in her quotation, continually provide us with an appreciation of the marriage between the discourse on time and the formal framework of theatre itself. This marriage supplies the intellectual and aesthetic frissons which can make viewing a Chekhov play such an intense experience.

Moreover, once we as audience can reach to the meta-field of the play where these two levels interact, we are confronted, deliberately and ironically with an experience of timelessness. At these moments the experience of the play, its themes as activated in its live theatrical mode, provides insight into the universal. A performance of this play simultaneously pursues both aspects, time and timelessness, in order to make its different points. However, in so doing, and here is where the performance of this text can defy and transcend the human construct of time, we appreciate how and why Chekhov's art has a timeless and universal significance beyond its immediate period. In this way this play, so draped in the paraphernalia of its own time, succeeds in performance in providing us with a sense of our own mortality.

This discourse would seem to make a mockery of marking a centenary, and I can almost sense a wry smile from Chekhov. I think perhaps we should ask ourselves why we have the tradition of such celebrations, whether of writers or of their works. We might find we are both the deceivers and the deceived. After all, why celebrate the elapse of a period of time when it is the quality of the genius of a writer which ensures survival. Chekhov, I think, with all the strength of his irony taught us to be utterly suspicious of this deceptive and comforting construct that we call time.

NOTES

1. Cynthia Marsh, 'Performing Quotation: Masha's Lines from Pushkin in *Three Sisters*', Conference Paper, IFTR, Amsterdam, 2002; BASEES, Cambridge, 2003.

2. Jacques Derrida, *Limited Inc*, Northwestern University Press, Evanston, 1988, p. 56 and passim.

3. For example, see William Babula, '*Three Sisters*, Time and the Audience', *Modern Drama*, XVIII, 1975, pp. 365–369; C. J. G. Turner, 'Time in Chekhov's *Tri sestry*', *Canadian Slavonic Papers*, XXVIII, 1986, pp. 64–79; id., *Time and Temporal Structure in Chekhov*, Birmingham Slavonic Monographs, 22, University of Birmingham, 1994; B. Zingerman, 'Vremia v p'esakh Chekhova', *Teatr Chekhova i ego mirovoe znachenie*, Nauka, Moscow, 1988, pp. 5–62 ; and passim in many other studies.

4. It is difficult to find an adequate term here. I do not mean the *mise en scène*, which as well as implying the set design and décor of a production has now also acquired the wider meaning of all the activities which go into transforming a written text into a performance. I mean here the moment of realization of the written text before an audience.

5. In his study of time in Chekhov's works Turner makes a point about the amount of writing in the present tense which is to be found in Chekhov's short stories, and how dramatic in nature these stories were (Turner, 1994, pp. 1–23).

6. This term was used by Philip Auslander in his study, *Liveness* (Routledge, London, 1999). He juxtaposes it to 'mediatized' performance. I am using it here in the sense of the live, performed aspect of a written text.

7. My view is different here from that of Zingerman, nor do I equate this view of the 'moment' with that of the Symbolist poets. Zingerman draws a careful contrast to the Symbolists' preoccupation with the 'moment'. For them the moment in its timelessness was a window on eternity. Chekhov's characters, Zingerman argues, seize the fleeting moment only to survive the dreadful monotony of their lives (Zingerman, p. 28). My view is that these 'moments' are expressed in the dramaturgical form itself.

8. Andrew Sofer's *The Stage Life of Props* (University of Michigan Press, Michigan, 2003) is both a study of the function of props on stage and a history of the development of particular props. The two points most pertinent to the argument here concern his reference to the 'temporal contract' with the audience (p. 14) and his concept of 'contextual reanimation' (p. 4). The temporal contract refers to an implied agreement with the audience that this prop signifies this and / or this for the duration of this performance. Contextual reanimation is a means for understanding the significance of props: 'a thick description of the stage event as best as we can construct it, using such cues as verbal and stage directions, visual records of historical

performances, and (where available) eye witness accounts' (p. 4). Sofer counters the linguistic (semiotic) approach which dematerializes props on stage with the idea of the theatrical presence of the object, i.e. placing emphasis on its physicality on stage. My argument rests on the fact that I have grouped props which can be seen to have a role in putting forward the play's critique of the human construct of time.

9. The fact that the gifts all come from men, several of whom are admirers or putative ones, often goes unnoticed. It is also to be noted that the two men who compete for Irina's affections in the plot, Tuzenbakh and Solenyi, do not bring gifts. The fact that the gifts often tell us as much about the donors as the recipients is expected in a writer as subtle as Chekhov.

10. Act one (translation my own).

11. Act one, shortly after his first entrance.

12. I am grateful to Professor Harai Golomb for his comment that this was the interpretation offered by the acclaimed British National Theatre production, which Laurence Olivier directed in 1969.

13. Other instances include the two-locational opening to the play, other quotations (for example from Krylov, Lermontov, Gogol and from songs and newspapers) and the street musicians who enter the garden in act four.

ROBIN MILNER-GULLAND
AND OLGA SOBOLEVA

Translating and Mistranslating Chekhov

This article derives from a 'collective analysis' at the 2004 Neo-Formalist Conference; some twenty participants, chaired by the present authors, focused their discussion on the opening pages of the story *Ionych* (1898), while also referring to translation problems relating to Chekhov's plays. The purpose of our analysis was practical: to examine how the chief translators of Chekhov into English faced, or did not face, certain problems, rather than to make any significant contribution to translation theory, or indeed to offer quasi-definitive solutions to the problems we identified. We quote some of the *ad hoc* contributions made by those at the discussion in the body of this article, and wish to express our gratitude to all participants.

It was Vasilii Zhukovskii, himself a fine translator from a number of languages, who wrote the proverbial phrase: 'переводчик в прозе есть раб, переводчик в стихах—соперник' ('the translator of prose is the slave of the original, while the translator of verse is the rival').[1] The inference is, of course, that the prose translation should be as accurate as possible, whatever that might mean, whereas the verse translator enjoys a degree of poetic licence. This argument, however, can be taken a step further, for Zhukovskii's aphorism seems to underestimate the problems of translation in prose. In order to transfer the fullest possible meaning of an original text, every phrase and word of that original text, complete with its literal meaning, any ethnic

In *Chekhov 2004: Chekhov Special Issues in Two Volumes, Volume I: Aspects of Chekhov. Essays in Poetics: The Journal of the British Neo-Formalist Circle*, Volume 30. Andrew, Joe (ed.) and Reid, Robert (ed. and preface). (Keele, England: Keele University Students Union, 2005): pp. 116–132. Copyright © 2005 Robin Milner-Gulland and Olga Soboleva.

and cultural allusions and nuances it potentially carries, even its value in terms of sound and maybe its visual aspects are an inalienable part of the tonality. Consequently the perfect translation even of a single word is well-nigh impossible,[2] let alone the perfect translation of a complex work of art stretching over a hundred pages or more. Therefore one should perhaps rephrase the observation of the great poet by emphasizing the incontrovertible fact that every translator is inevitably the victim of the original. Ultimately, he/she simply cannot hope to achieve anything like the full effect of the original text and, therefore, must simply try to accept defeat gracefully—or, indeed, awkwardly, if the style of the original demands it. We shall return to the question of the 'impossibility' of translation at the end of this article.

It seems that Chekhov himself was a great supporter of such a position and was sceptical about translation of his works. Thus when speaking of his *Cherry Orchard*, he referred to the absence of Russian realities in foreign countries: 'французы ничего не поймут из Ермолая, из продажи имения' ('the French will understand nothing either about Ermolai or about selling the estate')[3] and in Germany 'нет ни биллиарда,[4] ни Лопахиных, ни студентов à la Трофимов' ('there is neither billiard russe, nor Lophakhins, nor students à la Trofimov').[5] Time proved him wrong; and the main argument against Chekhov's disbelief in the power of translation concerns the quintessential features of his characters and the humanistic content of his writings, in which Russian realities are only a vehicle for revealing the universal questions.

English readers were introduced to Chekhov largely through the works of Constance Garnett, who since 1893 had had great experience in translating the works of Goncharov, Ostrovskii, Tolstoi and Dostoevskii. In 1894 Garnett visited Russia, and her first translation of *The Seagull* could have appeared as early as that year, if she had received permission from Chekhov, for which she asked him in a personal letter. However, this came to nothing. Her translations of Chekhov's plays did not appear in print until 1912,[6] and the English audience could only enjoy his prose, which Garnett had been translating since 1903.[7]

The new era in translation of Chekhov's writings was marked by the works of literary scholars. In the sixties such specialists as David Magarshack and the notable scholar Ronald Hingley *(The Oxford Chekhov)* published their translations of Chekhov's works in an endeavour to address anew the question of inter-cultural communication and to bring the great Russian author closer to a contemporary audience. Hingley's works are valued for their graceful rendering of Chekhov's style, attention to the sub-text and an attempt to convey the contemporary relevance of Chekhov's writings through a succinct, 'no-nonsense' register of English. These translations were highly regarded by such a masterful stylist as Kornei Chukovskii, who, nevertheless, pointed out

Hingley's failure to reveal the colour of popular speech ('просторечие') in Chekhov's writing,[8] which, in his opinion, left it 'chemically pure' and without any flair.[9] Donald Rayfield's translation[10] is a recent and intriguing experiment that takes Constance Garnett's texts and 'updates' them through a great many corrections and amendments: he makes around eighty changes in the first three pages of *Ionych*, some merely concerning spelling etc., but several involving whole phrases.

It is not an easy task to translate Chekhov's works: his writings have an ability to speak on many levels with different effects. Therefore the main point of concern will be to conflate all the levels of meaning in the original text: the narrative, the socio-historical and the universally metaphoric. It should also be mentioned that it emerged in our discussion that the problems of translating the plays are far from identical with those associated with the short stories, though space forbids our going further into this here.

In order to look more closely at the specific problems regarding translation of Chekhov's writings the participants were requested to focus on the first part of his short story *Ionych*[11] (1898), as translated by four different authors: Constance Garnett (*Selected Tales by Tchehov*, 1912), David Magarshack (*Lady with Lapdog and Other Stories*, 1964), Ronald Hingley (*The Oxford Chekhov*, IX, 1975) and Donald Rayfield (*The Chekhov Omnibus: Selected Stories*, 1994).

When translating Chekhov, or any literary writer, the author encounters two main kinds of difficulties: in general terms (1) linguistic and stylistic problems, as well as (2) the question of intercultural communication.

1. Different source languages will, of course, present differing problems for the translator working into English, so perhaps a few words on some of the major differences between Russian and English might not come amiss. As Russian is a highly inflected language, it is considerably more economical in words than English and also far more flexible in terms of word order, which may greatly affect emphasis in the phrase.[12] Rosamund Bartlett, who recently translated a series of Chekhov's short stories (though not yet this one),[13] pointed out that when working on separate paragraphs of Chekhov's texts she tried to keep the same number of words as in the original. She considers conciseness an important feature of Chekhov's style, and she had tremendous difficulties in finding an equivalent in English. The translation of Russian verbs can sometimes be surprisingly tricky, as there is no multiplicity of compound tenses as in English; at the same time, this multiplicity is not always as helpful as it might be. Even more troublesome can be the conditional mood, as there is no distinction in Russian between 'I would do something' and 'I would have done something'. In this context it is worth mentioning the key phrase, repeated several times in the ending of Chekhov's *Three Sisters*—'Если бы знать' (often, but inadequately, rendered 'If only one

could know')—which presents insuperable difficulty for translators. English seems unable to imitate the 'unfinalized' nature of this phrase's grammatical structure; hence any version of it can only circumscribe its potential.[14]

Syntax and punctuation are a more general problem, at the level of style or 'correct' language. Rosamund Bartlett suggested that special attention should be paid to the use of 'многоточие'[15] and semicolons in Chekhov's texts. In distinction to commas and colons, the usage of which is prescribed by Russian grammar (Joost van Baak), the latter result from meaningful choices by the author and should be treated contextually with extreme care and attention. In this respect Eric De Haard drew attention to the opening sentence in the text of *Ionych*. What are we to do with participles and gerunds? Whether and how to chop up sentences? Here he would plead to leave it as 'heavy' as it is, with its broad scope and its slightly ironic authorially-coloured indirect discourse, which makes an appropriate introduction to the story.

As far as linguistic problems are concerned, the main difficulty arises from translating words that have double (sometimes multiple) connotations in Russian and for which there is no single equivalent in English. An example can be found in the very first line of the story *Ionych* (note that even before its first line, the title of the story itself presents problems, to which we shall return below). The word 'приезжий' has a double connotation of 'a visitor' (chosen by Garnett and Hingley) and of 'a person who lived only a short time in the town' (preferred by Magarshack). In Chekhov's text neither of these translations would be perfect equivalents for 'приезжий', which implies both meanings. However the latter seems to be contextually more appropriate. This becomes clear if one looks at the first and third paragraphs of the text. At the beginning of the story it is mentioned that all 'приезжие' were advised to make acquaintance with the Turkins; in paragraph three the same idea is projected onto Dr Startsev 'и доктору Старцеву . . . тоже говорили, что ему необходимо познакомиться с Туркиными' ('and Dr Startsev . . . also was told that he had to make their acquaintance'): this 'тоже' ('also') clearly refers Dr Startsev to the group of 'приезжие', but at the same time he cannot be called 'a visitor'.

The same kind of difficulty presents itself in the word 'изумлялись' in the passage when Kotik receives congratulations from the audience on her playing the piano: 'Все окружили ее, поздравляли, изумлялись, уверяли, что давно уже не слыхали такой музыки' ('they all crowded round with their congratulations and admiration, declaring that they hadn't heard such a performance for years'). In Russian 'изумлялись' suggests admiration mixed with a pleasant surprise. If the element of surprise is omitted (as in Magarshack and Hingley, where the word 'admiration' is chosen) then the translator is making a stylistic mistake: Chekhov's ironic comment on the guests that are taken by 'surprise' every time they hear Kotik's performance is completely lost.

There are, of course, words whose limited connotations mean that they can be satisfactorily translated into English; and if the translator chooses to modify them then it should rather be considered as an infelicity to the original (e.g. 'возле губернатора' is not necessarily next door 'to the Governor's official place' [Magarshack]); in Hingley we read: 'charming families with whom one might make 'friends' instead of 'acquaintance' (знакомство); 'Vera—a slim and pretty woman' instead of 'good looking' (миловидная); 'любил шутить и острить' is conveyed as 'he rather liked his fun'—in the latter example inaccuracy is more perceptible, because an observation in the original text is replaced by a value judgement in the translation.

At the same time, in the words of Joe Andrew, even these apparent textual inaccuracies can often be argued as valid. For example, the first paragraph in the Garnett translation 'with whom one might make acquaintance' would sound a bit odd to modern readers: this antiquated form is now completely superseded by a more colloquial 'make friends'. Hingley's choice, therefore is justified as an attempt to reach out to the contemporary audience. On the other hand, as suggested by Cynthia Marsh, a crude modernization of the classic text is not necessarily a good idea. It would be far more appropriate stylistically to render the prose of the nineteenth century Russian writer in a coherent English speech of the same period: something that Constance Garnett, Chekhov's contemporary, was better equipped than ourselves to achieve.

2. The problem of intercultural communication in translation is highly important. First, because it partly incorporates linguistic and stylistic aspects and secondly, because the way in which the translator approaches this question demonstrates his/her attitude to the concept of translation in general.

Every literary text is culturally and historically loaded; it contains a multitude of signs that are bearers of culture, through which the foreign reader can familiarize himself/herself with it. By preserving these signs the translator invites the reader to plunge deeper into the culture and the time when the text was written, assuming that those interested in the text would be equally keen on learning more about the culture. When these signs are omitted or modified, the text loses its authenticity, but becomes more accessible to the general public. Thus Hingley's translation of Chekhov, in which the, characters have no patronymics, most specific cultural details are eliminated and phraseologisms are replaced by corresponding English equivalents, certainly brings the text closer to the mass reader, and in the case of the plays is intended to result in 'performable' versions.

This dilemma has led to the development of two schools of translators. On one side there are the literalists, who place priority on preserving the integrity of the text, and may have to use extensive notes to seek to explain at least some of the effects that the author was creating in the original. On the other hand, the proponents of free translation hold that the task of the translator is to provide a version that seeks to convey to the reader the 'spirit' of a work. For them, this may frequently involve seeking to create in the target language some equivalent to language-specific verbal effects, even if it necessitates choosing counterparts that are absent from the original text. Each side has some compelling arguments in defence of its own approach to the problem of literary translation. Because of the nature of the problem, it is highly unlikely that the question will ever be resolvable, especially when one has to take into consideration the country-specific approach to the phenomenon. Thus, Boris Christa pointed out that he was very much surprised that in England few people paid attention to the theory of translation.[16] The latter is a well developed branch of literary studies; it delineates the exact objectives of a translator in any particular case: e.g. in drama translations all stage directions should be conveyed with maximum precision; in a literary text the idiomatic expressions and phraseologisms should be kept. Willem Weststeijn and Wolf Schmid affirmed that an anglicized translation like Hingley's would be unacceptable in Holland and Germany where the academic tradition demands preservation of all culture-specific references with comments on them in the notes.

Cynthia Marsh, on the other hand, explained that the English were more cavalier in this respect. The aim of a translator is to make the original user-friendly for the contemporary audience, and the communicability of the text is of prime importance. The question of the 'contract with the reader' is a complex problem, and it all depends on what kind of audience the translation was aimed for (Robert Reid). Although a literary text should be valuable as a source of cultural and educational information, there is a limit to the number of comments that one can put in the notes without a risk of turning it into a research article. In his essay entitled 'Rebuilding the Bridge at Bommel' J. Holmes[17] represents the translator's choice pattern as being drawn from two axes: 'exoticising versus naturalising' and 'historicising versus modernising'. Choices made along the first axis concern the translator's decision either to retain a specific element of the original linguistic context or to replace it with one that will in some way match the target context. Choices made along the second axis reflect the decision either to evoke the time-bound language usage of the original or to render the original more up to date in terms of the period in which the translator works.

Obviously different concepts require a different degree of alteration, and it is difficult to predict which way the movement between different languages would go. However the common points of concern can be easily delineated. These will include: denotative words with no equivalents in the foreign language; connotative lexis based on cultural references in the country of the original; phraseologisms and idiomatic expressions, humour and discourse structure.

When translating culture-specific words with no equivalent in the foreign language, the translator tries to find an approximation with which the denotative meaning of a word is interpreted in a given context. This category of words is often represented by small details that do not interfere with the narrative, but give a cultural flavour to the text. For example, at the end of part one of *Ionych* we read that Dr Startsev 'прошел девять верст . . . ему казалось, что он с удовольствием прошел бы еще верст двадцать' ('after his six-mile walk . . . he felt he could have walked another fifteen with pleasure'). Unfortunately, none of the translators keeps the word 'верста'. It is difficult to deny that in this context the approximation of 'верста' to a 'mile' gives the right idea of a distance (if the conversion is performed correctly).[18] However the reader might be interested in the fact that 'верста' was the main measure of distance in the pre-revolutionary Russia (which would be certainly helpful for reading all Russian eighteenth / nineteenth century authors); and, perhaps, add it to the list of such distinct Russian cultural markers as 'самовар' or 'сарафан' that no longer require any translation. As it happens 'верста' is almost exactly equivalent to a kilometre. This would make a fine translation in Australia, where it is an official unit of distance, but not in Britain and the USA. However 'verst' is a word to be found in English dictionaries and perhaps should be used here—even if at the risk of 'exoticism'.

Another point of concern will be the names. Should the names be de-Russianized? Should one take away patronymics: e.g. 'Mrs Turkina' (or 'Mrs Turkin', as postulated out by Eric de Haard, following Nabokov)[19] instead of 'Vera Iosifovna', etc.? Patronymics are characteristic of Russian culture. A patronymic is very important in establishing an appropriate register in people's relations; at the same time, when used on its own (in Chekhov's time mostly among people of relatively low origin) it also brings in a sense of familiarity and kinship. The latter is implied in the title of the story *Ionych*, which conveys the unfavorable development of the hero: when Dr Startsev, Dmitrii Ionych, merges completely with the philistine atmosphere of the town of 'S', the inhabitants start calling him simply 'Ionych', showing that he has indeed become one of them. This notion is lost in Hingley's translation. In his text all characters, including Dr Startsev, are deprived of patronymics. The translator finds his way around the idea of 'personality transformation': in his text the sense of familiarity is conveyed by the fact that the inhabitants start addressing Dr Startsev simply as 'Doc'. This, however, cannot be accepted as a successful solution: firstly, the keynote of the story is lost in the title, which is important; and, secondly, the form 'Doc' as an abbreviation from 'Doctor' is something completely alien to Russian culture and would have never been used in the time of Chekhov; it is scarcely natural nowadays in (British)

English. Rayfield, incidentally, drops Garnett's meticulously included patronymics, but keeps the title 'Ionych'.

The question of names brings us to the second category of problems—the system of connotative references rooted in the cultural memory of the country of the original text. Thus, as suggested by Eric de Haard, 'Startsev' itself is a meaningful name in Russian, derived from the word 'старец'—an old, wise man or religious elder (an irony on Chekhov's part?). Should one go so far as to 'translate' proper names, as in a recent Dutch translation of Dostoevskii's *Notes of a Madman,* where Poprishchin (from Russian 'поприще' ['occupation']) became 'Mr Career'? On the one hand, adapting the names to the target culture can often involve over-clarification, i.e. rendering clear what was meant to be slightly disguised in the original. On the other hand, there are examples when this intention can lead to false allusions and misinterpretation. In Hingley's translation the name Pava, by which the footman Pavlusha is called in the Turkin family, is conveyed as 'Peacock', which would have a connotation of vanity. The latter has no justification in the text: 'Pava' simply makes the name sound less 'paysan' than Pavlushka. Furthermore, the word 'pava' in Russian means a female bird and could be hardly used for a boy. The same kind of criticism can be applied to Hingley's translation of the diminutive 'Kotik', the familiar name of Ekaterina Ivanovna. Hingley presents the character as 'Pussy', evoking a series of false, perhaps scabrous connotations in the English speaking audience; equally, to be informed in the first sentence that a point in favour of the people of 'S'—was that 'they had balls' (Garnett and, incredibly, Rayfield) might today provoke unnecessary giggles. These particular examples, therefore, do not deal with clarification as much as with intercultural misinterpretation. For 'Kotik', the abbreviation 'Cat' could probably be successfully used today—but was unusual, we believe, even in the 1960s.

A literary text, 'open' by definition, is transferred into another language, in which some semantic 'doors' are shut, while others, not apparent in the original text, are opened. A new text is born, which, in comparison with the original text, has an aura of meaningfulness not caught by the translators. A vivid example of this would be the title of the folk song which is heard in the background when Vera Iosifovna finishes reading her novel. It is not coincidental that Chekhov mentions the title of the song—'Лучинушка'. It certainly appeals to the cultural memory of Russian readers. The words of the song ('от работы спинушка ноет и болит / а лучина моя, лучинушка не ясно горит' ['the back is sore and aching after hard work / and my little splinter of wood is scarcely shining']) are well-known and would appear as an ironic comment on the pathetic aspirations expressed in the hostess' novel: 'и эта песня передавала то, чего не было в романе и что бывает в жизни'. The keynote of the comment would be lost if the translator just mentions the folk-song (as in Magarshack) and does not explain its content (for example, in a footnote)—as in Garnett, who mentions 'Lutchina' without any reference to the meaning of the word (Rayfield revises this as 'Oh, my old torch'), and in Hingley who translates the title as 'Rushlight' (a fair equivalent, though in fact 'лучина' is a spill or splinter of wood).

The question of translation of common quotations, phraseologisms and idiomatic expressions is inevitably more complex. Thus, for example, the quotation from Prince Potemkin 'Умри, Денис, лучше не напишешь' (words that were originally addressed to Fonvizin, after he wrote his Недоросль [*The Minor*]) is translated directly in Garnett's and Magarshack's versions ('Die, Denis, you won't write anything better'). However it sounds too heavy and does not seem to enter smoothly into the words of Mr Turkin (nevertheless this is quintessential for the character who naturally expresses himself through quotations, puns and verbal tricks). Furthermore, in Garnett's translation there are no comments on the origin of the quotation, so its sense remains obscure to the reader; in his revision Rayfield adds a footnote, however. Magarshack includes his comments in the text, which makes the phrase even more awkward and ponderous. Hingley, on the other hand, replaces the whole expression with a suitable English equivalent ('A thing of beauty is a joy for ever'), which sounds much more felicitous.

The same can be said about 'Здравствуйте пожалуйста', with which Turkin greets all his guests. This expression means 'look who is here!' These words are appropriate when Turkin greets Startsev (he is naturally surprised to see him on his doorstep), but when it appears that every single guest who habitually comes to visit the Turkins is greeted in the same way, the words appear as an ironic comment on the host. Unfortunately none of the translators, trying to stay as close to the Russian text as possible, has succeeded in conveying the meaning of the phrase ('How do you do, if you please' in Garnett; 'Good afternoon, how are you, please' in Magarshack, 'Pleased to meet you, I am sure' in Hingley and 'Hello and welcome' in Rayfield's revision of Garnett); and in this case an English idiomatic equivalent would be, perhaps, a more elegant solution.

It must be also noted that much of the humour in *Ionych* is even less translatable. Russian culture, like any culture, has its own unique sense of humour, the challenge of translating Chekhov's wit into an English idiom may be the main reason why there have been so many translations, not one of which seems entirely satisfactory. And no matter how good a translation is, it will never catch, for example, the irony in Chekhov's description of Kotik playing the piano, the unsophisticated puns of Mr Turkin or the whole spectrum of associations evoked by 'Жанчик'—an affectionate diminutive applied to a middle-aged man (the former is accentuated by Magarshack as 'Jean, my sweet', the latter—by Garnett, as 'Petit Jean')[20] in a pretentious

French form and with a clear phonetic allusion to 'зайчик' ('little hare')—a nickname of a little child (Hingley gives up and omits the entire utterance).

To refine meanings, all cultures have particular discourse patterns. The principles and strategies people use to organize their discourse shift from culture to culture (and of course within the culture). The usage of different discourse patterns may lead to confusion and misinterpretation in intercultural communication. There are different communication styles across cultures (direct and indirect, elaborate and succinct, instrumental and affective, and others), and an important cultural dimension of communication proposed by E. Hall is that of context[21]—the degree to which communication is explicit and verbal (low-context) or implicit and nonverbal (high-context). Members of low-context cultures usually open their message with the main point and then develop arguments in support of it (deductive strategy). Clarity, directness, and precision are valued. Messages are explicit and as logical as possible, without digressions and deviations (linear logic). Members of a high-context culture relate information freely taking into account the context of communication—environment, situation, background knowledge and even mood. They do not rely on words only; their messages contain more implicit meanings (see discussion of 'Лучинушка' above). Inductive patterns for the introduction of topics are preferable.[22] English culture bears more low-context characteristics, while Russian culture tends to be more high-context. Compare, for example, the inductive pattern in Chekhov's text 'Пройдя двенадцать верст и потом ложась спать, он не чувствовал ни малейшей усталости' to the deductive pattern 'On going to bed, he felt not the slightest fatigue after six miles walk' (Garnett) or 'После приема больных, Старцев отправился в город' to 'Startsev set out for town after surgery' (Hingley). The use of inappropriate discourse patterns may lead to confusion and misinterpretation in intercultural communication: therefore one would think that whatever is the discourse pattern in the original, it would be better to switch to the one that is appropriate to the language in which the text is translated, otherwise the text will appear incoherent to the readers (Cynthia Marsh, Jane Gary Harris).

The idea of cultural relativism can be traced back to Wilhelm von Humboldt who already in the eighteenth century realized that the majority of human concepts are 'so inextricably woven into the individuality of their language that they can neither be kept suspended between all languages on the mere thread of inner perception nor can they be carried over into another language without alteration'.[23] The cultural competence of foreign readers is different from that of native speakers, and the translator should fill the gap between these differences, either in the text or in the meta-text. Literary translation, therefore, is a continuous and continuously tested challenge, an unperfectible process of approximation. As we can see there are certain successes and failures, some connotative links are lost and new ones are established. However all these references, either potentially implied or subjectively imposed, suggest a new reading of the text and inevitably evoke new possibilities for its interpretation. Any translation is to a certain degree domestication, as well as an estrangement ('остранение'), and it is mainly through seeing translated reflections of the text that we can try to appreciate, the original concept. But are translations really 'mirrors'? More likely 'snapshots'—tied to a moment in time, apparently precise yet lacking proper perspective, slightly blurred in background, sometimes so narrowly framed that one hardly recognizes the setting.

As our discussion continued, it became obvious that behind any problems of how lexical details, culture-specific references etc. could be, have been or should be translated loomed a more shadowy, but greater issue: what (or whose) Chekhov is the object of attention? Not everyone's Chekhov is the same and that is as true among Russians as non-Russians. One example may suffice: that of D. S. Mirskii, a subtle scholar, connoisseur of literature. For Mirskii, Chekhov was a 'singularly even writer' in the tradition of Turgenev (whose Russian he deemed superior): Chekhov's, 'at a time when the spoken language was losing its organic raciness', was consequently more level and less rich, which 'makes Chekhov the least difficult of Russian writers to translate'.[24] This differs at every point from the view of the present authors (and, we think, of most of those at the discussion)—for them Chekhov is protean, as much lyrical as he is prosaic, a master of shifting tonalities, of subtle gradations of humour and seriousness, curiously intractable to translation, indeed. Among the translators we have examined, incidentally, Hingley would seem to be the one who most consistently projects his 'own' Chekhov, and an idiosyncratic one: businesslike, laconic, 'modern' (for its date—the 1960s). It leads to a brilliant and persuasive opening of his *Dr Startsev* (i.e. *Ionych*), that soon becomes facetious and even rather flip as Chekhov's tone shifts when describing the evening reading at the Turkins: consistently referring to Mrs Turkin's Novel with a jokey capital 'N', for example. From the interesting remarks he makes at the beginning of the Oxford Chekhov project it is clear Hingley knew just what he was doing. Rayfield similarly has interesting remarks on his revision of the Garnett versions (Constance Garnett herself seems never to have written about her working methods).

Anyone who has thought much about translation has sooner or later bumped up against an inevitable paradox: (a) translation is of its nature impossible[25] as we have seen even a single word, let alone a phrase or whole literary work, exists within a unique web of cultural references specific to a single language and the culture it articulates; (b) translations continue to be made, to be taken as carrying authority and in some way as conveying an authentic core of the meaning (and thus can be criticized—evaluated as 'better' or 'worse'); indeed our culture would have collapsed without them. To prefer (even with the greatest reservations) the latter viewpoint means that one must be at bottom an 'essentialist' as regards language, meaning and mental processes generally (rather than a pure 'formalist', for whom meaning can inhere only in its specific means of expression).[26] There are several reasons why such a point of view is ultimately unavoidable—among them the existence of communicative codes other than language—but it would be inappropriate to argue the question at length here. Suffice it to say that the very fact of our gathering to discuss, 'translating and mistranslating Chekhov' implied our commitment to the possibility of translation. But by the same token that possibility has not been, and can of its nature never be, perfectly realized. We all construct 'Chekhovs'—probably fluid, mutable ones—in our minds, to which words are only a sort of embodiment. The situation is really no different across the language boundaries from what it is within a language community; everyone, native speaker or not, has an idiolect, a mental framework, into which any utterance (especially one as complex as a work of literature) has to be conceptually 'translated'. At the same time every work of literature, even every utterance and every new speaker, changes the overall configuration of the language as a whole—by however little. So, of course, do translations—versions of Chekhov, however defective or meritorious, become by their very publication factors within the sphere of English language and culture. Translation is important, perhaps by virtue of the very imperfection of its 'unfinalized' nature.

NOTES

1. V. Zhukovskii, 'O basne i basniakh Krylova' (1809), *Sobranie sochinenii,* ed. V. P. Petushkova, Khudozhestvennaia literatura, Moscow-Leningrad, 1960, IV, p. 410.

2. The shortest poem in classic Russian literature appears to be G. R. Derzhavin's obituary for Suvorov, the single word 'жил' (thanks to G. S. Smith for pointing this out). The modernist Vasilisk Gnedov, of course, wrote his *Поэма конца (Endpoem)*, which was wordless—but the two words of the title should doubtless be taken into consideration. One of us once attempted to publish a translation of Gnedov's poem into English (the result was not a success). Of course, 'жил' presents its own problems for an adequate translation into English.

3. A. P. Chekhov, *Polnoe sobranie sochinenii i pisem. Pis'ma,* ed. Nikolai Bel'chikov, 1983, XI, Nauka, Moscow, p. 284.

4. Although the game came to Russia from Europe, the 'billiard russe' differed considerably from the Franco-Italian version: the 'billiard russe' had pockets that were usually absent in the European version of the game.

5. Chekhov, op. cit., p. 55.

6. Martin Fell's translation of four of Chekhov's plays (George Calderon, London, 1912) was followed by *Plays by Anton Tchekoff* translated by Julius West (Duckworth and Co, London, 1916). Patrick Miles, however, claims that at the

beginning of the century Garnett's translations of Chekhov's plays (published only in 1923: *A. Tchekhov, Plays,* translated from the Russian by Constance Garnett, Chatto and Windus, London, 1923, I–II) were widely circulated in manuscript, and in 1911 her translation of *The Cherry Orchard* was used for a production of the play in London (Miles, 'Chekhov na angliiskoi stsene', trans. by V. A. Riapolova, in *Literaturnoe nasledstvo*, Nauka, Moscow, 1997, C, 1, p. 494).

7. About these translations see: M. A. Shereshevskaia, 'Chekhov v Anglii' in ibid., p. 377.

8. Ibid., p. 405.

9. K. Chukovskii, 'Vina ili beda?', *Literaturnaia gazeta*, 3 August, 1963, p. 9.

10. Donald Rayfield, *The Chekhov Omnibus: Selected Stories (The Everyman Library)*, Tuttle Publishing, London, 1994.

11. First published in the monthly Literary Supplements to the journal *Niva* (September, 1898).

12. 'The cat killed the rat' is a simple sentence whose ordering in English cannot really be varied. The Russian equivalent requires only three words, as Russian has no definite or indefinite articles (a feature which causes Russians translating into English more difficulties than it does an English native speaker), but those three words can quite plausibly be ordered in any of the six mathematically feasible ways, sometimes giving the sentence a new emphasis which needs even more words in English: 'It was the cat that killed the rat' for example.

13. Rosamund Bartlett, *About Love and Other Stories (Oxford World's Classics)*, Oxford University Press, Oxford, 2004.

14. In this context one should also mention the problems in translation of the endings of all Chekhov's plays, the more so since final words carry particular significance: 'отдохнем' in *Uncle Vania* has the connotation of 'having a rest' as well as 'acquiring peace', and it is practically impossible to find an English equivalent that comprises both meanings.

15. Robin Milner-Gulland pointed out that there was a particular problem with 'многоточие', for this Russian punctuation mark has no generally accepted name in English, and is much less common.

16. See, for example, Thodore H. Savory, *Art of Translation*, Vintage / Ebury, London, 1969.

17. James Holmes, 'Rebuilding the Bridge at Bommel: Notes on the Limits of Translatability', *Dutch Quarterly Review of Anglo-American Letters*, II, 1972, pp. 65–72 (66).

18. There are two figures in the text: 'девять верст' and 'весрт двадцать'. Of course, 'верста' equals 3500 feet and a mile equals 5280 feet; therefore 'девять верст' is equal to 5.97 miles and 'весрт двадцать', is approximately 13.3 miles. All three translators, nevertheless, make a mistake in one figure or another. In Garnett we read: 'he felt not the slightest fatigue after six miles walk. On the contrary, he felt as though he could with pleasure have walked another twenty' (there is also another mistranslation 'весрт двадцать' is not 'another twenty', but 'approximately twenty'). The same can be found in Hingley who gives the figure of six miles, which is followed by 'another fifteen miles'. Magarshack suggests five and twelve miles, which is closer to the right answer, but not quite accurate.

19. 'In the old days, to be sure, great lyrical poets or the incomparable prose artist who composed "Anna Karenin" (which should be transliterated without the closing "a"—she was not a ballerina) could cheerfully ignore the left-wing progressive

philistines who requested Tiutchev or Tolstoi to mirror politico-social soap-box gesticulations instead of dwelling on an aristocratic love affair or the beauties of nature' (V. Nabokov, *Strong Opinions*, Weidenfeld and Nicolson, London, 1973, p. 112).

20. Rayfield revises it as 'Jean, my dear'—however, there is an obvious danger that an English reader might not perceive 'Jean' as a French name at all.

21. E. Hall, *The Dance of Life: The Other Dimension of Time*, Garden City, New York, 1983, p. 47.

22. R. Scollon and S. W. Scollon, *Intercultural Communication: A Discourse Approach*, Blackwell Publishers, Oxford, 2001, p. 81.

23. Carl Wilhelm von Humboldt, *Wilhelm von Humboldts Werke*, Albert Leitzmann, Berlin, 1903–1936, IV, pp. 21–23.

24. D. P. Mirskii, *Modern Russian Literature*, Oxford University Press, Oxford, 1925, pp. 87–88.

25. A view particularly associated with the philosopher W. V. Quine (see, for example, 'On the Reasons for Indeterminacy of Translation', *Journal of Philosophy*, LXVII, 1970, pp. 178–183).

26. The faith people have put across the ages in the validity of translation is a subject worthy of study in itself. Nowadays this seems particularly true of natural scientists. One small example: recently Steven Rose, an excellent writer and himself a specialist on mental processes, reviewing a book translated from Dutch, wrote 'the translators have done a superb job of capturing its freshness of style' (*Guardian Review*, 11 December, 2004). Did he compare the English text with the Dutch original? If not, was his judgement purely intuitive?

PEKKA TAMMI

Against Narrative ("A Boring Story")

1. Against . . .

> [Narrative] is so familiar and ubiquitous that it is likely to be
> overlooked, in much the same way as we suppose that the fish will
> be the last to discover water. . . . [W]e organize our experience
> and our memory of human happenings mainly in the form of
> narrative—stories, excuses, myths, reasons for doing and not doing,
> and so on. (Bruner 1991: 4)

The celebrated ubiquity of narrative in culture is both a fecund premise
and, I claim, the bane of narrative theory today. While not outright *against*
narrative, nor against theorizing about narratives, in this paper I nonetheless aim to remain fairly sceptical towards broad, overly eager uses of the
notion: not necessarily the most promising stance in a collection devoted to
narrative "as a way of thinking." No less ominously, my paper comes with
the subtitle "A Boring Story"—though this is also the title of the story by
Chekhov ("Skuchnaia istoriia," 1889) that I shall use to boost my argument,
once we are done with theory.

Everybody knows the lure of broad notions. One well remembers
such early, once eye-opening statements as those by Roland Barthes (1975:
235): "**Like life itself,** narrative is there, international, transhistorical,

Partial Answers: Journal of Literature and the History of Ideas, Volume 4, Number 2 (January
2006): pp. 19–40. Copyright © 2006 Hebrew University of Jerusalem. Reprinted by
permission of The Johns Hopkins University Press.

transcultural."[1] Or by Hayden White (1987: 1): "To raise the question of narrative is to invite reflection on the very nature of culture, and, possibly, even on the nature of **humanity itself.**" Hence, obviously, the tacit consensus prompting the vast expansion of the narrative-theoretical approach in current research everywhere, from literary narratology (where it all started) to social sciences, cultural and media studies, cognitive science, and a gamut of other, most diverse interdisciplinary arenas.[2]

It would hardly serve my purpose to go against interdisciplinarity in research (a sacred cow, if any). Certainly, the concept of narrative may travel, and, without doubt, it can be put to profitable uses outside studies of fiction—this is not my point here. Neither would there seem to be much need in the present context for retracing the emergence of the narrative "turn" in diverse disciplines, or the concomitant broadening and transformation of the initial concept.[3]

But let us look at some exemplars of the *overly* broad and, to my mind, overly enthusiastic usage, stemming from this very turn. First, from the psychologist Jerome Bruner, again, whose wording may still look reasonable at first blush:

> [O]nce the "cognitive revolution" in the human sciences brought to the fore the issue of how "reality" is represented in the act of knowing, it became apparent that it did not suffice to equate representations with images, with propositions, with lexical networks, or even with more temporally extended vehicles such as sentences. It was perhaps a decade ago that psychologists became alive to the possibility of **narrative as a form not only of representing but of constituting reality.** (Bruner 1991: 5)

The notion of narrative form *constituting* reality (in the same manner, that is, as a literary narrative constitutes fictional reality) is developed further in cognitive terms—recklessly, in my view—by Mark Turner in *The Literary Mind.* According to Turner's thesis, human thought in always involves not only narrative construction (surely an acceptable assumption), but also *literary* construction and hence construction of fiction, a claim to which I will return:

> Narrative imagining—story—is the fundamental instrument of thought. Rational capacities depend upon it. It is our chief means of looking into the future, of predicting, of planning, and of explaining. It is **a literary capacity indispensable to human cognition generally.** This is the first way in which the mind is essentially literary. (Turner 1996: 4–5)

From here there is but a step to claims like Alan Palmer's (in his *Fictional Minds*)—empty and, I think, actually harmful: "[T]heorists from various disciplines have suggested that life plans are scripted on fairy-tale patterns and that **in a sense we are all novelists**" (Palmer 2004: 186).

2. What Narrative?

Where is the harm? Or, why should we not like such claims?

A short answer would be that, as *literary* narratologists, we might not like quite this quick collapsing of the difference between literature (or fiction) on the one hand and non-literature ("life") on the other—a complex issue to be sure, and I will have more to say of it in a moment.

For a somewhat longer answer we still ought to take a look at how the notion of narrative has been understood in theory. What do narratologists have in mind when it is said that narratives are everyplace in our lives?

In what follows, I do not wish to enter the technical debate about defining narrative. (Debates about definitions remind me of a philosophical poem—by a Finnish poet—where the speaker visits a grocery store and drives the shopkeeper crazy by repeatedly asking to purchase a fruit, in general. Not an apple, or an orange, but a fruit.[4] In a similar manner, we might test general conceptions of narrative by asking, in a bookstore, in what section they keep narratives. The dim prospects of such an experiment notwithstanding, this has hardly hindered narratologists from trying, as we see below.)

Since I need it for my argument, I have compiled a roster of mainly standard definitions.

2.1. As Discourse

The most solid consensus, it would appear, prevails among those theorists who proceed to treat narrative as a discourse type, with definite textual features. At least an impression of a steady increase in precision emerges as we observe the formulas advanced by narratologists over the years—from a view of narrative as based on single events *(I walk)* to notions hinging on two events or more, or non-contradictory events, or temporal succession, sequence, causality, change, human agency, and so on.

And why not? Without doubt many of these efforts are successful in capturing our intuition of what it is that constitutes narrative discourse. The validity of any particular formulation is not my main issue here. Should we wish to practice narratology at all we need *some* definitions (if only to interrogate them, by brushing the definitions against actual narrative texts—which is the issue in this paper). I have in mind classical definitions like the following:

[A]ny narrative ... is a linguistic production undertaking to tell of **one or several events. ...** *I walk. Pierre has come* are for me minimal forms of narrative. (Genette 1980: 30)

For me, as soon as there is **an action or an event, even a single one,** there is a story because there is a transformation, a transition from an earlier state to a later and resultant state. "I walk" implies ... a state of departure and a state of arrival. (Genette 1988: 19)

[Narrative is] the representation of **at least two real or fictive events or situations in a time sequence, neither of which presupposes or entails the other.** (Prince 1982: 4)

[Narrative is] any representation of **non-contradictory events such that at least one occurs at time *t* and the other at time *t1*, following time *t*.** (ibid.: 145)

[I]n a "true" narrative as opposed to the mere recounting of a random series of changes of state, these situations and events also make up a whole, **a SEQUENCE the first and last major terms of which are partial repetitions of each other,** a structure having—to use Aristotle's terminology—a BEGINNING, a MIDDLE, and an END. (Prince 1987:59)

[Narrative (fiction) is] the narration of **a succession of [fictional] events.** (Rimmon-Kenan 1983: 2)

At the lowest level of simplification, narrative is **a sequence that is narrated.** (Cobley 2003: 7)

[N]arrative is a representation of a **causally related series of events.** (Richardson 2000: 168)

[Narrative is] accounts of **what happened to particular people in particular circumstances and with specific consequences.** (Herman 2003: 2)

[N]arrative is essentially **a verbal representation of things in time, and more specifically of changes of state caused by physical events.** (Margolin 2003: 284)

[Narrative is] the mental or textual representation of **a causally linked sequence of events involving individuated and human-like agents.** (Ryan 2004: 14)

2.2. As Speech Act

When narrative is defined not as a set of features, but as an *act* (by the teller)—the famous speech-act definition by Barbara Herrnstein-Smith—at bottom, this still coincides with many of the above formulations. Telling as such is not sufficient. We also expect there to be succession and sequence, for in a standard narrative the act of telling takes place only after *something happened* (a problematic criterion, as we see when we reach Chekhov). And, as recently suggested by James Phelan, the telling should come with a *purpose* and, presumably, with some *consequences*. Hence causality, too:

> [W]e might conceive of narrative discourse most minimally and most generally as verbal acts consisting of **someone telling someone else that something happened.** (Herrnstein-Smith 1981: 228)
>
> [N]arrative itself can be fruitfully understood as a rhetorical act: somebody telling **somebody else on some occasion and for some purposes that something happened.** (Phelan 2005a: 118)

2.3. As Cognitive Schema

It has also been suggested, in Wittgensteinian spirit, that instead of searching for necessary and sufficient conditions, "narratologists might do better to reconsider their strategy of pithy definitions . . . and to think of narrative instead as a language game" (Radium 2005: 201). In this view, narrative may just as well be regarded as all overall cognitive schema, imposed on any discourse by *the reader* (Monika Fludernik), or even by *the narratologist* (William Nelles):

> [N]arrativization applies one specific macro-frame, namely that of *narrativity*, to a text. When readers are confronted with potentially unreadable narratives, texts that are radically inconsistent, they cast about for ways and means of recuperating these texts as narratives. . . . [Narrativization is] **making something a narrative by the sheer act of imposing narrativity on it.** (Fludernik 1996: 34; see also Fludernik 2003)
>
> Narrativity . . . is the product of a tropological operation by which the metaphor of narration is applied to a series of words on a page. . . . **Narratological analysis is thus a performative discourse that makes a text it analyzes a narrative.** (Nelles 1997: 116)

Liberating as such formulations might sound, from the standpoint of defining things they still beg the question. If narratives are what readers peruse, and what narratologists study, we should next start defining "narrativity," which may be no less cumbersome a task. What is it, more precisely, that we impose on texts? Whether one wished it or not, we are once more led back—in a circular route—to ponder the *features* already isolated in previous definitions (all of them coined by narratologists, we remember).

2.4. The Bottom Line

Consequently, the narrative-theoretical bottom line would still seem to remain with the classical, broad conceptions. One of these, a particularly authoritative one, we find on the opening page of the recently-published *Routledge Encyclopedia of Narrative Theory:*

> [Narrative is] a basic human strategy for **coming to terms with time, process, and change.** (Herman et al. 2005: ix)

A strategy (for the teller and the reader alike). But one designed specifically for coping with temporal process, succession, sequence, and causality (change). About these, after more than three decades of narratological toil, there appears to exist a fairly unflinching theoretical consensus.

3. Consequences

This is where scepticism steps in. In my view, such sweeping formulations—no matter how lucid or innocuous in themselves—carry two streaks that have become particularly conspicuous in the aftermath of the narrative turn. Neither bodes well for *literary* narratology, which is my principal concern here.[5]

From this angle, harping on broad definitions may lead:

(i) either to stretching the notion disproportionately, until it snaps, losing all differentiating characteristics: if narrative equals *life itself* (as Barthes had it) the literary narratologist may be left with no particular object of analysis;

(ii) or, conversely, the expansion of narrative-theoretical approaches to domains like social sciences or cultural studies may lead to lopsided privileging of the "natural," quotidian, *realistic* type of narrative: the type resting staunchly on sequence, succession, causality, or closure which many of the accepted definitions just cited seemed to favour—again, a less than promising development for literary narratology.

Let us dwell for a while on these two complaints.

3.1. On Losing the Difference

As to the first point, it has been taken up by some narrative theorists themselves, alarmed by current misuses of narratological terms. So Gerald Prince remarks, with understandable irritation, that, in the present (post-narrative-turn) usage, "narrative" has been rather liberally employed:

instead of "explanation" or "argumentation" (because it is more tentative); one prefers "narrative" to "theory," "hypothesis," or "evidence" (because it is less scientistic); or speaks of "narrative" rather than "ideology" (because it is less judgmental); one substitutes "narrative" for "message" (because it is more indeterminate). (Prince 1999: 45)

Narrative as *ideology*. It is in such it broad sense that, for example, the famous Lyotardian "grand" narratives—dear to students of culture—are often made to stand for *any* supposedly dubious, homogenizing constructs: nationality, gender, belief in the progress of science, and so on.[6] Or think of the related notion of *identity* as narrative, another pet topic of cultural studies. Think only of popular slogans like the one quoted from Oliver Sacks—surely a well-meaning phrase, but narratologically a mess: "[E]ach of us constructs and lives a 'narrative,' and . . . this narrative is us, our identities" (cit. Eakin 2004: 122; Strawson 2004: 435).[7]

These uses of the concept are harmful because of their disproportionate broadness. Nothing is differentiated here, neither *life*, nor *narrative*, nor *us*. (Nor does it seem clear to me, no matter how hard one looks, that our belief in science, say—whether dubious or not—ought to be resolved via *narratological* means. These are frankly cultural or ideological matters. Do we need the concept of narrative here at all?)

But what is worse, from my present angle, is taking the next irresponsible step. Having first lumped narrative together with life, we add insult to injury by labelling all this *fiction* (in the manner of "we are all novelists"). According to the tacitly accepted theory here, if something can be called a narrative—and, as we just saw, almost anything can—it is fiction as well.[8]

Let us just look at the next excerpt, again taken from Mark Turner's *The Literary Mind:*

> Although literary texts may be special, the instruments of thought used to invent and interpret them are basic to everyday thought. **Written works called narratives or stories may be shelved in a special section of the bookstore,** but the mental instrument I call narrative or story is basic to human thinking. (1996: 7)

Everything is wrong here—starting with the assumption that there are, indeed, special shelves in bookstores for "narratives" (remember that Finnish poem!). Clearly Turner has "fiction" in mind, which is wrong again, if one bluntly assumes that this would cover all narrative writing.

And everything would be wrong in the following pronouncement, too, *if* it came from a narrative-theoretical text book (as it well might, I fear).

Instead, it occurs in *Mao II,* a novel by Don DeLillo: "News of disaster is the only narrative people need. The darker the news the grander the narrative" (1992: 42).

This *could* have been uttered by one narratologist or another, carried away by broad definitions. But DeLillo writes novels, of course. In a novel—in fiction—you are allowed to state anything. In a theoretical work you are not, which pretty well comprises what I have been arguing so far.

3.2. On Privileging the "Natural"

We come to my second complaint, having to do with the bias in narrative studies towards privileging sequence, temporal progression, causality. One could also talk of privileging the natural, quotidian, or *realistic* modes of narrative, if by "realism" we mean anything like a narrative *leading to closure,* the formula once proposed by Catharine Belsey.[9]

That such an overly general, top-down approach may be doubtful was already indicated by none other than Hayden White when he queried the propensity, in historiographical writing, "to have real events display the coherence, integrity, fullness, and closure of an image of life that is and can only be imaginary" (White 1987: 24). He went on to observe:

> The notion that sequences of real events possess the formal attributes of the stories we tell about imaginary events could only have its origin in wishes, daydreams, reveries. **Does the world really present itself to perception in the form of well-made stories, with central subjects, proper beginnings, middles, and ends, and a coherence that permits us to see "the end" in every beginning?** (ibidem)

For White, privileging coherence and closure goes hand in hand with a penchant for drawing a *moral* out of every story: "Could we ever narrativize without moralizing?" (25).

Of late, Shlomith Rimmon-Kenan has discerned a related bias: a tendency to overlook the *non*-sequential, *non*-causal, fragmentary modes of narration in the work done on authentic illness narratives. A close textual study may yield an altogether more differentiated picture, she suggests:

> In ill subjects . . . [narrative structuring] contains **phases of disintegration and fragmentation as well as moments pulling toward continuity and coherence, and these may even be simultaneous.** Fragmented narratives may become unintelligible, and hence risk remaining unheeded. Wittingly or unwittingly, they also subvert the cure-promising authority, thus provoking anxiety

which sometimes leads to their being "rewritten" by physicians and other care-givers. It is for these reasons that I feel an ethical commitment to such narratives, both as lived experience and as written texts. Furthermore, the possibility of fragmentation seems to me to lay bare the ill subject's vulnerability, thereby suggesting the limitations, perhaps even the *hubris* of the better-structured narratives. (Rimmon-Kenan 2002b: 22)

This is keenly observed, and I will yet return to illness narratives when I reach the case study from Chekhov.

What is being interrogated here, by Rimmon-Kenan as well as White, is precisely the broad and facile, if well-intentioned, notion of narrative as a way of triumphing over the discontinuity and indeterminacy of life through the simple feat of constructing linear, causally coherent sequences—narrative as therapy or cure, or narrative as a moral lesson.

These remarks concern non-fiction. Possibly, such a bias may still be acceptable from the perspective of social sciences, which study patently natural (or at least non-fictional) narratives. It may be right for cultural studies, often treating narratives as straightforward carriers of ideological content, with no specific narratological interest. But, again, for studying *literary* narratives such a one-sided approach can take us only so far.

3.3. On Doing It Otherwise: Towards Weak Narrativity

All of which leads me to my argument. For we should now ask whether it is not the capacity of literary fiction—unlike that of standard narratives evoked by theorists—to deal specifically with the *impossibilities*, the paradoxes and problems, of our human efforts to order experience. This is why even innocuous, seemingly precise definitions may appear to us suspect when they single out narrative as *the* strategy for "coming to terms" with time, process, and so on. For here we must instantly add, when discussing literature: or *not* coming to terms.

To phrase the question in still other terms: is it not the specific function of literary narratives to *do it otherwise*—by rendering problematic, by subverting, or by making strange in a thousand and one ways all those sweeping formulations thought up by theorists on the basis of standard, natural cases?

Therefore, the way to go for literary narratology, I argue, is squarely in the opposite direction from that taken in the wake of the narrative turn—away from general model-building and standard definitions, towards studying, rather, the subversive and strange, previously *un*theorized or insufficiently theorized cases: the glorious exceptions to the rules that classical definitions have been altogether too sweeping to recognize.

When such a route has been followed in recent ("postclassical") research, the studied texts have often been chosen from overtly experimental, avant-garde fiction of the Beckettian, or Pynchonian (or Nabokovian) variety.[10] It is this mode of blatantly anti-narrative experimentation that Monika Fludernik seems to have in mind when she writes that, in reading Beckett, for example: "Critics are confronted with a slippery edge on which they rightly hesitate to tread for fear of losing their mental balance. . . . In the wake of this loss of referentiality, rationality, consistency, and experientiality—where does one go?" (Fludernik 1996: 304; for a larger discussion of non-natural and experimental narratives see her chapters 6 and 7, 222–310).

This might sound somewhat alarming, but, as a matter of fact, we need not venture quite that far. One suspects that problematic, subversively strange, or indeterminate narrativity of the kind we are after here does not concern just avant-garde, experimental literature. Possibly, such an impulse is *always already* there, as it were, underlying even seemingly realistic, straightforward, and linear fiction.

Here—and this will be my all but last recourse to theory—I wish to borrow a concept from Brian McHale who has spoken (with regard to a more restricted set of texts, it is true) of *weak narrativity*. With this notion McHale indicates the literary strategy of conveying an *illusion* of narrative sequence, linearity, causality, closure—the features narrative theorists have been running circles around—while at the same time frustrating the reader's trust in the emergence of a coherent narrative. Referring to his examples chosen from a set of contemporary, postmodernist narrative poems McHale writes:

> Weak narrativity involves . . . telling stories "poorly," distractedly, with much irrelevance and indeterminacy, in such a way as to *evoke* narrative coherence while at the same time withholding commitment to it and undermining confidence in it; in short, having one's cake and eating it too. (McHale 2001: 165; see also McHale 2004: 259–260 and 2005)

I find this useful, since narrative is here no longer an overriding schema imposed on texts, as it tended to be in top-down theoretical approaches. Neither is narrative absent; it is placed delicately under erasure: reading a text you see an emerging narrative, and at the same time you do not.

This strategy may occur anyplace in literature (not only in postmodernist texts discussed by McHale)—which allows me to move on to the example from Chekhov. Something very similar is going on in his story. Having sufficiently expounded against narrative, let us now see what it writer of fiction like Chekhov would have to say of all this.

4. "A Boring Story"

The story by Anton Chekhov—not only a "boring" story,[11] but a poignant and funny one as well, of a burnt-out Professor in a Russian university—can be read as, among other things, a meditation on narrative, and, if you will, on narrative theory.

Theorists, we remember, persist in their view of narrative as an instrument for *coming to terms with time, process, and change.* As to Chekhov's narrator, he comes to terms with none of these, which is also effective in turning the story into a fictional illness narrative. Let it be added that as a fictional story of illness the Chekhov text corresponds singularly well to the pattern described by Rimmon-Kenan—a pattern consisting of (I quote again) "phases of . . . fragmentation as well as moments pulling toward . . . coherence, and these may even be simultaneous" (Rimmon-Kenan 2002b: 22). In his own manner, Chekhov is having his narrative cake and eating it too.

4.1. Indeterminacy of Sequence

"A Boring Story" starts with a transparent narratological trick, ostensibly in the heterodiegetic, third-person mode:

> There is in Russia an eminent professor, a Nicholas Stepanovich Such-and-such—a mail of great seniority and distinction. So many medals, Russian and foreign, does he possess that when he wears them his students refer to him as an icon-stand. He knows all the best people, having been on terms of intimacy with every celebrated Russian scholar of the last twenty-five years at least. His present life offers no scope for friendship. But if we speak of the past the long list of his famous friends ends with names like Pirogov, Kavelin and the Poet Nekrasov, who all bestowed on him an affection sincere and warm in the extreme. He is a member of all Russian and three foreign universities, and so on and so forth. (92)

Only after this does the narrator lay his cards on the table: "All this, and a lot more that might be said **makes up my so-called name**" (ibid.).

He then goes on to supply a patently depressing portrait of himself—an aging man with bad nerves, bad teeth, plagued by thoughts of the approaching death:

> What of the bearer of this name—of myself, in other words? I present the spectacle of a sixty-two-year-old man with bald head, false teeth and an incurable nervous *tic*. I'm every bit as dim and ugly as my name is brilliant and imposing. My head and hands

tremble with weakness. Like one of Turgenev's heroines, I have
a throat resembling the stringy neck of a double bass, my chest
is hollow, my shoulders are narrow. When I speak or lecture, my
mouth twists to one side. When I smile, senile wrinkles cover my
whole face, and I look like death. There is nothing impressive about
my wretched figure, except perhaps that, when I suffer from my
nervous *tic,* a special look comes over me—one bound to provoke
in those who observe me the grim, arresting thought that "the man
will soon be dead, obviously." (92–93)

It is the self-portrait of your proverbial burnt-out academic, ruminating on
the frustrations of his personal and public life.[12]

And from here on, the narrative proceeds not only in the homodiegetic,
frankly first-person mode, but (this is Chekhov's true narratological trick)
consistently in the *present tense,* already anticipating the tactic of simultaneous narration in subsequent writers from Kafka to Beckett, for example, or
J. M. Coetzee, singled out and thoroughly studied by contemporary researchers such as Dorrit Cohn.[13] Evidently, the "weak" form of narrativity—ensuing
from our sense of indeterminate temporal sequence coupled with direction-
less causality—has more than a little to do with such narrative simultaneity,
as here *the narrator himself has no way of knowing how the story will turn out.*
(There would also be an analogy to simultaneous modes in non-fictional narration, as in sports broadcasts, which in many ways resemble the case at hand.
No more than Chekhov's Professor, does the announcer in a baseball broadcast know which way the events will turn: an unexpected affinity that might
bear some more probing.) [14]

Nor can the reader of the story determine with any certainty the nature
of the Professor's speech act as a teller. Does the Professor actually utter any
of this? There occurs constant, paradoxical oscillation in the narrative between
signs of a written document (presumably a diary)[15] and records of all immediate mental monologue that may, perhaps, remain not wholly verbalized. On
occasion, we find unmistakable anticipations of an unnamed audience and its
responses, as well as metanarrative commentary on the act of telling: "Should
you need to know" (97); "I shall confine myself here to four visits only" (105);
"Shameful its it is, I'll describe . . ." (130), and so on. At the same time, these
are counterpoised and made problematic by the sheer immediacy of interior
monologue: "What shall I do? Call my family? No, there's no point" (134);
"The corridor clock strikes one, then two, then three" (137); "A light tap on
the door. Someone wants me" (140)—such a sense of indeterminacy in the
telling culminates in the parting scene with Katya that is made to conclude
the story: "Farewell, my treasure!" We can hardly know how the Professor

ever manages to narrate the simultaneous scene, and as readers of the story we are not supposed to know.

But this is not all. After the prelude to the story it soon becomes apparent that the Professor is not only narrating simultaneously—telling about it while living—but also, and still more problematically, telling what occurs in his life *repeatedly*, every day, or from one week or month to another. Here is still one of Chekhov's covert narrative ploys. In narratological research this device has been termed *iterative narration:* "narrating one time . . . what happened n times," as Gérard Genette puts it in *Narrative Discourse* (1980: 116; cf. 118–119).

Such a narrative strategy apparently tallies well with the "boring" quality of the story. (*Boring* might be the middle name of McHale's "weak" narrativity.) Neither subsequent to the narrated action, nor literally simultaneous (since the action is repeated), the Professor's position as the teller appears to float insecurely outside the constraints of all natural narrative schemas. We now notice that most of what we read about consists of reiterating the routines of the narrator's existence, even though these are disguised as singular events, succeeding each other: routines like morning teas with his wife and family (94–96), walks to the university and preparing for the lectures (96–99), meetings with colleagues and pestersome students (102–105), and other occurrences taking place *n* times during the first half of the story.

Take, for example, the description of the Professor's lecturing routine:

> I know what I shall lecture about, but just how I shall lecture, what I shall start with, where I shall end—that I don't know. I haven't a single sentence on the tip of my tongue. But I only have to glance round my lecture hall, built in the form of an amphitheatre, and utter the timeworn phrase "last week we were discussing —," for sentences to surge out of my inner self in a long parade—and the fat is in the fire! I speak with overwhelming speed and enthusiasm, feeling as if no power on earth could check the flow of words. (100)

And so on—the description continues for two pages. This is how it goes for the Professor, from one week to another, one may surmise, and has been going for the past thirty years.

But then—wait. Not everything is repeated. Or at least the following occasion would seem to be of a more singular kind:

> In the middle of a lecture tears suddenly choke me, my eyes begin smarting, and I feel a furious, hysterical urge to stretch forth my arms and complain aloud. I want to cry aloud that fate has sentenced

me, a famous man, to capital punishment, that within six months someone else will be officiating in this lecture theatre. I want to shout that I've been poisoned. New thoughts, hitherto unfamiliar, have been blighting the last days of my life, and they continue to sting my brain like mosquitoes. Meanwhile my situation seems so appalling that I want all members of my audience to leap from their seats in terror and rush panic-stricken to the exit with screams of despair.

Such moments are not easily endured. (102)

This no longer seems routine—for the speaker or for the audience—but a genuinely singular, heart-stopping experience. Still, the narrator says— paradoxically: *Such moments* are not easily endured.

There may still be an untold number of other moments like this, even though the very particular mode of telling makes the episode look singular. Here we find a variant of Genette's *pseudo*iterative, which is routine and singular, immediate and iterative at the same time, with the precise location of the related events in the narrative sequence left indeterminate and floating.

This, it seems, is what the peculiarly Chekhovian weak narrativity is all about. Such oscillations between singular—iterative could be amply illustrated especially with episodes from the latter portion of the story, where the Professor proceeds to dwell on his relations with his young protégée, his stepdaughter Katya. Here we constantly come across iterative passages embedded within singulative scenes or, conversely, signs of singularity within the iterative. (Chekhov performing his quiet narratological acrobatics: compare, for example, the prolonged descriptions of Katya's calls to her stepfather, their daily dialogues, or the Professor's own, compulsive visiting, all encapsulated within single particularized scenes, 105–111 and 116–125).

Our sense of the narrator's insecure temporal location culminates when we come to the poignant conclusion. Here the Professor, persistently maintaining the present tense (indeed, as in a sportscast) reports his supposedly final parting from Katya. Partings always *feel* singular and final, whether or not they are so. It is a poignant, pathetic conclusion—not on the part of Chekhov, of course, but for the hapless narrator who is in no position to tell how the story of his life might proceed from here:

Katya stands up and holds out her hand—smiling coldly, not meeting my eyes.

"So you won't be at my funeral?" I want to ask.

But she doesn't look at me. Her hand is cold and seems alien. I accompany her to the door in silence.

Now she has left me and is walking down the long corridor
without looking back. She knows I'm watching her, and will
probably turn round when she reaches the comer,

No, she hasn't turned. Her black dress has flashed before my
eyes for the last time, her steps have died away.

Farewell, my treasure! (141–142)

4.2. Indeterminacy of "Point"

Having reached the conclusion, we are left to inquire about the *point*, or the
thematic sense of all this. What is Chekhov driving at in his story? Or what
was I driving at in placing the text in the context of narrative-theoretical
notions?

Surely, at least one of Chekhov's points (and mine, too) would be that
such a narrative strategy is not "driving at" anything in particular. Readers of
Chekhov are familiar with an overall impression of non-causality in his stories.[16] There is *no* progression in the narrative towards a determinate theme,
nor closure, nor a "solution" put forward from the controlling position of the
narrator. The narrator—to recapitulate—comes to terms neither with time,
nor process, change, nor anything else in his life.

Rather, just as the mode of narration in Chekhov's story keeps oscillat-
ing between paradoxical positions, immediacy, singularity, and iteration, the
narrator, too, appears to be hesitating between competing interpretations of
the story of his life. Here is one interpretation—the Professor telling Katya:

Now my dreams have come true, as you see. I've received more than
I dared to hope. For thirty years I've been a well-loved professor,
I've had excellent colleagues, I've enjoyed honours and distinction.
I've loved. I've married for love, I've had children. **When I look
back, in fact, my whole life seems a beautiful and accomplished
composition.** (119)

This, we could add, is the standard narratological view of life "as narrative"
that Chekhov is commenting on a century in advance. I am not claiming
(and neither is Chekhov) that such a theory could not be valid—to a point.

But here we have another, contending interpretation, also given by
Chekhov's narrator:

And rack my brains as I will, broadcast my thoughts where I may, I
clearly see that there's something missing in my wishes—something
vital, something really basic. My passion for science, my urge to
know myself, together with all my thoughts and feelings, and the

conceptions which I form about everything—**these thinks lack any common link capable of bonding them into a single entity.** Each sensation, each idea of mine has its own separate being. Neither in my judgments about science, the stage, literature and my pupils, nor in the pictures painted by my imagination could even the most successful analyst detect any "general conception," or the God of a live human being.

And if one lacks that, one has nothing. (139)

In other terms: what is lacking in his life is, precisely, narrativity. As I have attempted to show, this is the situation rendered in the peculiarly "weak" narrative design of Chekhov's story.

Thus, to rephrase the bottom line once more, life may *not* be shaped as a narrative, after all. Or it is *not only* a narrative. It also involves indeterminacy and oscillation between boring routine, repetition, and singularities, some of them pathetic and even heart-breaking. And it is this domain in between, I have been claiming, that is the province of narrative fiction. For literary narratologists, this reserves a paradoxical position, leading us to raise doubts against theories that supply the very props of our enterprise. Most definitely, this is the domain of Chekhov who is *against narrative* in his story from the inside, as it were, while telling us about it.

Notes

1. I use boldface throughout to emphasize the key phrases. Italics in the quoted texts are the authors'.

2. Over two decades ago Shlomith Rimmon-Kenan (1983: 1) opened her textbook on *Narrative Fiction* by pointing out that—fiction aside—"[n]ewspaper reports, history books, . . . films, comic strips, pantomime, dance, gossip, psychoanalytic sessions are only some of the narratives which permeate our lives." For her recent and—if I read correctly—somewhat less optimistic treatments of the interdisciplinary concept of narrative see Rimmon-Kenan 2002a and 2006.

3. Such retracings are aplenty. Aside from the entry on "Narrative Turn in the Humanities" (Kreiswirth 2005) in *Routledge Encyclopedia of Narrative Theory*, see, for instance, Kreiswirth 2000; Richardson 2000; Herman 2003 and 2005; Fludernik 2005. See also the very thorough account of narrative across media (other than literature) in Ryan 2004.

4. The Finnish poem, entitled *"Looginen kertomus"* ("A Logical Tale"), appears in Manner 1980: 286–287. Significantly, it transpires that the shopkeeper is named Plato.

5. For two other recent critiques of the narrative turn see Lamarque ("On Not Expecting Too Much from Narrative," 2004) and Strawson ("Against Narrativity," 2004). For drawing my attention to the latter—too late for me to change my title—I am indebted to James Phelan, who his also taken up Strawson's case against narrative identity in his editorial to *Narrative* (Phelan 2005b). My present angle is

more modest. What I want to specify are the consequences of these developments for the analysis of literary fiction.

6. See, for instance, Cobley (2003: 184–187) for a more tolerant overview.

7. The quote comes from Sacks's *The Man Who Mistook His Wife for a Hat* (1985).

8. Marie-Laure Ryan aptly terms this the *panfictional* fallacy. Ryan writes: "The frequently heard phrase 'the narratives of science' . . . carries the implication that scientific discourse does not reflect but covertly constructs reality . . . according to the rules of its own game in a process disturbingly comparable to the overt working of narrative fiction. Calling a discourse 'a narrative' or 'a story' in order to question its claim to truth amounts to equating narrative with fiction" (Ryan 2005a: 345; cf. Ryan 2005b).

9. "['Realism' is] characterized by *illusionism*, narrative which leads to *closure*, and a *hierarchy of discourses* which establishes the 'truth' of the story" (Belsey 1991: 70).

10. The coordinates for postclassical narratology have been lucidly drawn by Herman (1999: 2) its well as in the following by Margolin: "literary narrative . . . does pay disproportionate attention to marginal/exceptional cases, to unusual varieties, to breakdowns or failures of one or more of these categories, and to components . . . which have not yet been successfully handled by a set of rigorous theoretical concepts and claims" (2003: 288). For an exemplary, book-length approach to classical and postclassical concepts "in the extreme narrative circumstances of [Pynchon's] *Gravity's Rainbow*" see Hägg (2005: 80). I have myself attempted to study Nabokov's narratologically subversive ways in Tammi 2003 and forthcoming.

11. "Or "A Dreary Story," as the Ronald Hingley translation has it. For practical purposes, all references are to Hingley's English version (Chekhov 1998), and page numbers will be given in the text.

12. For an existential (eminently non-narratological) interpretation of the Professor's state of mind see Lev Shestov's seminal essay "Creation from Nothing" ("Tvorchestvo iz nichego," 1908).

13. The classical analysis of Coetzee's *Waiting for the Barbarians* (1980) is in Cohn 1999: 96–107. Cohn (97n.) expressly names Chekhov (and Kafka) as precursors of the simultaneous tactic. In her earlier study (Cohn 1978: 193–195), "A Boring Story" is also taken up as a borderline case between narration and monologue. On the high incidence of present-tense narration in contemporary Anglo-American fiction see Fludernik 1996: 249–256 and passim.

14. For shrewd narratological remarks on simultaneity in sportscasts see Ryan 1993. Cf. also Carrard 2005.

15. "The story carries the subtitle "From an Old Man's Memoirs" ("Iz zapisok starogo cheloveka"), with a nod towards the long tradition of *Zapiski* in Russian literature—cf. Gogol', *Zapiski sumashedshego* (*Memoirs of a Madman*, 1834), another early exemplar of simultaneity in narration. Chekhov's narrator also refers to his "**jottings** *[zapiski]* and musings" (127).

16. See the classical discussion in Chudakov's 1971 *Poetika Chekhova;* cf. especially the last chapter (245–278), where the issue is broached in other than narrative-theoretical terms. My remarks on "A Boring Story" were designed to supply some narratological addenda to these findings.

Works Cited

Barthes, Roland. 1975 [1966]. "An Introduction to the Structural Analysis of Narrative." Trans. Lionel Duisit. *New Literary History* 6/2: 237–272.

Belsey, Catherine. 1991 [1980]. *Critical Practice.* London and New York: Routledge.

Bruner, Jerome. 1991. "The Narrative Construction of Reality." *Critical Inquiry* 18/1: 1–21.

Carrard, Philippe. 2005. "Sports Broadcast." In Herman, Jahn, and Ryan 2005, pp. 563–564.

Chekhov, Anton, 1998. *Ward Number Six and Other Stories.* Trans. Ronald Hingley. Oxford: Oxford University Press.

Chudakov, A. P. 1971. *Poètika Chekhova.* Moscow: Nauka.

Cobley, Paul. 2003 [2001]. *Narrative.* London and New York: Routledge.

Cohn, Dorrit. 1978. *Transparent Minds: Narrative Modes for Presenting Consciousness in Fiction.* Princeton, N.J.: Princeton University Press.

———. 1999. *The Distinction of Fiction.* Baltimore: The Johns Hopkins University Press.

DeLillo, Don. 1992 [1991]. *Mao II.* London: Vintage.

Eakin, Paul John. 2004. "What Are We Reading When We Read Autobiography?" *Narrative* 12/2: 122–132.

Fludernik, Monika. 1996. *Towards a "Natural" Narratology.* London and New York: Routledge.

———. 2003. "Natural Narratology and Cognitive Parameters." In *Narrative Theory and the Cognitive Sciences,* ed. David Herman. Stanford: CSLI Publications, pp. 243–267.

———. 2005. "Histories of Narrative Theory (II): From Structuralism to the Present." In *A Companion to Narrative Theory,* ed. James Phelan and Peter J. Rabinowitz. Oxford: Blackwell, pp. 36–59.

Genette, Gérard. 1980 [1972]. *Narrative Discourse: An Essay in Method.* Trans. Jane E. Lewin. Ithaca, N.Y.: Cornell University Press.

———. 1988 [1983]. *Narrative Discourse Revisited.* Trans. Jane E. Lewin. Ithaca, N.Y.: Cornell University Press.

Herman, David. 1999. "Introduction: Narratologies." In *Narratologies: New Perspectives in Narrative Analysis,* ed. David Herman. Columbus: Ohio State University Press, pp. 1–30.

———. 2003. "Introduction." In *Narrative Theory and the Cognitive Sciences,* ed. David Herman. Stanford: CSLI Publications, pp. 1–30.

———. 2005. "Histories of Narrative Theory (I): A Genealogy of Early Developments." In *A Companion to Narrative Theory,* ed. James Phelan and Peter J. Rabinowitz. Oxford: Blackwell, pp. 19–35.

———, Manfred Jahn, and Marie-Laure Ryan, eds. 2005. *Routledge Encyclopedia of Narrative Theory.* London: Routledge.

Herrnstein-Smith, Barbara. 1981 [1980]. "Narrative Versions, Narrative Theories." In *On Narrative,* ed. W. J. T. Mitchell. Chicago: University of Chicago Press, pp. 209–232.

Hägg, Samuli. 2005. *Narratologies of Gravity's Rainbow.* Joensuu: University of Joensuu.

Kreiswirth, Martin. 2000. "Merely Telling Stories? Narrative and Knowledge in the Human Sciences." *Poetics Today* 21/2: 293–318.

———. 2005. "Narrative Turn in the Humanities." In Herman, Jahn, and Ryan 2005, pp. 377–382.

Lamarque, Peter. 2004. "On Not Expecting Too Much from Narrative." *Mind & Language* 19/4: 393–408.

Manner, Eeva-Liisa. 1980, *Runoja 1956–1977.* Helsinki: Tammi.

Margolin, Uri. 2003. "Cognitive Science, the Thinking Mind, and Literary Narrative." In *Narrative Theory and the Cognitive Sciences*, ed. David Herman. Stanford: CSLI Publications, pp. 271–294.

McHale, Brian. 2001. "Weak Narrativity: The Case of Avant-Garde Narrative Poetry." *Narrative* 9/2: 161–167.

———.2004. *The Obligation toward the Difficult Whole: Postmodernist Long Poems*. Tuscaloosa: The University of Alabama Press.

———. 2005. "Narrative in Poetry." In Herman, Jahn, and Ryan 2005, pp. 356–357.

Nelles, William. 1997. *Frameworks: Narrative Levels and Embedded Narrative*. New York: Peter Lang.

Palmer, Alan. 2004. *Fictional Minds*. Lincoln: University of Nebraska Press.

Phelan, James. 2005a. *Living to Tell about It: A Rhetoric and Ethics of Character Narration*. Ithaca: Cornell University Press.

———. 2005b. "Editor's Column: Who's Here? Thoughts on Narrative Identity and Narrative Imperialism." *Narrative* 13/3: 205–210.

Prince, Gerald. 1982, *Narratology: The Form and Function of Narrative*. Berlin: Mouton.

———. 1987. *A Dictionary of Narratology*. Lincoln and London: University of Nebraska Press.

———. 1999. "Revisiting Narrativity." In *Grenzüberschreitungen: Narratologie im Kontekst / Transcending Boundaries: Narratology in Context*, ed. Walter Grünzweig and Andreas Solbach. Tübingen: Gunter Narr, pp. 43–51.

Richardson, Brian. 2000. "Recent Concepts of Narrative and the Narratives of Narrative Theory." *Style* 34/2: 168–175.

Rimmon-Kenan, Shlomith. 1983. *Narrative Fiction: Contemporary Poetics*. London: Methuen.

———. 2002a. "Towards . . . Afterthoughts, Almost Twenty Years Later." In *Narrative Fiction: Contemporary Poetics* (2nd ed.). London and New York: Routledge, pp. 135–149.

———. 2002b. "The Story of 'I': Illness and Narrative Identity." *Narrative* 10/1: 9–27.

———.2006. "Concepts of Narrative." *COLLeGIUM*, forthcoming.

Rudrum, David. 2005. "From Narrative Representation to Narrative Use: Towards the Limits of Definition." *Narrative* 13/2: 195–204.

Ryan, Marie-Laure. 1993. "Narrative in Real Time: Chronicle, Mimesis, and Plot in the Baseball Broadcast." *Narrative* 1/2: 138–155.

———. 2004. "Introduction." In *Narrative across Media: The Languages of Storytelling*, ed. Marie-Laure Ryan. Lincoln: University of Nebraska Press, pp. 1–40.

———. 2005a. "Narrative." In Herman, Jahn, and Ryan 2005, pp. 344–348.

———. 2005b. "Panfictionality." In Herman, Jahn, and Ryan 2005, pp. 417–418.

Shestov, Lev. 1908. "Tvorchestvo iz nichego (A. P. Chekhov)." In *Nachala i kontsy: Sbornik statei*. St. Petersburg: Stasiulevich, pp. 1–68.

Strawson, Galen. 2004. "Against Narrativity." *Ratio* 17/4: 428–452.

Tammi, Pekka. 2003. "Risky Business: Probing the Borderlines of FID. Nabokov's *An Affair of Honor (Podlec)* as a Test Case." In *Linguistic and Literary Aspects of Free Indirect Discourse from a Typological Perspective*, ed. Pekka Tammi and Hannu Tommola. Tampere: Department of Literature and the Arts. University of Tampere, pp. 41–54.

———. 2006. "Exploring *Terra-Incognita*." In *FREE-language-INDIRECT-translation-DISCOURSE-narrative*, ed. Pekka Tammi and Hannu Tommola, forthcoming.

Turner, Mark. 1996. *The Literary Mind*. New York: Oxford University Press.

White, Hayden. 1987 [1980]. "The Value of Narrativity in the Representation of Reality." In *The Content of the Form: Narrative Discourse and Historical Representation.* Baltimore: The Johns Hopkins University Press, pp. 1–25.

OLIVER TAPLIN

Greek Tragedy, Chekhov, and Being Remembered

My conclusion may well seem a familiar one, but I hope to explore some less frequented ways of approaching it. So I'll start with the conclusion, which is well-epitomized in the *Iliad* by the poetic future of Hector in what James Redfield called his "tragedy." I am thinking especially of his last lines before he is fatally wounded, when he realizes he is about to die:

> Then let me not die without a last effort and without fame *(kleos)*, but achieving something great, and worth knowing by future generations *(essomenoisi pythesthai)*.
>
> —*Iliad* 22.304–305

The point is that every time the poem is performed or read—or even when the lines are quoted, as here and now—Hector's aspiration is fulfilled. All the audiences from the first coining of the lines down through us and into the foreseeable future are *essomenoisi*. But it is not Hector's brave stand alone which wins the future *kleos* for him: this also requires the survival of the poem. The aspiration is one for the poet as well as the hero. If the poem is not worth repeating, then its characters will fade away with it, leaving no trace.

Arion: A Journal of Humanities and the Classics, Volume 13, Number 3 (Winter 2006): pp. 51–65. Copyright © 2006 Oliver Taplin.

So as well as the bravery there has to be the telling, the articulation, the craft and the vividness. If you will tolerate the shorthand, it is the "beauty" of the poetry that salvages Hector from oblivion. And maybe there is a subliminal reminder of that a few lines later when Achilles' spear is about to transfix Hector's throat (317–319): it is as bright as Hesperos, "the most beautiful *(kallistos)* star in the sky." The spear is not only the gift of the gods to Peleus; it stays shining *kallistos* within a memorable scene of poetry. There is nothing intrinsically beautiful about violent death—it does not in itself deserve the attention of future audiences. It is the poetry that turns the pain—the blood, the smell, the disgusting horror of physiological mutilation—into something we may want to hear about, something *essomenoisi pythesthai*. The future, I am suggesting, rests with people in some sense *wanting* to know about the suffering, and finding it "beautiful."

* * *

A development of this rationale of tragedy is, then, my destination. To start with, I shall explore three trains of thought that, in my mind, have been converging on it. First, one leading from my current research, which is on the bearing on tragedy of fourth-century vase painting, mainly paintings from the Greek West (so-called "South-Italian"). I am hoping, in that research, to show how quite a few of the vases with mythological narratives have very interesting, though varied and complex, relations with what was likely to have been the most familiar way of telling heroic myth at that time in that part of the world—tragedy, that is. Fortunately, for my purposes here, the much-contested question of what relations there were, if any, can be bypassed, because, whether or not the vases invoke tragedies, what is indisputable is that the occasion they were made for was primarily if not exclusively funerary. The fact that they were all found in tombs—whether by archaeologists or by *tumbaroli*—does not necessarily show that they were commissioned or made for funerary use; but many of those that are most relevant are too large for any symposiastic or practical use—many even have holes in the bottom, and so could never have held liquid.

These vases are conspicuous objects. Many of them stand over 75 cm high, some even up to 125 cm; they are skillfully potted and ornamented; the pictures are carefully drawn and painted, using purple, white, and gold as well as black. And they are covered in elaborate figured scenes, not using standard mass-produced sketches—in fact quite often displaying unusual iconographies. These are, then, classy items, not cheap or inconspicuous, ornaments for prestige funerals. And, given their funerary setting, what seems surprising is that so many of their mythological scenes are "tragic" in content—whether or not directly connected with an actual tragedy. There are scenes of violence, danger, distress, and disruption, often including premature and unnatural death. There has been a gathering movement (best articulated by Luca Giuliani) to search them for suggestions or associations that will afford some comfort to the bereaved—*consolatio* material. And with some scenes this is not hard: Orestes and Iphigeneia among the Taurians suggests family reunion and future safety; Orestes and Electra at the tomb of Agamemnon exemplifies devotion to a dead father (though it is not so reassuring for mothers!); Andromeda rescued by Perseus shows the triumph of courage and love; Niobe turning into stone is a model of grief and remembrance. Much ingenuity, often pretty selective, is expended on finding crumbs of comfort in the stories chosen. But some of them are too uncomfortable, surely, to be rescued: Medea triumphant over Jason and the bodies of her sons; Hippolytus unable to control his horses; Lycurgus madly slaughtering his wife and children; Neoptolemos treacherously assassinated at Delphi. If these scenes are consolatory in some way then it is not because there is anything reassuring about the terrible sufferings depicted.

Yet, however horrific the events, however much the agents and victims suffer, the painting is never disfigured—that is to say that it is never ugly or disgusting or degrading. I suppose that this contrasts with much modern storytelling, especially in film. Realism says that if the events are ugly, they should be seen in their ugliness—this is true to life. What the vase-paintings do is to take the horrors of the heroic past and turn them into artifacts of beauty. The vases may not be to modern taste, but they were clearly meant to be seen as objects of beauty. Out of the agony and conflict and death is salvaged an artwork that has form, color, gracefulness, even a certain calm perhaps. They suggest—at least this is my train of thought—they suggest that, although human life is full of grief, especially of death and bereavement, it is not *utterly* nasty and brutish. And it *may* not merely all be swallowed up in the greater shapelessness. The artist has rescued something amazing and alerting from the terrible events of the mythical past: analogously we, the mourners at this funeral in the present, should be assured that human life can, despite everything, be seen, if it is turned to the right light, as something with color, shape, and form. We are encouraged to resist the feeling that it is all entirely senseless, amorphous, to be snuffed out without trace or meaning. In this way the hard fact of the suffering is not hidden or disguised or denied, but it is given a future, one that offers a certain restorative strength through the paying of attention to art—whether this be regarded as some kind of truth, or as a pleasure, or merely an analgesic.

* * *

My second approach route is through the planting of aetiologies—aetiologies of names, institutions or, as most often, cult locations and practices. By this term I mean the kind of "just so stories" which give an explanation set in the distant past for something which still exists in the audience's present. An archetypal example is the story that Achilles tells Priam at *Iliad* 24.614–617 about how Niobe, as she wept over her dead children, was turned into a rock with a stream running down it. That rock, says Achilles, is still visible "now" on Mount Sipylus—and it is, indeed, still a tourist sight near the (now Turkish) town of Manisa to this day.

Although aetiologies are pretty common in tragedy, I am not aware of a satisfactory discussion in terms of *why* they are there, asking what they may contribute to the overall significance of the tragedy as a whole for its audiences. They are especially often declared by the Euripidean *deus ex machina*, a device that tends to give the modern reader the impression of an artificial wrapping up, so that the aetiologies appear to be merely part of this last-minute cosmetic patching. But they are far from exclusively Euripidean. There is the hero-cult of Oedipus in *Oedipus at Colonus* and of Ajax in *Ajax*—some others are arguable in Sophocles, but not so clear. Aeschylus' *Eumenides* is awash with aetiologies, and phrases about "all of future time" appear again and again. There is the alliance between Athens and Argos; the homicide court on the Areopagus; the vote of Athena; the cult of the Erinyes assimilated to that of the Semnai; the honesty of Athenian jurors; the future prosperity and fertility of the city—even, arguably, the incorporation of tragedy into Athens. It is interesting, then, that *Seven against Thebes*, although also the third play of a trilogy, has no aetiology, at least none that is at all clearly signaled in our text. There is little comfort: the city is saved, but the emphasis is on the obliteration of the royal house.

This downbeat closure to *Seven against Thebes* may serve as a transition back to a particularly telling Euripidean play, *Trojan Women*. The gods have deserted Troy. There is no future cult promised; the city will be burnt to the ground; there will be no surviving males, not even any monument. Even the *name* of Troy will be obliterated without trace. This is a repeated motif in the laments of the final scene. First there is the chorus at 1291–1292:

The great city, no city, has perished, and Troy no longer exists.

Then addressing the temples and the city itself, they say (1319):

You will fall to the earth and become without a name.

And again 1322–1324, just a few lines from the end:

The name of our country will disappear.
Everything will go one way or another.
Wretched Troy no longer exists.

I do not need to labor the point: *anonymoi . . . onoma de gar aphanes eisin,* at the end of a play in which the double names of *Ilios* and *Troia* (Troy) have been spoken dozens of times. Even as they lament the obliteration of the name of Troy, they are in fact perpetuating it. They press DELETE, and what they do is SAVE. And this point is in fact spelled out, with a Homeric explicitness that is rare in tragedy, at 1240–1245. Hecuba says:

> So nothing rested with the gods, except my suffering, and Troy, especially hated among cities. We made sacrifices in vain. And yet if the god had not turned everything upside-down, we would have disappeared without trace, and would not be put into poetry, subjects for the bards of future generations.

So there *is* a hidden aetiology, one without the help of any explicit declaration, in *Trojan Women:* the future of Troy in poetry. As long as the poetry is preserved and read by humans, heard and talked about, the aetiology is fulfilled and renewed. But what is it that earns the future in poetry for Troy? Not the event of being sacked—many cities have been destroyed and left no name and no poetry. I think the answer has to be the *quality* of the suffering, and the expression of that quality, its articulation. Greek tragedy narrates terrible events—pain, death, undeserved misery, horrors—yet it never falls silent; and it never descends into inarticulacy, or even into the unmetrical. The characters talk about their sufferings, even debate about them; the chorus always gathers its witness and forms it into song and dance.

So the things in human life that threaten to descend into the meaningless, the anarchic, ugly and unspeakable, offer instead poetry, music, and dance. This is some comfort—or at least the offer of it. I do not need to claim that it truly, ultimately, lifts our suffering out of the harsh reality of the world: but it does hint that the amorphousness and cacophony might, if seen and heard in the right way, have form and even beauty. There is a phrase in the aetiology delivered by Artemis in *Hippolytus* which expresses my point well. Phaedra has perished in self-disgust and vindictiveness; Hippolytus has come to a horrible end, and we see his mangled body before our eyes; his father is bereaved through his own curse; Athens herself has lost a future leader. Despite all this cruel suffering, the marriage customs of Trozen will symbolize the salvaging of something: Hippolytus, as Artemis tells him, will have great "honor" *(timê)*: for all time the young women there will cut their hair and lament him before their wedding (1428–1430):

> In recompense for these sufferings I shall give you high honors in this land of Trozen: before their wedding virgin girls shall cut their locks

for you; and through long ages you shall reap the high grief of
their tears.

    And so the poetry-creating care *(mousopoios merimna)* of
unmarried girls shall

      for ever be concerned with you, and Phaedra's desire for you
will not disappear

        without a name in silence.

He will be the object of *mousopoios merimna,* and Phaedra's fierce love will
not be silenced either, deleted without a name.

    Now, we ordinary citizens who watch tragedy cannot expect to have *our*
names preserved in poetry. Far from that, we hope that our sufferings will
never be so terrible or so extraordinary as to be worthy of special memorial.
These are the privileges of the great heroes—extraordinary yet hardly envi-
able. I suppose that the question now is whether there is any equivalent for us,
the common-or-garden audience, whether there is some analogy or transference between our obscure lives and the dark-shining beauty and poetry of the
lives of the tragic heroes.

* * *

These questions were revolving in my mind when I saw Chekhov's *Three
Sisters* last year—in fact twice, in two different productions. And it was
perhaps Chekhov who gave me the impetus for the connections I am making here between tragedy and the future. Chekhov liked to call his plays
"comedies"; and quite apart from all the many other differences of tone and
form from the Greek plays, the characters are not drawn from the heroic
past but from the ordinary bourgeois present. They and their names are fic-
tions. *Three Sisters* is set in a large town in the middle of nowhere—it does
not even get given a name. The three sisters and their brother moved there
from Moscow when their father was promoted in the army and sent off to
command the local brigade. There are very few people of any culture or education there, apart from the army officers. They belong to the era of the idle
rich, although things are changing. Near the very beginning a lieutenant,
Baron Tuzenbakh, talks of the dawn of a new age: "I'm going to work, and
in twenty-five or thirty years time everyone will work. Everyone."[1] But the
recurrent talk of what the future has to bring comes above all from the newly
posted battery-commander Vershinin. He has hardly arrived on the scene
and he is already dwelling on the unpredictability of the future, about how
you cannot know what will seem, in retrospect, "significant and important
. . . or what will seem pathetic and absurd." When Masha, one of the sisters,
complains of the uselessness of their knowing three foreign languages—"we
know too much," she says—Vershinin launches into a speech (182):

Oh, what a thing to say! [laughs] You know much too much. I don't think there exists, or ever could exist, a town so dull and dreary that it has no place for intelligent, educated men and women. Let's suppose that among the hundred thousand inhabitants of this town—oh, I know it's a backward, rough sort of place—there's no one else like you three. Well, you obviously can't hope to prevail against the forces of ignorance around you. As you go on living you'll have to give way bit by bit to these hundred thousand people and be swallowed up in the crowd. You'll go under, but that doesn't mean you'll sink without trace—you will have some effect. Perhaps when you're gone there will be six people like you, then twelve and so on, and in the end your kind will be the majority. In two or three hundred years life on this earth will be beautiful beyond our dreams, it will be marvelous. Man needs a life like that, and if he hasn't yet got it he must feel he's going to get it, he must look forward to it, dream about it, prepare for it. That means he must have more vision and more knowledge than his father or grandfather ever had. [laughs] And here are you complaining you know too much.

MASHA [takes off her hat] I'm staying to lunch.

IRENA [with a sigh] You know, what you've just said ought really to be written down.

So, according to this, even assuming that we sink without trace, that does not necessarily mean that we shall have no effect on the world: this is an appealing attempt to salvage some light from the impending threat of overwhelming dark. In the second Act Vershinin has a discussion with the Baron (196–197):

VERSHININ Let me see. Well, for instance, let's try and imagine life after we're dead and buried, in two or three hundred years, say.

TUZENBAKH Very well then. When we are dead, people will fly around in balloons, there will be a new style in men's jackets and a sixth sense may be discovered and developed, but life itself won't change, it will still be as difficult and full of mystery and happiness as it is now. Even in a thousand years men will still be moaning away about life being a burden. What's more they will still be as scared of death as they are now. And as keen on avoiding it.

VERSHININ [after some thought] Now how can I put it? I think everything on earth is bound to change bit by bit, in fact already is changing before our very eyes. Two or three hundred years, or a thousand years if you like—it doesn't really matter how long—will bring in a new and happy life. We'll have no part in it of course, but it is what we are living for now, working for, yes and suffering for. We're creating it, and that's what gives our life its meaning, and its happiness too if you want to put it that way.

An attempt is made, then, to give some meaning to the suffering—and an attempt to find some restorative consolation. But, in a counter-movement to this, things only get worse for the three sisters. Their brother makes a bad marriage and squanders their inheritance, and with it any chance of returning to Moscow. Olga settles for becoming a provincial headmistress; the married sister Masha falls in love with the unattainable Vershinin; the youngest Irena agrees to marry the Baron even though she does not love him. And then, finally, on the day of the fourth and last act, the whole army brigade is leaving, posted to Poland. Vershinin and Masha have to part forever. Then comes the stage direction, "the muffled sound of a distant shot is heard": the Baron has been killed in a pointless duel over a trivial offence.

With the stage direction: "The three sisters stand close together" (236–237), the closing dialogue begins:

MASHA Oh listen to the band. They're all leaving us, and one has gone right away and will never, never come back, and we shall be left alone to begin our lives again. We must go on living, we must.

IRENA [puts her head on Olga's breast] What is all this for? Why all this suffering? The answer will be known one day, and then there will be no more mysteries left, but till then life must go on, we must work and work and think of nothing else. I'll go off alone tomorrow to teach at a school and spend my whole life serving those who may need me. It's autumn now and it will soon be winter, with everything buried in snow, and I shall work, work, work.

OLGA [embraces both her sisters] Listen to the band. What a splendid, rousing tune, it puts new heart into you, doesn't it? Oh, my god! In time we shall pass on forever and be forgotten. Our faces will be forgotten and our voices and how many of us there were. But our sufferings will bring happiness to those who came after us, peace and joy will reign on earth, and there will be kind words and kind thoughts for us and our times. We still have our lives ahead of us, my dears, so let's make the most of them. The band's playing such cheerful, happy music, it feels as if we might find out before long what our lives and sufferings are for. If we could only know! If we could only know!

. . .

CHEBUTYKIN [singing softly] Tararaboomdeay, let's have a tune today. [reads the newspaper] None of it matters. Nothing matters.

OLGA If we could only know, oh if we could only know!

CURTAIN

There is there is one particular clause here that pierces with its poignancy: "Our faces will be forgotten and our voices *and how many of us there were.*" This is Chekhov's equivalent of "and the name of Troy will be lost." It is the defining mark of the sisters that they are three. When Vershinin first arrives in Act One only two of the sisters are in the room: "But there should be three of you sisters. I remember three little girls. Can't remember your faces, but that your father Colonel Prozorov had three little girls I remember quite clearly."

And, recalling the "Tragedy of Hector," it will *not* be forgotten "how many of us there were," not even though they are fictional characters. The three sisters are even numbered in the very title of the play. Every time the play is performed—or even quoted in a talk—they are not forgotten. This is in an oblique way a kind of aetiology. And it is this, I think, that gives a sense of hope to the way we hear Olga's aspiration to want to know what our fives and sufferings are for. With our realistic and world-weary intellects we may think that her speech is merely so much sentimentality: that very attitude is voiced by Chebutykin in a kind of counterpoint—"What does it matter? Nothing matters." Yet who wants to align themselves against Olga with an idle, drunken, and exhausted old parasite?

* * *

So, to return to Greek tragedy and to conclude. The quality of the suffering and the quality of its expression become words and spectacle and music and dance, and people go to the theater to experience them. In everyday life we have to get on with things, and most of us hope for the best. We cannot find the energy to live if we are forever peering into the abyss and demanding the meaning of it all, forever confronting the all-too-real possibility that life is meaningless and inexplicable. During the course of watching a tragedy, the audience is exposed to extreme human suffering; they are encouraged to ask for explanation, yet not allowed any easy answers or redemptions. During the course of watching a tragedy we see with unmuddied clarity that the gods may not be just or repay their debts; that marriages and families may not be reliable; rulers may not be good; the search for knowledge may not bring wisdom or understanding. And more and worse. We have to endure these all too real possibilities. Then we emerge from the theater to carry on with our everyday human lives, with everyday resilience and hope. The worst can happen, we see. But it may not happen—and we should press on with our own lives.

The way that the terrible sufferings of the tragic characters are still turned into the beauty and form of tragedy is imbibed and taken away in a diluted draft by the everyday members of the audience (note the metaphor of imbibing, rather than the purgation of Aristotelian *katharsis*). Human creativity, in collaboration with the human ability to appreciate poetry, the visual arts, music and dance imparts the energy to live. This combination emboldens us to keep DELETE at bay. And so, although the tragedies are set in the past they turn us, their audiences, with renewed strength to SAVE, to face the future.

NOTE

1. Translations from Chekhov are taken from *Five Plays*, trans. Ronald Hingley (Oxford 1998).

AUTHOR'S NOTE

This article is based on a talk given to a Seminar on "Futures," held in Corpus Christi College, Oxford, in 2004. I am grateful for the perceptive comments made there.

STUART YOUNG

A Blind Spot:
Chekhov's Deepest Horizons

Chekhov's drama has traditionally been associated with detailed, even cluttered, naturalistic settings.[1] Occasionally, as in the final act of *Uncle Vanya*, set in Vanya's room, the description of the stage is indeed elaborate. Generally, however, Chekhov's directions are "laconic,"[2] certainly compared with those of Ibsen and Strindberg. The scenic elements are carefully, scrupulously selected and are often emblematic: according to Meyerhold, Chekhov insisted that "the stage reflects the quintessence of life and there is no need to introduce anything superfluous on to it."[3]

Chekhov's description of the setting for Act Two of *The Cherry Orchard* is invested with particular symbolic weight.[4] Therefore, as Beverly Hahn insists, it "demands the most absolute precision for its effect":[5]

> Open fields. An old chapel—long abandoned and dilapidated. Near it a well, large stones which were evidently once tombstones, and an old bench. A road can be seen leading to the Gayev estate. On one side loom dark poplars, and there the cherry orchard begins. In the distance is a row of telegraph poles, and far, far away, on the horizon, can be dimly made out a large town, which is visible only in very fine, clear weather. The sun will soon set.[6]

Journal of Dramatic Theory and Criticism, Volume 21, Number 2 (Spring 2007): pp. 65–78.
Copyright © 2007 Stuart Young.

This setting contains a particularly curious detail, a detail more intriguing perhaps than the celebrated, enigmatic "breaking string" that sounds for the first time in this act: "far, far away, on the horizon, can be dimly made out a large town, which is visible only in very fine, clear weather." The description is, of course, especially challenging for the designer: how to convey that impression of just-visibility and that exceptional distance? Perhaps it is more pertinent to ask: have you ever beheld that town and that horizon? I have seen perhaps ten *Cherry Orchards*, and I have yet to espy either town or horizon.

As with so much else in Chekhovian theatrical tradition, the failure to show that expansive landscape and horizon can be traced back to Stanislavsky, who was schooled in the late nineteenth-century aesthetic of illusionism as exemplified by the productions of the Saxe-Meinengen company and André Antoine. Consequently, the Russian director and his designer Viktor Simov routinely elaborated in excessive detail the essential scenographic elements specified by Chekhov, "encasing the plays in a highly detailed, representational, physical world".[7] As Edward Braun notes, the precision and specificity of Chekhov's directions for the second act of *The Cherry Orchard* were lost on Stanislavsky.[8] The tension between encroaching modernity and provincial stasis was largely absent from the Moscow Art Theatre set, which, as Nick Worrall remarks, represented a more emphatically pastoral landscape, in the manner of the painter Levitan.[9] Missing was the row of telegraph poles in the distance, while introduced were haystacks, a silver birch and two fir trees; and the tumble-down chapel that Chekhov describes became a much grander, more prominent presence, centre stage left. Moreover, Stanislavsky accompanied all this with one of his usual soundscapes: rustling leaves, crackling branches, croaking frogs, and corncrakes. To Chekhov's annoyance Stanislavsky also toyed with the idea of having a train cross upstage during the act; at least this would have conveyed the aspect of technological advance signified by the telegraph poles. As for that horizon, a ridge rising in the background actually served to foreshorten the distance and confine the landscape, and Stanislavsky's prompt copy states, "The town is not yet visible in the heat haze."[10] Moreover, an evening mist rises from the ravine—an image that, with unintended irony, nicely encapsulates Stanislavsky's obfuscating of Chekhov's dramaturgy.

Stanislavsky is not the only one guilty of negligence or misunderstanding here. Sometimes the possibility of our seeing that horizon is precluded by the translator. Among translations into English, David Mamet's and, surprisingly, Trevor Griffiths's versions of the play acknowledge neither the town nor the horizon.[11] Pam Gems notes the "outline of a town," but it is merely in "the distance," not "far, far away" (there is no mention that the town is visible only in very fine, clear weather); and she does not refer to the horizon.[12]

Yet Chekhov was particularly adamant about the setting and the horizon that he envisaged. Presumably ever mindful of Stanislavsky's proclivities, while revising the play he wrote to Vladimir Nemirovich-Danchenko that he had "reduced the décor . . . to a minimum" and he asked that in Act Two "you give me genuine green fields and a road and *a sense of distance unusual for the stage*."[13] This insistence on the horizon and the view to it acquires greater significance when set alongside an important speech of Lopakhin's later in the act: in something of a *profession de foi*, Lopakhin speaks of God's having given us the "deepest horizons."[14] This subtle but resonant echo points to the way in which, in Chekhov's plays, scenography operates in an extremely "intricate and complicated" relationship with character, stage business and props;[15] dramatic action and dialogue are deliberately, often ironically, juxtaposed with visual images.[16]

The nature of this relationship is perhaps disguised because of the extent to which Chekhov moves from the "fixed," "closed" spaces of Ibsen's realistic drama and Strindberg's early, naturalistic plays,[17] with their single-point perspective, to spaces that are more fluid, open and "multidimensional."[18] Described in meticulous detail, the single settings of plays such as *Hedda Gabler, Ghosts* and *Dance of Death (Part One)* feature carefully constructed locations which serve to emphasize and signify aspects of the central characters' plight.[19] On the other hand, although settings like the nursery in *The Cherry Orchard* certainly have powerful resonance for the characters, and although details such as the third-act fire in *Three Sisters* heighten the drama, their significance is not firmly fixed by an authorial voice. Rather, as is appropriate for plays which elevate the ensemble above a central role or roles, meaning is left more open to interpretation by both characters and spectators,[20] and that sense of a shifting perspective is facilitated in all Chekhov's major plays because we see those characters in a series of different locations.

Arnold Aronson credits "modern and postmodern" productions, which have broken emphatically with Stanislavskian naturalism in favor of syncretic, poetic designs, with enabling the "Chekhovian landscape" to "thrive" by capturing the fundamental qualities of the plays' scenography: the "implied transparency of walls, fluidity of space, juxtaposition of near and far and symbolic use of familiar items."[21] According to Aronson, Chekhov is a Symbolist playwright for whom "the concrete elements of the external world were manifestations of emotional states of being," "not a documentary recording of domestic décor"; Chekhov's "settings are virtual roadmaps to the psyche."[22] However, although Chekhov may have insisted that "the stage is art" and that it "demands a degree of artifice,"[23] and although his dramaturgy moves beyond naturalism and allows a fluid, shifting perspective, it does not necessarily follow that he is more interested in "the evocation of a state of mind" or "emotional states of being" than in "the details of real life."[24] Nor does it follow that he seeks to create a space that is primarily existential, even ahistorical or apolitical. As Peter Holland argues, a disdain for "naturalism in its fullest sense . . . does not contradict a Chekhov whose aim is . . . to analyze society directly."[25] Indeed, the significance of the "concrete elements of the external world" in Chekhov's plays is not merely subjective but derives from a "specific historicity and precise sociological imagination" that require some substantiation.[26]

Designs which distill the plays' "poetic essences"—perhaps synthesizing the various locations in a single set—might recognize the extent to which Chekhov has moved from the static Ibsenian drawing-room to something more fluid and polyphonic, and they may capture the dichotomy and counterpoint between public and private spheres. They may also express a "Bergsonian awareness that reality stands outside time" or show the plays to open, as Andrey Bely suggests, "an aperture into Eternity."[27] However, such designs, like most conventional, naturalistic stagings, have generally continued to emphasize unduly emotional resonance and *nastroyeniye* (mood), and therefore have overlooked the precise way in which Chekhov envisages the scenography to function. Consequently, some of these distillations ignore or override Chekhov's own selection of the crucial scenic elements. It is not unusual, for instance, for the lake to disappear altogether from view in *The Seagull*, often to be located hypothetically somewhere in the direction of the audience. On the other hand, as in Giorgio Strehler's, Anatoly Efros's and Andrei Serban's *Cherry Orchards*,[28] often cherry trees—or their blossom—have assumed an especial prominence beyond the discreet presence indicated in Chekhov's descriptions of each act's settings.

To examine the intricate and complicated role that scenography plays in Chekhov, let us return to that elusive horizon. Of course, the notion of Chekhov's distant horizons seems like an oxymoron. If we think of Chekhov in terms of horizons at all, they tend to be very narrow ones: his plays are usually seen as claustrophobic. Therefore, because "Chekhov's characters are often trapped in a life or philosophy that is represented by the concrete elements of a house,"[29] they are all too easily hermetically sealed in the fourth-wall, naturalistic world that the Moscow Art Theatre and its adherents have fashioned for them.[30] Certainly the characters are frequently self-absorbed and inward looking. Even when they look outwards, as Vershinin and Trofimov do most obviously, they are generally dismissed as dreamers rather than identified as visionaries; they apparently take refuge in fantasy and illusions to compensate for personal inadequacy and unhappiness. Yet, although the characters themselves are often oblivious, Chekhov's focus extends considerably beyond their narrow circles.

The conceit of the stage encapsulating the world in miniature is, of course, older than Shakespeare's Globe, but this is often disguised in realistic and naturalistic theatre, which, especially when it confines action to a "fixed" room, seems to value the particular over the emblematic. Therefore, we are often encouraged to celebrate Chekhov's characters for their special, quirky individuality rather than their representativeness. However, just as *Hedda Gabler* is emblematic of a wider bourgeois world, so *The Cherry Orchard* can be seen as capturing in microcosm a whole society on the brink of "convulsive change."[31] (Indeed for Richard Eyre this is what makes the play the greatest of the twentieth century.[32]) Trofimov makes the point explicitly at the end of the act, when he tells Anya, "All Russia is our orchard."[33]

Although reference to the horizon is most explicit in *The Cherry Orchard*, allusion to a much wider world beyond the immediate context of the drama is there in the other plays too, even in the most insular, *Uncle Vanya*. In the final act of *Three Sisters* the play suddenly opens out to the Prozorovs' garden, with a long avenue of firs affording a view of a river and a wood beyond. The canvas implicitly extends even further with the passage of soldiers through the garden reminding us of the imminent departure of the brigade for Poland.[34] Of course, that extended world is evoked not only by elements of setting and stage action, but by the references in the plays' dialogue to other people and places: in *The Cherry Orchard* to Ranevskaya's aunt in Yaroslavl, her lover in Paris, and Lopakhin's business in Kharkov; in *Three Sisters* to Balzac's marriage in Berdichev, and a smallpox epidemic in Tsitsikar; and in *The Seagull* to Dorn's visit to Genoa, and Arkadina's and Nina's performances in Kharkov and Moscow. A more distant backdrop still is signaled by a visual detail in the final act of *Uncle Vanya*, seemingly the most "chamber" of the plays. Hanging on the wall of Vanya's room is a map of Africa, which, the stage description notes, "is obviously out of place here."[35] (Another interesting challenge for a designer: to suggest the out-of-placeness of the map!) Eventually, towards the end of the act, when Astrov reluctantly takes his leave, he acknowledges the map: he goes up to it, looks at it, and says, "It must be scorching in Africa now."[36]

Where these wider prospects are registered at all, they tend to be understood as metaphors for the characters' personal plight, or as highlighting the characters' existential predicament or their suffering, even conferring a tragic dimension on that suffering. So, J. L. Styan somewhat lamely posits that the "useless and incongruous" map of Africa in *Uncle Vanya* is "suggestive of the vague and muddled horizons of Vanya's thinking."[37] For Rokem, Chekhov's "open" doors, pointing to other worlds and possibilities, simply emphasize that his "heroes are caught somewhere between paralysis and despair."[38] In a similar vein Aronson concludes that "what is clearly most significant for Chekhov" in the setting for the last act of *Three Sisters* is "the vista stretching into the distance with its implication of continuity and the promised land that the sisters can never reach"; "The freshness or freedom of the outside world is tantalisingly visible yet inaccessible."[39]

Aronson's understanding is symptomatic of a more general inclination to read the entire scenography of *Three Sisters*—its sequence of changing settings—somewhat in the Ibsenian manner as a direct, physical correlation of the sisters' story. Hence Hahn reasons that the sisters' "gradual loss of power in their own house is externalized in the visual details" of these settings:[40] in the darkening, more ominous mood as the action shifts from the sunny daylight of Act One, first to the winter evening of Act Two and then the deepest night of Act Three, and from the grand, spacious interior of the first two acts—the drawing-room and adjoining ballroom—to the rather claustrophobic bedroom shared by Olga and Irina. The sense of increasing despair is also apparently emphasized by the fire raging in the town, visually represented by the red glow at a window visible through a doorway. Accordingly the outdoor setting of Act Four, with only the terrace of the house visible on the right, is commonly interpreted as making literal the sisters' effective expulsion from the house. Consequently, for Hahn, the "receding perspectives of the long avenue of firs, the river and the forest" express the profound sadness that characterizes the play: they "give more the feeling of a crisis being over than of anything being solved."[41]

Such reasoning, like the failure to register or represent adequately the wider frames of reference and horizons, derives from the readiness of performers and audiences alike to take their cue from the characters' own accounts of themselves and to indulge the navel-gazing. (That is why those miseries can easily assume tragic proportions.) Because the irony operating in the plays is often muted in productions, we fail to perceive the bathos of such lines as Irina Prozorova's "my soul is like an expensive piano that is locked and the key lost."[42] However, Chekhov's dramaturgy should work to prompt us to apply the corrective perspective that the characters are unable to bring to their predicament and problems. This is evident in the use of counterpoint in the construction of scenes: for example, at the beginning of *Three Sisters*, the upstage laughter and ridicule of Solyony by Chebutykin and Tuzenbakh comments ironically on Olga's and Irina's fanciful talk of going to Moscow.

More than is generally appreciated, setting is another device Chekhov uses, especially in his last two plays, to comment ironically on the characters and their propensity to look inwards. It is just possible that the wider view to the horizon upstage actually places the downstage drama and apparent misery in a different perspective, indeed in perspective *per se,* ensuring that the struggles and suffering of the characters are not permitted to loom disproportionately large.[43] In other words, looking outwards can alter our looking inwards.

Therefore, the setting for Act Four of *Three Sisters,* for example, can be understood rather differently from the way in which Hahn and Aronson read it. The fire of Act Three provides a clue to this. The turmoil created by the fire generates hysteria and fatigue which precipitate the series of emotional outbursts and crises involving the sisters and then Andrey. Olga complains that she has aged ten years in this single night. However, although she and her siblings are distressed, there are many others in the town who are patently much worse off, as Olga herself has actually told us: Kirsanovsky St has evidently burnt to the ground and its inhabitants are presumably destitute, and the Kotilins and Vershinins have had to flee their homes. Meanwhile, all Fedotik's belongings have been destroyed, but, in marked contrast to Irina's self-pitying anguish that her life is running out, the junior officer laughs and dances at his misfortune! It is surely significant, too, that, from early in the act, we can see the dawn progressively breaking.[44]

The setting for Act Four of *Three Sisters,* with its path through the Prozorovs' garden to the river and beyond, not only points towards more distant places—Poland, where the brigade is being posted, and of course Moscow—but it allows the world beyond the sisters' circle to enter the scenic space of the play. Although financial constraints doubtless often prevent productions from realizing this, Chekhov envisages that, during the act, miscellaneous townspeople and five or six soldiers walk through the garden en route to the river. The passers-by, who create a "vivid and active" world around the sisters,[45] include, in particular, two street musicians. Those two itinerants may intrude less brusquely and dramatically than the passerby in Act Two of *The Cherry Orchard;* however, lest we romanticize them as part of the picturesque scenery, Anfisa remarks, "Poor wretches. They're not playing because their stomachs are full."[46] The musicians' destitution *may* be an analogue for the dispossession of the three sisters' house by Natasha, but of course, like the victims of the fire, their privation is actually much greater. It is noteworthy, too, that it is Anfisa who makes these remarks about the musicians. She has been evicted by Natasha from the house and is living with Olga at the school, yet she declares that there is "no-one happier than I."[47] Therefore, Anfisa's cheerful resilience and the street musicians' plight not only put the miseries of the sisters and Andrey into perspective but they may become an implicit rebuke of the Prozorovs' self-centeredness.

Similarly, like Trofimov in *The Cherry Orchard,* but more concretely, Astrov in *Uncle Vanya* reminds us of the world beyond the perimeter of the Serebryakov estate and so offers a wider perspective, and tacit judgement, on the troubles of the self-absorbed members of the household. At the very beginning of the play we learn of the typhus epidemic, poverty and squalor at Malitskoye, and later in Act One we are told of the damage to an entire ecosystem: the destruction of forests, rivers, the habitats of animals, and the climate. At this point Astrov is called away to attend to a worker in a nearby factory who has been injured.[48]

The society-in-microcosm in *The Cherry Orchard* is on the threshold of profound change—albeit a transformation that proved more profound in retrospect—and in the play Chekhov juxtaposes three principal ideological standpoints: that of the gentry landowners faced with the imminent loss of their estate and way of life; the radical, revolutionary—implicitly Marxist—position espoused by Trofimov; and the new capitalist class personified by the son-of-a-serf-turned-businessman, Lopakhin. The political and philosophical debate between these three positions is not presented polemically. That is not Chekhov's style. Even if it were, considerations of censorship made it difficult to be more direct,[49] and this was presumably unnecessary for the play's original Russian audience. The debate becomes most explicit in Act Two.

It is significant that, for this act, the action moves from the nostalgia-ridden nursery of Act One to the open country beyond Ranevskaya's estate. The symbolic resonances of the outdoor setting are clear. As Braun observes, the telegraph poles, the road and the town on the horizon are a synecdoche for the recent industrial and technological progress now encroaching on Ranevskaya and Gayev's world,[50] which is evoked, in the foreground, by the dilapidated chapel, a well, and large stones which look like tombstones. For Hahn the backdrop gives "an urban perspective to the pastoral image, foreshadowing the end of a country idyll."[51]

In this act, Francis Fergusson remarks; Chekhov actually shows us an important "moment of change in society" and here we see most starkly the characters' attitudes and responses to that change.[52] Therefore, the expansive landscape of *The Cherry Orchard*'s second act could be seen as endorsing Gayev's perception that Nature is indifferent to human fate.[53] On the other hand, the landscape speaks positively of the possibility of progress, a literal representation of the transformation of the countryside that Lopakhin and Trofimov advocate. Although the telegraph poles bring the unwelcome reminders of Ranevskaya's lover in Paris, even Gayev appreciates the benefits of technological advances: in his very first speech in Act Two, he remarks on the convenience of the new railway. In the light of Chekhov's insistence on an exceptional sense of distance for this scene, it is surely significant that, when the three ideological positions are presented and contrasted most sharply towards the end of the act, Lopakhin actually utters the word "horizon." He does so after Trofimov's long, impassioned speech condemning the intelligentsia for its ignorance, empty philosophizing, and failure to build crèches and libraries. Somewhat undercutting Trofimov's rhetoric, Lopakhin then very briefly and matter-of-factly reports his own real work in the present—he's up at five every morning—and proffers his own vision: "Lord, you have given us huge forests, boundless fields, the deepest horizons, so, living here, we ought really to be giants."[54]

The sun is now setting, if indeed it has not set already; so, perhaps the view to that town on the horizon has dimmed? Nevertheless, the backdrop gestures both at the wider world to which Trofimov refers in his indictment of the Russian intelligentsia and at the expanse and vast horizons that Lopakhin invokes. Therefore, the sale of the cherry orchard, which is presented as an unthinkable catastrophe by Ranevskaya and Gayev and often as a tragedy by productions and commentators from Stanislavsky onwards, is placed in a different perspective when considered in terms of Russian society as a whole and the changes occurring in it. Surely the audience's response to the ideological debate and to the issue of the fate of the cherry orchard is critically affected by the setting?

This argument may seem to privilege unduly Lopakhin's point of view, but Chekhov regarded him as the "central" figure in the play,[55] intended Stanislavsky to play the role and was disappointed that he did not,[56] and amended the text to make the businessman more sensitive and sympathetic.[57] Lopakhin was not to be a vulgar kulak, but, according to the actor Leonid Leonidov, Chekhov saw him as a cross between a merchant and "a professor of medicine at Moscow University."[58] Moreover, as John Tulloch points out, Lopakhin's lines and his proposal for transforming the orchard echo the sentiments and arguments of the contemporary scientist Il'ya Menchikov, whom Chekhov greatly admired.[59] Stephen Baehr also notes Chekhov's own belief in progress, as expressed in a letter to his publisher:[60] "I have believed in progress since childhood, and can't not do so."[61]

Lopakhin's "horizons" speech is placed just before two brief but highly significant incidents which show the wider world intruding more emphatically and disturbingly into the foreground: the first vibration of the famous breaking string and the sudden appearance of the mysterious passer-by. The far-off sound of a breaking string, seemingly coming from the sky, is described by Hahn as the "sound of social transition."[62] Notwithstanding its mysterious, ethereal quality, the effect is to give that expansive landscape-in-transition a greater material and historical reality: Lopakhin explains the sound as a cable snapping in the mines, while Firs interprets it as a portent of doom, recalling the momentous emancipation of the serfs. According to Vladimir Kataev, the breaking string "conjures up [Russia's] vastness and a sense of time sweeping past."[63] The episode of the breaking string prompts Ranevskaya, who has found Lopakhin's talk of giants rather alarming, to suggest that they go inside, but, before they are able to retreat to the house, they are interrupted by the equally mysterious and troubling passer-by, whose dress and quotations of Nekrasov and Nadson identify him as a radical escaping from prison or exile. Both the sound of the breaking string and the stranger in effect emerge from that vast background landscape; Chekhov wrote to Knipper that the sound "must ... be felt as coming from a very great distance."[64]

The way in which the scenography of the first two acts of *The Cherry Orchard* juxtaposes an enclosed social order with a more complex, changing, technological world serves to endorse Georg Lukács's argument—taken up by Braun—that Chekhov's plays present a conflict between subjective intentions and feelings, and objective reality.[65] In the same vein, Griffiths argues that *The Cherry Orchard* deals "not only with the subjective pain of property-loss but also and more importantly with its objective *necessity*."[66] Although, ironically, Griffiths's translation fails to report Chekhov's setting satisfactorily, the landscape of Act Two, with its unusually wide horizon, helps to establish that objective reality.

Just as the deeper structures of Chekhov's realism are not conveyed by excessive naturalistic detail, neither (as has been argued above) are they necessarily signaled by more abstract, synthesizing or reductive designs. Peter Brook's *Cherry Orchard*, for example, with its assortment of carpets, offered no horizon beyond that of the theatre itself.[67] Meanwhile, productions such as Adrian Noble's for the Royal Shakespeare Company in 1995–1996, which cast Ranevskaya's house as the central character in the drama,[68] offer a purely subjective perspective that not only obscures the "specific historicity" of Chekhov's world, but also disguises the contrapuntal relationship between setting, action, and character. Serban's 1977 and 1992 *Cherry Orchards* certainly opened up the stage,[69] using a cyclorama to suggest a larger panorama;[70] however, the abstraction of the productions' designs implied an existential void rather than a physical, material expanse.

One non-naturalistic production which did present the landscape of *The Cherry Orchard*'s second act particularly interestingly was that directed by Manfred Karge and Matthias Langhoff at Bochum's Schauspielhaus in West Germany in 1981. The production bore the heavy imprint of the directors' East German politics: the play was updated to the 1920s and Chekhov's landowners and their entourage, equated with the self-seeking profiteers of the Soviet New Economic Period, were viewed through the lens of Erdmanesque/Mayakovskian satire.[71] The scenography naturally reinforced this unsympathetic conception of the characters, and consequently the set for Act Two lacked some of the poetic indeterminacy that Senelick identifies in the outdoor location.[72] However, that set represented a playful, witty, and imaginative response to the challenge posed by Chekhov's stage directions. It featured a white wall extending across the width of the stage. Four large-ish doorways in the wall afforded views of an expansive, receding landscape on a photographic backcloth far upstage. The four apertures worked cunningly to draw attention to and create a degree of intrigue about the background, and they potentially exaggerated the sense of distant vastness, especially because the wall was positioned well downstage. Of course, whereas Chekhov's description of the landscape suggests a subtler transition, the wall signified an emphatic division between the Gayev estate and the wider world beyond. That demarcation was underlined by the prominence of a railway track, which Chekhov does not specify but which features conspicuously in the play's dialogue, especially in Lopakhin's speeches. Coming to an abrupt halt in the foreground of the backcloth, the railway suggested the imminence of the onslaught of industrialization and, with it, economic and social change. Meanwhile, by confining most of the action to a relatively shallow strip downstage, the scenography seems to have emphasized the tenuousness of the characters' situation and the hopelessness of any resistance to larger historical forces. The passer-by made a most startling, and Brechtian, entrance into this space. In this instance he did actually emerge from that vast landscape: played by Karge, he came from behind the backcloth, lifting it high as he did so.[73] Although, in line with the mise en scène as a whole, the second-act set may have been rather reductive in its interpretation of the text,[74] nevertheless it captured very effectively something of the Chekhovian interplay between foreground and background, thereby potentially pointing to the way in which Chekhov's drama "confront[s] and communicate[s] the dialectical relationship between . . . the private and the public" that Rokem identifies as a vital function of theatre.[75]

If there is any doubt that Chekhov intends his theatre to enable us to see beyond the immediate preoccupations of the foreground to the wider horizon, it is spelt out for us in *The Seagull*. At the beginning of the play, the curtain rises to reveal a rough stage, presumably centre stage or upstage centre. That stage stands astride a wide path leading to the lake in the background, and its curtain actually hides the lake from view. Commentary on the metatheatrical and metadramatic aspects of *The Seagull* focuses on the device of the play-within-the-play and the allusions to *Hamlet*, but overlooks how that stage-within-the-stage functions physically. Too often, as with *The Cherry Orchard*, productions miss the significance of Chekhov's description of the set, which is important not simply for the self-reflexive image of the curtain within the curtain: the rough, makeshift stage rudely disrupts the romantic illusion of the receding, bucolic vista so carefully engineered within the proscenium arch theatre.[76]

Treplev, whose play is about to be performed on this stage, famously advocates that "new [theatrical] forms are needed."[77] Whether or not Chekhov satirizes Treplev's particular attempt to create those new forms in a pseudo-Symbolist (or Decadent) mode, it seems reasonable to assume his endorsement of the ambition, which, after all, he sought to achieve with his own plays. Treplev tells his uncle that, in the hidebound, contemporary theatre, when the curtain goes up you see a room with three walls, within which the actors try to drag out of trite lines and scenes some moral platitude that might come in useful about the house. On the other hand, when the curtain rises on his stage, it "will open directly on a view of the lake and the *horizon*,"[78] as indeed it does for Nina's performance of the play-within-the-play.

In the course of *The Seagull* the action retreats to rooms with three walls and the lake disappears from literal view. That scenic progression seems to parallel Treplev's loss of his sense of vocation and faith in himself, his losing sight of the horizon he speaks about with such optimism at the beginning of the play. Although Chekhov's characters may lose sight of, or fail to perceive at all, that far-off horizon, we, the audience, should not, because it allows us to see those characters' situations—and perhaps our own—in perspective. By seeing the background in productive interplay with the foreground, we may see beyond ourselves and may re-imagine our life and our world. Treplev, the theatrical-literary visionary, may have lost his way, but his rough stage never-theless endures as a powerful image of the way in which the theatre can both rudely challenge our preconceptions and open up for us a more expansive perspective. If only productions allow them, Chekhov's plays demonstrate what the theatre can do so well: set subjective desire against objective neces-sity and so enable us to look both inwards and outwards, to see the deepest horizons that Lopakhin envisions.

Notes

1. Arnold Aronson, "The Scenography of Chekhov," *The Cambridge Companion to Chekhov,* ed. Vera Gottlieb and Paul Allain (Cambridge: Cambridge University Press, 2000) 135.

2. Freddie Rokem, *Theatrical Space in Ibsen, Chekhov and Strindberg: Public Forms of Privacy* (Ann Arbor, Mich.: UMI Research Press, 1986) 29.

3. *Meyerhold on Theatre*, trans. and ed. Edward Braun (New York: Hill and Wang, 1969) 30.

4. Edward Braun remarks that the settings in *The Cherry Orchard* are "more significant in their detail and more clearly synecdochic than in any of the earlier plays." Edward Braun, *"The Cherry Orchard," The Cambridge Companion to Chekhov* 114.

5. Beverly Hahn, *Chekhov: A Study of the Major Stories and Plays* (London: Cambridge University Press, 1977) 25.

6. Anton Chekhov, *Polnoye sobraniye sochineniy i pisem* [Complete collection of works and letters], 30 vols., soch. [hereafter *Works*] 13 (Moscow: Nauka, 1986) 215. This and all subsequent quotations from this edition of the plays are my translations, as are quotations from Chekhov's letters.

7. Aronson 137.

8. Braun 114.

9. Nick Worrall, "Stanislavsky's Production Score for Chekhov's *The Cherry Orchard* (1904): A Synoptic Overview," *Modern Drama* 42 (1999): 525.

10. I. N. Solov'eva, ed., *Rezhissërskiye ekzemplyari K. S. Stanislavskogo*, vol. 3, 1901–1904 (Moscow, 1983) 339.

11. Anton Chekhov, *The Cherry Orchard*, trans. David Mamet (New York: Samuel French, 1986) 26; Anton Chekhov, *The Cherry Orchard*, trans. Trevor Griffiths (London: Pluto Press, 1981) 18.

12. Anton Chekhov, *The Cherry Orchard*, trans. Pam Gems (Cambridge: Cambridge University Press, 2000) 37.

13. Chekhov, *Pol. sob. soch., pis'ma* [hereafter *Letters*] 11 (1982) 243. Letter of 22 August 1903. My italics.

14. Chekhov, *Works* 13:224.

15. Rokem 32.

16. See Hahn ix.

17. Stanley Vincent Longman, "Fixed, Floating and Fluid Stages," *The Theatrical Space*, Themes in Drama 9, ed. James Redmond (Cambridge: Cambridge University Press, 1977) 152.

18. Rokem 35.

19. For example, Ibsen specifies that the drawing-room in *Hedda Gabler* has doors opening, on one side, into a hall and, on the other, onto a veranda and the garden, while upstage center there is a smaller room, Hedda's private space. At times during the play's four acts, in close correspondence to the heroine's predicament, curtains screen off both the view through the French windows and Hedda's upstage cabinet. Together with changes in lighting and properties, the constriction of the scenic space and the loss of the sense of access to the outside world provide a visual metaphor for Hedda's plight: "The theatrical space within . . . becomes the symbol of the powerful repression that the heroine suffers." (Hanna Scolnicov, "Theatre space, theatrical space, and the theatrical space without," *The Theatrical Space* 18.) Similarly, the set for *Dance of Death (Part One)* makes literal the prison in which Alice and the Captain find themselves trapped in their relationship: their drawing-room is the interior of a circular fortress tower, beyond which can be seen, through two doors upstage, the seashore and military batteries, where a sentry is permanently on duty.

20. Rokem 32.

21. Aronson 146–147.

22. 134–135.

23. Quoted by Meyerhold, *Meyerhold on Theatre* 30.

24. Aronson 134.

25. Peter Holland, "Chekhov and the resistant symbol," *The Theatrical Space* 237.

26. Trevor Griffiths, preface, *The Cherry Orchard*, trans. Griffiths, v.

27. Laurence Senelick, *The Complete Plays*, by Anton Chekhov, trans., ed. and annotated by Senelick (New York: W. W. Norton and Co., 2006) 975; Andrey Bely, *"The Cherry Orchard," Russian Dramatic Theory from Pushkin to the Symbolists: An Anthology*, trans. and ed. Laurence Senelick (Austin: University of Texas Press, 1981) 92.

28. Strehler directed *The Cherry Orchard* at the Piccolo Teatro, Milan, in 1974; Efros directed the play at the Taganka, Moscow, in 1975; and Serban directed it at the Vivian Beaumont Theatre in New York in 1977, and for the Romanian National Theatre, in Bucharest and Moscow, in 1992.

29. Aronson 145.

30. For *Three Sisters*, for example, Stanislavsky "sought to concentrate heavily around Chekhov's heroes such a crushing and stifling atmosphere—expressing itself everywhere, even in the tiniest details." M. N. Stroeva, "*The Three Sisters* in the Production of the Moscow Art Theatre," *Chekhov: A Collection of Critical Essays*, ed. Robert Louis Jackson (Englewood Cliffs, N. J.: Prentice Hall, 1967) 133.

31. Richard Eyre, *Directors' Theatre: Sixteen Leading Directors on the State of Theatre in Britain Today*, by Judith Cook (London: Hodder and Stoughton, 1989) 33.

32. Eyre, *Directors' Theatre* 33 and personal interview, 6 June 1985.

33. Chekhov, *Works* 13:269.

34. This expansive view was conveyed very clearly in Karl Ernst Herrmann's set for Peter Stein's production for the Schaubuhne, Berlin, in 1984. See Laurence Senelick, *The Chekhov Theater: A Century of the Plays in Performance* (Cambridge: Cambridge University Press, 1997) 259–260.

35. Chekhov, *Works* 13:105.

36. 114.

37. J. L. Styan, *Chekhov in Performance: A Commentary on the Major Plays* (Cambridge: Cambridge University Press, 1971) 132.

38. Rokem 51.

39. Aronson 137, 145.

40. Hahn 303.

41. 305.

42. Chekhov, *Works* 13:180.

43. Styan 274.

44. Chekhov, *Works* 13:161.

45. Styan 213.

46. Chekhov, *Works* 13:183.

47. 183.

48. Of course, a further indictment on the Serebryakov circle is that their melodramatic antics result in the neglect of the estate and of the doctor's duties and projects.

49. On 19 October 1903, Chekhov wrote to Olga Knipper about the difficulty of "depicting" Trofimov's problems with the authorities. Chekhov, *Letters* 11:279.

50. Braun 114–115.

51. Hahn 25.

52. Francis Fergusson, "*The Cherry Orchard:* A Theater-Poem of the Suffering of Change," *Chekhov: A Collection of Critical Essays* 155, 152.

53. "Oh glorious Nature, you shine with eternal radiance, so beautiful, so indifferent . . . ," remarks Gayev in the wake of Lopakhin's speech about the horizons. Chekhov, *Works* 13:224.

55. Chekhov, letters to Knipper and Konstantin Stanislavsky, 30 October 1903, Chekhov, *Letters* 11:290, 291.

56. Chekhov, letters to Stanislavsky, 30 October 1903, and to Nemirovich-Danchenko, 2 November 1903, 291, 293.

57. Braun 116.

58. Chekhov, quoted by the actor L. M. Leonidov, *Chekhov i teatr: Pis'ma, fel'etoni, sovremenniki o Chekhove-dramaturge* [Chekhov and the theatre: letters, articles and comments by contemporaries on Chekhov the playwright], by E. D. Surkov (Moscow, 1961) 351.

59. John Tulloch, "'Going to Chekhov': Cultural Studies and Theatre Studies," *Journal of Dramatic Theory and Criticism* 13.2 (1999):27.

60. Stephen L. Baehr, "The Machine in Chekhov's Garden: Progress and Pastoral in *The Cherry Orchard*," *Slavonic and East European Review* 43 (1999):99.

61. Chekhov, letter to Alexey Suvorin, 27 March 1894, Chekhov, *Letters* 5 (1977): 283.

62. Hahn 17.

63. Vladimir Kataev, *If Only We Could Know: An Interpretation of Chekhov*, trans. and ed. Harvey Pitcher (Chicago: Ivan R. Dee, 2002) 288.

64. Chekhov, letter to Knipper, 18 March 1904, Chekhov, *Letters* 12 (1986):65.

65. Braun 111.

66. Griffiths vi.

67. Brook directed the play at the Bouffes du Nord, Paris, in 1981, revived it there in 1983, and recreated the production at the Brooklyn Academy of Music, New York, in 1988.

68. Tulloch 41.

69. Arthur Bartow, *The Director's Voice: Twenty-one Interviews* (New York: Theatre Communications Group, 1988) 288.

70. See Senelick, *The Chekhov Theatre* 297. Santo Loquasto's design for the New York production was replicated by Mihai Maescu for the Romanian National Theatre (344).

71. See Henning Rischbieter, "Kommt Uns Nur Noch Die Farce Bei?: Karge/Langhoff Inszenieren Tschechows 'Kirschgarten' in Bochum," *Theater Heute* 22 (1981) 31.

72. Senelick, *The Complete Plays*, by Chekhov 975–976.

73. Rischbieter 31.

74. Senelick describes the production as "an aggressive reduction of the GDR's ideological attitude to the West." *The Chekhov Theatre* 256.

75. Rokem 75.

76. Styan 21.

77. Chekhov, *Works* 13:8.

78. 7. My italics.

Chronology

1860   Anton Pavlovich Chekhov born January 17 in Taganrog, Crimea, to Pavel Yegorovich, a grocer, and Eugenia Morozov. Chekhov's grandfather had bought his way out of serfdom just twenty years earlier.

1875   Chekhov's father, forced into bankruptcy, flees Taganrog for Moscow. Chekhov's family is evicted from their home, but Chekhov decides to remain in Taganrog to complete his high-school education.

1879   Chekhov moves to Moscow. There he rejoins his family and enrolls in the University of Moscow to study medicine.

1880   Begins contributing humorous short stories and sketches to magazines in Moscow and St. Petersburg under the pen name Antosha Chekhonte.

1884   Begins medical practice.

1886   "Vanka" published. Begins fruitful correspondence with Dmitrii Grigorovich, a well-established Russian writer.

1887   *Ivanov*, Chekhov's first play, is produced in Moscow to mixed reviews.

1888   Wins the Pushkin Prize for Literature from the Russian Academy of Sciences. "The Steppe" published.

1889	*The Wood Demon,* an early prototype for *Uncle Vanya,* closes after three performances. Chekhov's brother Nikolai dies of tuberculosis.
1890	Travels to Siberia to report on the Sakhalin Island penal colony. During his research there, he interviews up to 160 people a day.
1891	When famine hits the nearby Russian provinces, Chekhov works to relieve the cholera epidemic that ensues among the serf population. This work becomes material for his short story written concurrently, "The Peasants."
1892	"Ward No. 6" published.
1894	"Rothschild's Fiddle" and "The Student" published.
1896	*The Seagull* produced at the Alexandra Theatre in the fall to disappointing crowds.
1897	*Uncle Vanya* published. First diagnosed with consumption, or pulmonary tuberculosis, a disease that will eventually prove fatal.
1898	"Gooseberries" published.
1899	Moves to Yalta with his family after his father's death. *Uncle Vanya* opens in Moscow to large audiences. *The Seagull,* which failed in its first production, reopens at the Moscow Art Theater, also, with success. "Lady with Lapdog" published.
1901	*Three Sisters* published. Marries Olga Knipper, a member of the Moscow Art Theater troupe.
1902	"The Bishop" published.
1903	"The Betrothal" published.
1904	*The Cherry Orchard* produced in January to great acclaim. Chekhov dies on July 2 in Germany, of pulmonary tuberculosis at age 44.

Contributors

HAROLD BLOOM is Sterling Professor of the Humanities at Yale University. He is the author of 30 books, including *Shelley's Mythmaking* (1959), *The Visionary Company* (1961), *Blake's Apocalypse* (1963), *Yeats* (1970), *A Map of Misreading* (1975), *Kabbalah and Criticism* (1975), *Agon: Toward a Theory of Revisionism* (1982), *The American Religion* (1992), *The Western Canon* (1994), and *Omens of Millennium: The Gnosis of Angels, Dreams, and Resurrection* (1996). *The Anxiety of Influence* (1973) sets forth Professor Bloom's provocative theory of the literary relationships between the great writers and their predecessors. His most recent books include *Shakespeare: The Invention of the Human* (1998), a 1998 National Book Award finalist; *How to Read and Why* (2000); *Genius: A Mosaic of One Hundred Exemplary Creative Minds* (2002); *Hamlet: Poem Unlimited* (2003); *Where Shall Wisdom Be Found?* (2004); and *Jesus and Yahweh: The Names Divine* (2005). In 1999, Professor Bloom received the prestigious American Academy of Arts and Letters Gold Medal for Criticism. He has also received the International Prize of Catalonia, the Alfonso Reyes Prize of Mexico, and the Hans Christian Andersen Bicentennial Prize of Denmark.

SAVELY SENDEROVICH is professor of Russian Literature and Medieval Studies at Cornell University, Ithaca, N.Y. He has published studies in Russian literature, folklore and the history of culture. His books include *Chekhov s glazu na gla* (St. Petersburg, 1994) and *Georgii Pobedonostsev v russkoi kul'ture* (Moscow, 2002).

MAGGIE CHRISTENSEN is instructor in English at the University of Nebraska, Omaha. She has written on Fay Weldon and Jorge Luis Borges in addition to Chekhov.

ADRIAN HUNTER is a senior lecturer in English studies at the University of Stirling in Scotland. He has published editions of James Hogg's *The Private Memoirs and Confessions of a Justified Sinner* (2001) and Stephen Crane's *Maggie* (2006). His *Cambridge Introduction to the Short Story in English* was published in 2007.

JEFFERSON J. A. GATTRALL is lecturer in Russian and Slavonic Studies at the University of Sheffield, U.K. His 2005 dissertation at Columbia University was "Cult of Image: Literary Portraits of Jesus in European and American Prose, 1831–1895." He has published on Chekhov and Dostoevsky.

KERRY McSWEENEY is professor of English at McGill University. His most recent books include *Supreme Attachments: Studies in Victorian Love Poetry* (1998), *The Language of the Senses: Sensory-Perceptual Dynamics in Wordsworth, Coleridge, Thoreau, Whitman, and Dickinson* (1998), *What's the Import? Nineteenth-Century Poems and Contemporary Critical Practice* (2007), and *The Realist Short Story of the Powerful Glimpse: Chekhov to Carver* (2007).

KJELD BJØRNAGER was associated with the Slavic Institute, University of Aarhus, Denmark. His 1978 dissertation was "Elena Guro and the Urbanism of Russian Modernism," and he has published on modern Russian literature.

CYNTHIA MARSH is professor of Russian drama and literature in the School of Modern Languages and Cultures at the University of Nottingham, U.K. The focus of her research is Russian theatre. She has published mainly on Chekhov and Gorky. Her most recent book is *Maxim Gorky: Russian Dramatist* (2006).

ROBIN MILNER-GULLAND is associate tutor in the Centre for Continuing Education and research professor at the University of Sheffield, U.K. She is widely published in journals featuring articles on Russian literature.

OLGA SOBOLEVA is a program coordinator at the London School of Economics and Political Sciences. Her research interests are in comparative nineteenth- and twentieth-century literature; she also published *The Silver Mask: Harlequinade in Symbolist Poetry of Blok and Belyi* (2007).

PEKKA TAMMI is professor of English at the University of Tampere, Helsinki. He wrote *Russian Subtexts in Nabokov's Fiction: Four Essays* (2001) and, with Hannu Tommola, edited *Free language, Indirect Translation, Discourse Narratology: Linguistic, Translatological and Literary-Theoretical Encounters* (2006).

OLIVER TAPLIN is professor of classical languages and literature at Magdalen College, Oxford University. He wrote *Literature in the Greek and Roman Worlds: A New Perspective* (2000).

STUART YOUNG is program coordinator at the University of Otago, Dunedin, New Zealand. He is also a director, translator and reviewer specializing in Russian drama, particularly Chekhov.

Bibliography

Allen, David. *Performing Chekhov.* London: Routledge, 2000.

Barricelli, Jeane-Pierre, ed. *Chekhov's Great Plays: A Critical Anthology.* New York: New York University Press, 1981.

Bartlett, Rosamund. *Chekhov: Scenes from a Life.* London: Free Press, 2005.

Bely, Andrei. "The Cherry Orchard." In L. Senelick, ed. and trans. *Russian Dramatic Theory from Pushkin to the Symbolists: An Anthology.* Austin, TX: University of Texas Press, 1981.

Bentley, Eric, and Theodore Hoffman. *The Brute, and Other Farces.* New York: Grove Press, 1958.

Bitsilli, Petr M. *Chekhov's Art: A Stylistic Analysis.* Trans. T. W. Clyman and E. J. Cruise. Ann Arbor, MI: Ardis Press, 1983.

———. "From Chekhonte to Chekhov." In V. Erlich, ed. *Twentieth-Century Russian Literary Criticism.* New Haven: Yale University Press, 1975.

Bogayevskaya, Ksenia. Introd. "Tolstoy on Chekhov: Previously Unknown Comments." *Soviet Literature* 1 (1980).

Bristow, Eugene K. *Anton Chekhov's Plays.* Norton Critical Edition. New York: Norton, 1977.

Brustein, Robert. "Anton Chekhov." *The Theater of Revolt: An Approach to the Modern Drama.* Boston: Little, Brown, 1964.

Calder, Angus. "Literature and Morality: Leskov, Chekhov, Late Tolstoy." Ch. 8, *Russia Discovered: Nineteenth-century Fiction from Pushkin to Chekhov.* New York: Barnes & Noble Books, 1976.

Chudakov, Alexander P. *Chekhov's Poetics.* Trans. E. Cruise and D. Drags. Ann Arbor, MI: Ardis Publishers, 1983.

175

Chukovsky, Kornei. *Chekhov the Man.* Trans. P. Rose. London: Hutchinson and Co., 1945.

Conrad, Joseph. "Sensuality in Chekhov's Prose." *Slavic and East European Journal* 24, n.2 (Sum. 1980): 103–117.

Debreczeny, Paul. "The Device of Conspicuous Silence in Tolstoy, Chekhov, and Faulkner." In Victor Terras, ed. *American Contributions to the Eighth International Congress of Slavists.* Vol. II: *Literature.* Columbus, OH: Slavica, 1978.

————, and Roger Anderson, eds. *Russian Narrative and Visual Art: Varieties of Seeing.* 1994.

————, and Thomas Eekman, eds. *Chekhov's Art of Writing: A Collection of Critical Essays.* Columbus, OH: Slavica Publishers, 1977.

De Maegd-Soep, Carolina. *Chekhov and Women: Women in the Life and Work of Chekhov.* Columbus, OH: 1987.

Dunnigan, Ann, trans. *Chekhov: The Major Plays.* New York: 1964.

Eekman, Thomas, ed. *Critical Essays on Anton Chekhov.* Boston: G. K. Hall & Co., 1989.

Emeljanow, Victor, ed. *Chekhov: The Critical Heritage.* London, Boston & Henley: Routledge & Kegan Paul, 1981.

Erenburg, Ilya. "On Re-reading Chekhov." In *Chekhov, Stendhal and Other Essays.* Ed. and trans. by A. Bostock and Y. Kapp. Leningrad: Iskusstvo, 1962.

Ermilov, Victor. *Anton P. Chekhov: 1860–1904.* Trans. Ivy Litvinov. Moscow: Foreign Language Publishing House, 1953.

Finke, Michael C. *Seeing Chekhov: Life and Art.* Ithaca, N.Y.: Cornell University Press, 2005.

Frydman, Anne. "'Enemies': An Experimental Story." *Ulbandus Review* 2 (1979): 103–119.

Ganz, Arthur. "Anton Chekhov: Arrivals and Departures." In ch. 2 of his *Realms of The Self: Variations on a Theme in Modern Drama.* New York: New York University Press: 1980.

Gorky, Maxim. "What Chekhov Thought of It." *English Review* 8 (1911): 256–266.

Gottlieb, Vera. *Chekhov in Performance in Russia and Soviet Russia.* Alexandria, VA: Chadwyck Healey, 1984.

Hahn, Beverly. *Chekhov: A Study of the Major Stories and Plays.* London: Cambridge University Press, 1988.

Hingley, Ronald. *A New Life of Anton Chekhov.* New York: Alfred A. Knopf, 1976.

Holland, Peter. "Chekhov and the Resistant Symbol." In J. Redmond, ed. *Drama and Symbolism.* Cambridge: Cambridge University Press, 1982.

Howe, Irving. "What Can We Do With Chekhov?" *Pequod* 34 (1992): 11–15.

Jackson, Robert L., ed. *Chekhov: A Collection of Critical Essays*. Englewood Cliffs, NJ: Prentice-Hall, 1967.

———, ed. *Reading Chekhov's Text*. Evanston, IL: Northwestern University Press, 1993.

Jarrel, Randall. *The Three Sisters*. New York: Macmillan, 1969.

Karlinsky, Simon. "Nabokov and Chekhov: Affinities, Parallels, Structures." *Cysnos* 10, n.1 (1993): 33–37.

Kirjanov, Daria A. *Chekhov and the Poetics of Memory*. New York: Peter Lang, 2000.

Koteliansky, S. S. and L. Woolf, trans. *Reminiscences of Anton Chekhov by M. Gorky, A. Kuprin, and I. A. Bunin*. New York: B. W. Huebsch, 1921.

———, ed. and trans. *Anton Tchekhov: Literary and Theatrical Reminiscences*. New York: 1927; rpt. New York: Blom, 1965.

———. *The Oxford Chekhov*, 9 vols. Oxford: Oxford University Press, 1965–1980.

Kramer, Karl D. *The Chameleon and the Dream: The Image of Reality in Chekhov's Stories*. The Hague: Mouton, 1970.

Lantz, Kenneth A. *Anton Chekhov: A Reference Guide to Literature*. Boston: G. K. Hall, 1985.

Lavrin, Janko. "Chekhov and Maupassant." *Studies in East European Literature*. London: Constable, 1929, 156–192.

Letters of Anton Chekhov. Trans. by Micheal H. Heim in collaboration with Simon Karlinsky. New York: Harper & Row, 1973.

The Letters of Anton Pavlovich Tchehov to Olga Leonardovna Knipper. Trans and ed. by Constance Garnett. New York: Benjamin Blom, 1966.

Letters on the Short Story, the Drama and Other Literary Topics by Anton Chekhov. Selected and ed. by Louis S. Friedland. 2nd. ed., rpt. New York: Dover Publications, 1966.

Magarshack, David. *Chekhov: A Life*. 1953; rpt. Westport, CT: Greenwood Press, 1970.

Manheim, Michael. *Vital Contradictions: Characterization in the Plays of Ibsen, Strindberg, Chekhov and O'Neill*. Brussels, Belgium: Peter Lang, 2002.

Mann, Thomas. "Anton Chekhov." *Mainstream* 12 (1959): 2–21.

Martin, David W. "Figurative Language and Concretism in Chekhov's Short Stories." *Russian Literature* 8 (1980): 125–150.

Matelaw, Ralph E., ed. *Anton Chekhov's Short Stories: Texts of the Stories, Background, Criticism*. New York: Norton, 1979.

Mathewson, Rufus W., Jr. "Intimations of Mortality in Four Chekhov Stories." In W. E. Harkins, ed. *American Contributions to the Sixth International Congress of Slavists*. Vol. II: *Literary Contributions*. The Hague: Mouton, 1968.

――― . "Thoreau and Chekhov: A Note on 'The Steppe'." *Ulbandus Review* 1 (1977): 28–40.

McSweeney, Kerry. *The Realist Short Story of the Powerful Glimpse: Chekhov to Carver.* Columbia, SC: University of South Carolina Press, 2007.

Moss, Howard. "Three Sisters." *The Hudson Review* 30 (1977–1978): 525–543.

――― . "Chekhov." In Donald Davie, ed. *Russian Literature and Modern English Fiction: A Collection of Critical Essays.* Chicago: University of Chicago Press, 1965.

Nemirovsky, Irene. *A Life of Chekhov.* Trans. E. de Mauny. London: Grey Walls Press, 1950.

Nilsson, Nils Ake. *Studies in Chekhov's Narrative Technique: "The Steppe" and "The Bishop".* University of St. Stockholm: Almqvist & Wiksell, 1968.

O'Connor, Frank. "The Slave's Son." Ch. 3. In *The Lonely Voice: A Study of the Short Story.* Cleveland & New York: Meridian Books, World Publishing Co., 1965.

O'Faolain, Sean. "Anton Chekhov or 'The Persistent Moralist.'" *The Short Story.* London: Collins, 1948.

Pahomov, George. "Essential Perception: Chekhov and Modern Art." *Russian, Croatian, Serbian, Czech and Slovak, Polish Literature* 35, n.2 (1994).

Parts, Lyudmila. *The Chekhovian Intertext: Dialogue with a Classic.* Columbus, Ohio: Ohio State University Press, 2008.

Pervuldrina, Natalia. *Anton Chekhov: The Sense and the Nonsense.* New York: Ottawa, 1993.

Rayfield, Donald. *Anton Chekhov: A Life.* London: HarperCollins Publishers, 1997.

――― . *Understanding Chekhov: A Critical Study of Chekhov's Prose and Drama.* Madison: University of Wisconsin Press, 1999.

Roken, Freddie. *Theatrical Space in Ibsen, Chekhov and Strindberg: Public Forms of Privacy.* Ann Arbor, MI: UMI Press, 1986.

Safran, Gabriela. *Rewriting the Jew: Assimilation Narratives in the Russian Empire.* Stanford, Cal.: Stanford University Press, 2000.

Scolnicov, Hanna. "Chekhov's Reading of *Hamlet*." In *Reading Plays: Interpretation and Reception.* Eds. Hanna Scolnicov and Peter Holland. New York: Cambridge University Press, 1991.

Senderovich, Savely and Munir Sendich, eds. *Anton Chekhov Rediscovered. A Collection of New Studies with a Comprehensive Bibliography.* East Lansing, MI: Russian Language Journal, 1987.

Speirs, Logan. "Tolstoy and Chekhov: *The Death of Ivan Ilych* and 'A Dreary Story'." *Oxford Review* 8 (1968): 81–93.

Strongin, Carol. "Irony and Theatricality in Chekhov's *The Seagull.*" *Comparative Drama* 15 (1981): 366–380.

Styan, J. L. "The Delicate Balance: Audience Ambivalence in the Comedy of Shakespeare and Chekhov." *Costerus* 2 (1972): 159–184.

Swift, Mark Stanley. *Biblical Subtexts and Religious Themes in Works of Anton Chekhov.* New York: Peter Lang, 2004.

Tait, Peta. *Performing Emotions: Gender, Bodies, Spaces, in Chekhov's Drama and Stanislavski's Theatre.* Aldershot, England: Ashgate, 2002.

Tolstoy, Leo. "An Afterword to Chekhov's Story 'Darling'." *What Is Art? and Essays on Art.* Trans. Aylmer Maude. London: 1938.

Tulloch, John. *Shakespeare and Chekhov in Production and Reception: Theatrical Events and Their Audiences.* Iowa City, Iowa: University of Iowa Press, 2005.

Valency, Maurice. *The Breaking String: The Plays of Anton Chekhov.* New York: Oxford University Press, 1966.

Van der Eng, Jan, Jan M. Meijer, and Herta Schmid, eds., *On the Theory of Descriptive Poetics: Anton P. Chekhov As Story-Teller and Playwright.* Lisse: Peter de Ridder Press, 1978.

Yachnin, Rissa. *The Chekhov Centennial: Chekhov in English: A Selective List of Works by and About Him,* 1949–1960. New York: Public Library, 1960.

Wilson, Edmund. "Seeing Chekhov Plain." *The New Yorker* 22 (November 1952): 180–198.

Winner, Thomas. *Chekhov and His Prose.* New York: Holt, Rinehart & Winston, 1966.

Yarmolinsky, Avrahm. *The Unknown Chekhov: Stories and Other Writings.* London, 1959.

———, ed. *The Portable Chekhov.* New York: Viking, 1947; 2nd ed., 1968.

Acknowledgments

Savely Senderovich. "*The Cherry Orchard:* Chekhov's Last Testament," *Russian Literature*, Volume 35 (1994/2009): pp. 223–242. Copyright © 1994/2009 Savely Senderovich. Reprinted by permission of the author.

Maggie Christensen. "Re-examining the 'Coldly Objective' Point-of-View in Chekhov's 'The Bet' and 'A Trifle from Life,'" *Eureka Studies in Teaching Short Fiction*, Volume 3, Number 1 (Fall 2002): pp. 56–63. Copyright © 2002 Maggie Christensen. Reprinted by permission of the author.

Adrian Hunter. "Constance Garnett's Chekhov and the Modernist Short Story," *Translation & Literature*, Volume 12, Number 1 (Spring 2003): pp. 69–87. Copyright © 2003 Adrian Hunter. Reprinted by permission of the author.

Jefferson J. A. Gattrall. "The Paradox of Melancholy Insight: Reading the Medical Subtext in Chekhov's 'A Boring Story,'" *Slavic Review: American Quarterly of Russian, Eurasian, and East European Studies*, Volume 62, Number 2 (Summer 2003): pp. 258–277. Copyright © 2003 University of Illinois. Reprinted by permission of the publisher.

Kerry McSweeny. "Chekhov's Stories: Effects or Subtexts?" *Modern Language Studies*, Volume 34, Numbers 1–2 (Spring–Fall 2004): pp. 42–51. Copyright © 2004 Kerry McSweeny. Reprinted by permission of the author.

Kjeld Bjørnager. "The Masculine Triangle in *Uncle Vania.*" *Chekhov 2004: Chekhov Special Issues in Two Volumes, Vol. 1: Aspects of Chekhov. Essays in Poetics: The Journal of the British Neo-Formalist Circle,* Volume 30. Eds. Joe Andrew and Robert Reid (ed. and preface). (Keele, England: Keele University Students Union, 2005): pp. 45–52. Copyright © 2005 Kjeld Bjørnager. Reprinted by permission of the author.

Cynthia Marsh. "Two-timing Time in *Three Sisters.*" *Chekhov 2004: Chekhov Special Issues in Two Volumes, Vol. 1: Aspects of Chekhov. Essays in Poetics: The Journal of the British Neo-Formalist Circle,* Volume 30. Eds. Joe Andrew and Robert Reid (ed. and preface). (Keele, England: Keele University Students Union, 2005): v, 253 pp. 104–115. Copyright © 2005 Cynthia Marsh. Reprinted by permission of the author.

Robin Milner-Gulland and Olga Soboleva. "Translating and Mistranslating Chekhov," In *Chekhov 2004: Chekhov Special Issues in Two Volumes, Vol. 1: Aspects of Chekhov. Essays in Poetics: The Journal of the British Neo-Formalist Circle,* Volume 30. Eds. Joe Andrew and Robert Reid (ed. and preface). (Keele, England: Keele University Students Union, 2005): pp. 116–132. Copyright © 2005 Robin Milner-Gulland and Olga Soboleva. Reprinted by permission of the authors.

Pekka, Tammi. "Against Narrative ('A Boring Story')," *Partial Answers: Journal of Literature and the History of Ideas,* Volume 4, Number 2 (January 2006): pp. 19–40. Copyright © 2006 Hebrew University of Jerusalem. Reprinted by permission of The Johns Hopkins University Press.

Oliver Taplin. "Greek Tragedy, Chekhov, and Being Remembered," *Arion: A Journal of Humanities and the Classics,* Volume 13, Number 3 (Winter 2006): pp. 51–65. Copyright © 2006 Oliver Taplin. Reprinted by permission of the author.

Stuart Young. "A Blind Spot: Chekhov's Deepest Horizons," *Journal of Dramatic Theory and Criticism,* Volume 21, Number 2 (Spring 2007): pp. 65–78. Copyright © 2007 Stuart Young. Reprinted by permission of the author.

Index